The Blackest Sheep

Also by Joanne L. Yeck

"At a Place Called Buckingham"

The Jefferson Brothers

"At a Place Called Buckingham," Volume Two

Peter Field Jefferson: Dark Prince of Scottsville & Lost Jeffersons

The Blackest Sheep

Dan Blanco, Evelyn Nesbit, Gene Harris
&
Chicago's Club Alabam

Joanne L. Yeck

♦♦♦
SLATE RIVER PRESS

Copyright © 2019 by Joanne L. Yeck

All rights reserved. Printed in the United States of America.

No part of this book may be reproduced in any manner whatsoever without written permission except in the case of brief quotations embodied in critical articles and reviews.

Yeck, Joanne L.
The Blackest Sheep: Dan Blanco, Evelyn Nesbit, Gene Harris & Chicago's Club Alabam/by Joanne L. Yeck
  p. cm.
Includes bibliographical references and index.
ISBN: 978-0-9839898-7-5 soft cover
ISBN: 978-0-9839898-8-2 ebook
1. Chicago, Illinois—History. 2. Nightclubs. 3. Prohibition. 4. Historic Buildings—Chicago. 5. Jazz. 6. Nesbit, Evelyn (1884-1967). 7. Cabarets. 8. Speakeasies.
I. Joanne L. Yeck, 1954 – II. Title.

Library of Congress Control Number: 2019936875

Book production by Braughler Books, LLC
braughlerbooks.com

Published by Slate River Press Ltd.
slateriverpress.com

For Gene Harris ~

Whom I could have met but didn't.

CONTENTS

PROLOGUE
Gene Harris   1

ONE
Dan Blanco & White City   3

TWO
The Cabaret Wars   13

THREE
Albert Bouche's Moulin Rouge Café   45

FOUR
Northern Lights: Shootout At The Roadhouse   51

FIVE
Dan Blanco, Evelyn Nesbit & Bill Rothstein's Moulin Rouge   61

SIX
E.C. Yellowley & The War On Booze   93

SEVEN
Chicago's Club Alabam: Presenting Evelyn Nesbit   111

EIGHT
Dixie Bound: Evelyn Nesbit & Gene Harris   127

NINE
"This Is A Night Club"   135

TEN
Happy Days Are Here Again   151

ELEVEN
Gene Harris' Club Alabam   159

TWELVE
Fashion Club Stables & The End Of An Era   175

EPILOGUE
Evelyn Nesbit ... Peace At Last   191

Notes   199

Selected Bibliography   215

Acknowledgements   219

Index   221

About the Author   231

Author's Note

The Blackest Sheep is a work of nonfiction which would have been impossible to write without the legacy of dozens of journalists, frequently published without bylines, working for daily newspapers. I am especially grateful to everyone who helped preserve Evelyn Nesbit's life story, including Nesbit herself. Nothing comparable survives for Dan Blanco or Gene Harris, not even business papers, and coverage of their lives in periodicals was sporadic. The book contains no invented or undocumented dialogue. All quotations originally appeared in a book, newspaper article, memoir, letter, or were garnered from interviews. Frequently, especially in the case of historical newspapers, names of people and places were published with contradictory spellings; these have been standardized. Additionally, within quotations, I have sometimes conformed spelling and punctuation for clarity's sake.

Gene Harris (1899–1964).
(AUTHOR COLLECTION)

Gene Harris' 1964 obituary was saved by his niece, Willa Yeck, and filed under "H" for Harris. His place in our family tree was revealed by this clue ... Gene Harris was survived by his sister, my grandmother, Mrs. Milan Sanger of Ames, Iowa.

GENE HARRIS DIES; MANAGED CLUB ALABAM

BY WILL LEONARD

Rush street's oldest resident is dead.

Gene Harris, who had been associated with the Club Alabam since 1925, died Friday night in Passavant hospital, where he had been in a coma since suffering a stroke a week ago in his home that adjoins the club.

Mr. Harris

The Club Alabam, under the genial Harris' management for 30 years, was believed to be oldest night club in the United States operated continuously under the same ownership. Scarcely changing thru the seasons, it had been a symbol and a reminder of what night life was like in the Prohibition era and the post-repeal period. Gene, who loved to sit with his customers telling stories or simply chatting, was synonymous with the Club Alabam.

Illness Factor in Closing

When he closed it last May

PROLOGUE

Gene Harris

The name Gene Harris meant nothing to me.

Following my mother's death, I discovered a surprising obituary in her filing cabinet dated December 27, 1964, which revealed that my grandmother had a brother, Gene Harris. A sister I had never heard about, Pauline Rose of San Bernardino, California also survived him. Who were these people?

As it turned out, my grandmother Minnie (Harris) Sanger and Gene Harris were half-siblings. Minnie and Gene shared the same father, my great-grandfather, Clay Harris. Ruth B. Wales was the mother of Gene and Pauline.

Gene's obituary ran on page three of the *Chicago Tribune*, indicating he was a prominent Chicago resident. Written by Will Leonard, author of the newspaper's weekly entertainment column, "On The Town," the article stated that, at the time of his death, Gene Harris owned the oldest single-proprietor nightclub in the city—Club Alabam. A raconteur of the first order, Gene Harris and his warm repartee were synonymous with the establishment. Born in Leon, Iowa, in 1899, seventeen years later he left the Midwest, determined to see the world. For decades, he entertained patrons with tales of his adventures.[1]

By the early 1960s, Club Alabam's business had thinned to a trickle. The once ubiquitous chorus line and pretty hostesses were gone. Harris kept his doors open, his iconic neon sign of a high-kicking showgirl illuminating Rush Street at night.

The obituary's details were tantalizing. Who was Gene Harris' original partner, Dan Blanco? What about his wife, "Babs," who once worked at the club? Not to mention that Gene was one of the country's leading breeders of Shetland ponies.

Great-uncle Gene's vagabond ways and his involvement in nightclubs, especially during Prohibition, were more than enough to qualify him as one of the family's black sheep. Despite his youthful waywardness, he emerged a stable, successful businessman and a beloved Chicago institution. His pony breeding business, based partly in his home town of Leon, kept him in contact with the extended Harris family. His Chicago residence, adjacent the club, was always open to adventurous cousins passing through the city. Why had my mother never mentioned him? Was there more to Gene's story?

Little did I know that following these slim threads of Uncle Gene's life would lead me to Chicago's first cabarets, gangster wars during the Roaring Twenties, and the breathtakingly beautiful Evelyn Nesbit, who once found herself at the heart of a great American scandal. The more I learned, the more Gene's story blossomed as a microcosm of Chicago's most colorful era, when the blackest sheep ruled the town and the nation eagerly followed their every step.

Bootleggers. Drug dealers. Gamblers. Showgirls. Cabaret stars—fresh, as well as faded. They all populated Jazz Age Chicago and could not have been further from Leon, Iowa and Gene Harris' unremarkable beginnings than the moon.

This exciting, sometimes dangerous nightlife, drew Gene Harris to Chicago in the early 1920s. How had Chicago evolved from a town filled with disreputable saloons into a city rich with sophisticated cabarets? Ultimately, understanding Gene Harris' mentor, Dan Blanco, would hold the key to unlocking the story of my great-uncle's life and the fascinating history of what would eventually become *his* Club Alabam.

CHAPTER ONE

Dan Blanco & White City

Dan Blanco, founder of Chicago's Club Alabam, was born Daniel Leblang on January 3, 1877, in Mazatlán, Mexico. As a small child, he immigrated with his parents to the U.S. and was naturalized when his father became a citizen in about 1885. A performer, songwriter, satirist, and cabaret host, at the turn of the twentieth century, Blanco headed an act adapted from French and German cabaret, suited to beer gardens and rathskellers. With Ragtime, Honky Tonk, and syncopated rhythms all the rage, groups like Blanco's were in vogue and in demand. These "rathskellerians" were small groups of young men who sang and danced around a pianist, engaging their audience in intimate settings. In America, however, they were often relegated to vaudeville where the limitations of a stage performance constrained the performers' movements. Rathskellerians needed to work the room, singing and frolicking among tables topped with beer and pretzels, teasing regulars, and joyfully singing old favorites, night after night. Blanco's act specialized in comedy, even including Yiddish routines, with an occasional nod to pathos or melodrama.

White City And The Rathskellerians

On May 27, 1905, White City, a $1,000,000 amusement park and Chicago's answer to New York's Coney Island, opened in the center of the city. A perfect venue for Dan Blanco and his troupe, White City was founded by Hungarian immigrant Morris Beifeld and touted as "Chicago's Brightest Spot" and the "World's Finest Amusement Resort." White City's diverse programming included a band concert, gondola rides, a fire show (a three hundred foot street scene, complete with police, pedestrians, and a burning building, ultimately saved by men from three fire companies!), and thrill rides that "bumped the bump." The famous and novel infant incubators, fresh from the Saint Louis World's Fair, were on display. Its attraction, Midget City, was extremely popular. There was a photograph gallery, an observation wheel, and a ballroom ready to accommodate 2,400 eager dancers. Located at 63rd Street and South Park Avenue on Chicago's South Side, over the years, White City would employ hundreds of entertainers, including Dan Blanco.

Early in its history, White City Amusement Park relied on a carnival-like atmosphere to attract customers. With this type of entertainment came performers, barkers, and roustabouts who often exhibited questionable morals. White City wasn't alone in this tactic. Showmen all over town cashed in on midway and sideshow attractions. By 1908, Chicago, situated in the center of America's circus territory, was home to more "freaks" than any other city in America. Some owned homes, others rented rooms. In the off-season, these specialty acts found supplemental work in Chicago's vaudeville and burlesque houses, as well as in dime museums.[2]

In the summer of 1909, while White City attempted to shift its attractions toward decent, family entertainment, the Chicago Law and Order League pressured showmen city-wide to consider their public influence, especially on Chicago's youth. League President Arthur Burrage Farwell found many amusements to be "immoral and degrading." Even if children did not peak behind the curtain, barkers shouted out intolerable enticements. Hoochee-coochee dancers came in for extra scrutiny, as did tableaus called "living picture shows."

President Farwell complained: "Women with scarcely anything on were to be seen wriggling themselves into the most suggestive and shocking pictures.... Some of these women did everything humanly possible to give an indecent exhibition short of stripping themselves entirely to committing acts which would not be tolerated on any stage in the world. These rotten shows ought to be kept closed."[3]

Bertha Faulk, a "Bare Bronze Beauty" featured at White City, became a test case of indecency. Arrested in her dressing room, Bertha was covered in gilt paint and very little else. The twenty-five-year-old German, unable to speak a word of English, explained that she had performed in principal cities of Europe and America without censor. When she appeared at Harrison Street Municipal Court, Judge Edberhardt's courtroom was packed with theatrical and park managers, as well as ogling spectators. Bertha was "dressed" for her role as a Bare Bronze Beauty, coated in bronze paint and wearing two "girdles." The jury decided that her costume violated no city ordinance, the acquittal relieving not only the owners of White City but also the managers of theaters and parks across Chicago.

Alcohol flowed freely in those days and, in addition to the bandstand, White City featured a rathskeller. Unlike similar basement taverns around Chicago, White City's rathskeller obeyed the city ordinances, sold liquor within legal hours, and offered a "clean" atmosphere, suitable to a "better" class of clientele. Dan Blanco's act, which featured his antics with a trio or quartet, became a popular fixture and his reputation for solid entertainment grew.

King Of The Mafia

In 1910, Dan Blanco's Rathskellerians made headlines with a pastiche of Italian opera called "King of the Mafia." Sporting a black mustache, a bandana tied around his head, Blanco burst out from behind an upright piano, waiving a stiletto.

> "I am the king of the Mafia,
> When I get mad I get daffia;
> I sink a stiletto right into your back,
> If I don't I'm a son of a gun.
> When I say I'm a goin' to keel
> You betcha your life I certainly weel;
> All of the guineas they call me Phil,
> I'm the king of the Mafia."[4]

The audience went wild. Apparently, in 1910, it was safe to poke fun at organized crime. At least for Dan Blanco.

Every evening, patrons encouraged waiters to take complimentary drinks to the merry players. They always declined. Blanco explained: "None of us drink. We can't afford to. We sing fifty songs here every evening. I write most of my songs. That "Mafia" song is mine and so is the "Good-by" number. Ernie Erdman at the piano is a composer and Otto Fisher there writes ballads and Slayter Brockman teaches stage dancing all day. We work here, but we don't drink here nor anywhere else. That's right."[5]

Dan Blanco was innovative and stayed current, bringing new songs to the Rathskeller as soon as they were published. Early in his career, when he and his syncopated singers perfected delivering popular tunes such as "Waltz Me Around Again, Willie," the notion of a European cabaret was virtually unknown in the American Midwest. Entertainers mingling with straight-laced guests edged on indecency. Blanco and his rathskeller antics introduced Chicago to the delights of this intimate form of entertainment. It wasn't long before similar acts appeared in cafés throughout the city's tavern-filled urbanscape.

By 1912, Chicago was hot for the somewhat indecent "Tango Soiree" and White City installed a cabaret in one of its big restaurants. In early June, White City's rathskeller was "in full blast," featuring Dan Blanco's quartet of Rathkellerians in their most successful season at the amusement park. That year, Blanco was joined by Ralph Drew, Fred Geraghty, and Ernie Erdman, comprising what the *New York Clipper* called a "great singing aggregation." They would play White City for the entire summer. The *Chicago Examiner* reported that these Rathskellerians De Luxe were "burning up" audiences with "classy songs." Their act was a blend of repartee and tunes, featuring Ernie Erdman's new hit, "You Don't Have to Bring Me Violets."[6]

Summer bookings at White City had to be supplemented with work during the colder months. In the off season, Dan Blanco continued to write songs, tend bar, and perform in Chicago's restaurants, cafés, and clubs. Described as a "versatile singing comedian," he also occasionally played out of town in vaudeville theaters billed as a "Character Comedian."

These jobs, when he was fortunate enough to get them, took him from the safe, middle-class confines of White City into a darker world. Long before 1920, when Prohibition was established nation-wide, Chicago at night was a rough and dangerous place. While there was not a steady stream of St. Valentine's Day Massacres, vice was widespread in the city during the first twenty years of the new century. Despite the fact that serving liquor was legal—providing the tavern owner had a license and poured during established hours—continuous lawbreaking kept authorities busy. From prostitution and gambling to gun fights and brawls, many of Chicago's entertainment venues provided a ready-made stage for criminal activity. These were the establishments that employed Dan Blanco and his eventual partner, Gene Harris.

During the 1910s, Blanco's experience working in the tougher parts of town certainly broadened his sphere of acquaintance and, ultimately, gave him the experience and confidence to open a café of his own.

A versatile vocalist, in 1910, Blanco performed with Bernie Adler, Bert White, and Charles Waller, billed as "Chicago's Real Entertainers," at the Alhambra Theater. Located at Archer Avenue and South State Street, the venue had recently been refurbished into a burlesque house. Blanco, Adler, White and Waller filled out the program for a two-act musical, "The Merry Whirl."[7]

In January of 1911, Adler, White, and Blanco were billed as "Three Famous Entertainers" at J. J. Jordan's Café at 2008 South Wabash Avenue. Advertisements encouraged perspective patrons to "Follow the Merry Crowd" to Jordan's establishment and enjoy its beautiful New Vine Room. Three years later, the *Chicago Daily Tribune* would call Jordan's café a "dive." Located in the city's "red light district" in the South Side Levee, this section of the First Ward was filled with row upon row of disreputable houses, stretching from 16th to 22nd Street, along Dearborn Street and Armour Avenue. Jordan's and other taverns regularly violated ordinances, serving liquor all night. This was the heart of a sinister Chicago, where entertainers of all stripes rubbed elbows with the underworld—from petty criminals to big time gangsters. Saloonkeeper J. J. Jordan was arrested on three counts of selling liquor without a license and Jordan's Café would finally close its doors in the summer of 1914, as part of a massive Levee cleanup.[8]

"Best in the World"

During the early months of 1913, Dan Blanco sang at O'Byrne's on North Clark Street. Despite its North Side location, in 1911, O'Byrne's was named in a vice inquiry as one of the many saloons that disgraced the city for violating police ordinances. In particular, like others on the list, O'Byrne's relied heavily on the complementary trade of prostitutes. Two South Side properties owned by gangster Andy Craig, German Village Café at 816 South State Street and The Tivoli at 846 South State Street, also made the 1911 list. A decade later, Blanco and Craig would be partners in their own establishment, a cabaret at the northern edge of the city limits called Northern Lights.

Dan Blanco's 1913 booking at O'Byrne's kicked off a stellar year for the entertainer. At thirty-five, he reached a new peak in popularity. He may have hired a press agent. Suddenly, his name was popping up in articles, as well as White City advertisements. *The Player*, a weekly publication that covered "Everything in Amusements," plugged both the resort, which was doing "splendid business," and its illustrious cast of entertainers. Dan Blanco and his Rathskellerians were singled out, along with pianist Stanley Murray, noting: "Blanco and his boys have broken all records by returning to the South Side amusement resort for their ninth year."[9]

In May, Blanco returned to White City's Rathskeller, situated below the Casino. That season, Sophie Tucker—"The Last of the Red Hot Mamas"—appeared in the park's Cabaret; The Great Raymond thrilled audiences with his personal charm, as well as his magic; and the Rathskeller became a free attraction, guaranteeing packed houses. The amusement park management praised the Rathskellerians, stating, "Don't Leave White City Without Hearing Them."

Dan Blanco's group, now nothing short of an institution, was billed as Chicago's Best Rathskellerians. Tom Boure, writing for the *American*, exclaimed: "Dan Blanco and His Four Rathskellerians deserve blue ribbons!" *Chicago Examiner*'s Richard Henry Little topped that claim, insisting that Dan Blanco and his "Quartette of World Beaters" were the "Best in the World."

> … While we applaud all the new things at White City, there was nothing that gave us so great joy as to drop down into the restaurant in the lower part of the Casino Building and find that our old friend, Dan Blanco, the King of the Mafia, is back on his throne. There is no entertainer in the United States or Europe quite as interesting as Dan Blanco. He has been at White City nine years, and mellows with the years and gets funnier and funnier with each passing season. He is as big a feature at White City as the high, light spangled tower, and he mustn't be overlooked.[10]

The Rathskellerian repertoire continued to combine hit songs of the day with the group's own compositions. *Inter Ocean* columnist Max H. Alexander wrote in his "Notes from Songdom," that Dan Blanco and his quartet were "a riot" singing "Love Me While the Lovin' Is Good."

In "Vaudeville Gossip," Max Alexander applauded Blanco and his collection of "boys" in more detail: "Dan Blanco and his four rathskellerians, composed of Stanley Murray (at the piano), Harry Walters, Charles Phillips and Vern Bristo, are making the hit of their lives and are fast becoming known as the best quartet in town. These boys have for the past three seasons been at White City, and from all appearances will be there for ten more if they wish it."[11]

The amusement park attracted the middle class. Fashion was modest. Even in the hottest weather, skirts were long, with a slim silhouette. Straw boaters and summer suits were ubiquitous. The Rathskellerians dressed the part, their cabaret act designed to please both ladies and gentlemen. Publicity pictured truly youthful Rathskellerians, ringing an ever-smiling, slightly paternalistic-looking Dan Blanco. Slicked down, collegiate hair was neatly parted. Pointed Fiberloid collars were clean and sharp.

During the summer of 1913, White City was trimmed with gold and green, featuring a model of the Panama Canal, eight feet wide and one hundred feet long—proclaimed to be the largest working model ever built of the canal. Wayne O. Adams, formerly a U.S. engineer in Panama, was on hand giving lectures, describing its construction. In the Casino, thrilling Tango Teas took place every afternoon at 5:00 p.m., followed by the cabaret at 6:00 p.m. Below the Casino, of course, were the riotous Dan Blanco and his Rathskellerians. That June, the group consisted of Harry Walters, Tonny Broad, Charles Phillis, and Stanley Murray, singing the currently popular "Motor Cycle Michael With Me," featuring a two-seater motorcycle.

Mid-summer, Dan Blanco's grinning portrait graced a full-page feature article promoting the city's parks: Sans Souci, Riverview, and White City. The 1913 season offered spectacular competition. Riverview staged the "Sinking of the Titanic" to rival White City's Panama Canal. Journalist Gene Morgan singled out White City's cabaret as novel in the Midwest:

> White City deserves honors as the pioneer in many amusement ideas. Last summer the first of the cabarets was installed in the big restaurants. It was a startling innovation—on the surface of it—and Chicagoans wondered whether such a bizarre, Parisian novelty as that could make headway in this conservative metropolis. The notion of having singers and entertainers

mingle with guests at the tables seemed to be—well, rather flighty, to say the least.¹²

Chicago fell in love with this "flighty" form of entertainment. The amusement park served as a testing ground for smaller venues and, by 1913, cafés across the city offered distinctive cabaret-style acts which proved a perfect match for Dan Blanco's sensibilities. No wonder he was flashing a big smile for the *Tribune's* camera; Morgan credited him for inspiring the "entertainer café:"

> Beneath the hall of the tango and the birthplace of the Chicago cabaret is the good old rathskeller. Like the "Venice" ride, the rathskeller hasn't changed a mite since White City first was built. Next summer Dan Blanco and his "rathskeller four" will celebrate their tenth anniversary in ragtime revelry at White City.
>
> When Blanco and his syncopated troubadours began in 1905 warbling "Waltz Me Around Again, Willie," the "entertainer" café was quite an unknown quantity in Chicago. The word cabaret meant to the initiated a French wine shop. Yet Dan "had" everything in the cabaret style back in the days of "Way Down in Mah Heart I've Got a Feeling for You," and that was years before New York adopted the ragtime café chantant and claimed it as one of the artistic emanations of the great metropolis.
>
> He is still faithful on the job, digesting the new songs as fast as the publishers turn them out, which is about one every forty minutes.¹³

Thinking ahead to the seasonal close of White City and the need for winter work, Dan Blanco placed a humorous classified ad in the *New York Clipper* column, 'Such is Life in Chicago," written "by Gad":

> **CLASSIFIED AD. DEPARTMENT.**
> Situation Wanted.—Young man, thirty years old, will accept position in vaudeville. Will leave city if desired, also wife, who is perfectly willing I should. Address Dan Blanco.¹⁴

At vaudeville's peak, Chicago was home to over two dozen houses. Talent like Dan Blanco could slip in and out of local bills. In November of 1913, Blanco appeared at Chicago's Folly, performing a comic "coon song" called "Down in Monkeyville." Popularized by vaudeville comedians Arthur Collins and Byron G. Harlan, the tune satirized unruly attendees at rathskeller shows, vaudeville, and cabaret. The Collins and Harlan recording on Edison Disc included patter in black dialect. Blanco's interpretation of the song is lost today.[15]

During 1914, Dan Blanco's star continued to rise. In the off season, he worked at Natalby's, a fashionable German restaurant which spanned 23–29 Randolph Street. A notice in the *Clipper* announced: "Dan Blanco, the 1914 Model Entertainer, is now taking down a nice weekly wad from Natalby's succeeding Fred Sosman."[16]

Dan Blanco returned to White City for the 1915 season. By November, White City's financial difficulties were crippling. The company owed on bonds amounting to $225,000. The landowner and lease holder, Chicago's meatpacking magnate J. Ogden Armour, pressed for funds when the management couldn't meet the rent. Samuel J. Kline was appointed receiver.

While negotiations for a transfer of ownership went on behind the scenes, in the spring of 1916, White City opened as usual, extending its season with an enormous, outdoor roller skating rink, said to be the largest in the West. 1,000 skates were available for rent. A veranda, filled with seats for spectators, was adorned with flags. Music was furnished by Maxham's Military Band. Popular shows included "The Review of Revues," a free musical mélange; "Neptune and His Daughters," a marine spectacle; "Aldo the Great;" and "The Mining Days of '40." Perennial pleaser Dan Blanco carried on in the Rathskeller, a favorite haunt of patrons.

White City promoted a safe and sane Fourth of July celebration and Joseph Beifeld, the brother of White City manager and showman Morris Beifeld, successfully negotiated a new, ninety-eight year lease from landowner J. Ogden Armour. While this business deal might not have directly affected contracts with talent, at the end of July, Dan Blanco announced that he had created a new cabaret act with long-time cohort Bernie Adler and Sidney C. Gibson (who previously entertained at Coney Island with his former partner, Fred Fisher). Before joining Blanco, Adler and Gibson played the Empress in Des Moines, Iowa. By autumn, the trio appeared at Collins', described as a fashionable and exclusive South Side cabaret.[17]

Adler and Gibson were well-known in Chicago, appearing privately in "soirees in the homes of Chicago's *beau monde*." Their repertoire included popular songs and sentimental ballads. Gibson performed peppy folk dances while Adler was an adapt whistler, described as "admirable in his accompaniments." A funny fellow, Gibson offered up original composition such as, "I am saving up my neck-ties to hang myself; all I need is two more."[18]

Was their popularity strong enough to draw crowds to the Chicago's South Side? Perhaps the city's "better class" did go slumming in order to catch the trio's act. There, Blanco inevitably rubbed shoulders with the elite of Chicago's underworld, quite a contrast with the middle- and working-class patrons of White City. In the months and years to come, these connections would prove invaluable as Blanco aspired to manage his own cafés and cabarets.

CHAPTER TWO

The Cabaret Wars

In April of 1917, the United States entered the fight in Europe, committing to The Great War. In Chicago, soldiers and sailors would be looking for a good time before shipping off or while on leave. The resulting, rapid proliferation of saloons and cafés offered Dan Blanco the ripe opportunity to step into managing his own venue, the Grand Café. Doubtless confident in his ability to capture an audience, at last Blanco would be independent and free to hire his talented friends. With years of cabaret experience, Blanco was renowned for a solid show. His partner, Ray McCloskey, who remains a bit of a mystery, may have contributed business acumen to the new venture, as well as capital. Their optimism was short-lived when the wartime economy did not prove to be a boon for Chicago's North Side cabarets.

On June 2, 1917, Blanco and McCloskey opened the Grand Café (a.k.a. New Grand Café and Dan Blanco's), located at 519 North Clark Street at the intersection of Grand Avenue and North Clark. Approaching forty, Blanco likely found performing song after song, night after night, an increasing challenge. The comparatively relaxed role of impresario was a perfect fit for the personable entertainer/songwriter. Now a local celebrity, his name alone would draw business. In addition to Dan Blanco's flashing smile and easy manner, the Grand Café featured well-known local singers (and perennial Blanco partners) Bert White and Bernie Adler. In step with the times, there was a syncopated band. That summer, vaudevillian Flo Kennedy, "The Little Girl with the Big Voice," was also featured on the bill. Bert White brought not only significant talent to the Grand Café, but also a vivid past and experience navigating the vicissitudes of cabaret business.

◆ ◆ ◆

Only three years earlier, Chicago reformers had launched a full-scale war against saloons and cabarets in the crime-ridden South Side Levee. In 1914, during a spree of police raids, which the *Chicago Examiner* called a crisis in the underworld, Bert White's short-lived saloon (formerly Roy Jones') was abruptly closed. Along with White's place, the police targeted long-term scofflaws, including the management at J. J. Jordan's, where White and Blanco previously performed; the Cadillac Hotel Café, run by Balme & Rothschild; and Colosimo's, owned by Big Jim Colosimo, boss of the South Side. The scandal surrounding Roy Jones' notorious red light district café, located at 2037 South Wabash Avenue, began in early April of 1914 when a man was murdered at his establishment.

On the night of April 8, James Franche, known in the criminal world as "Duffy the Goat," shot and killed Isaac Henagow of California. Reportedly, "The Goat" shot the man through the heart for suggesting that women had the right to vote. Ninety minutes later someone called the *Tribune* saying that there was a murder cover-up in progress at Roy Jones' widely-known South Side Café. When reporters arrived on the scene, the evening's entertainment was in full swing. Cabaret singers were performing Irving Berlin's "This Is the Life" and the second floor was packed. Proprietor Roy Jones maintained the shooting had taken place outside the establishment and admitted an injured man had been brought inside, taken upstairs, and then sent by ambulance to a nearby hospital. Witnesses on the street contradicted Jones' statement, saying the man was shot inside the café. Reporters questioned significant blood still evident on the second floor. There was none on the sidewalk outside. Murder suspect James Franche had fled with a female companion.

On April 10, Roy Jones, along with seventeen waiters and entertainers, were seized in a raid conducted by a dozen detectives and investigators sent from the State's Attorney's office. One entertainer and three waiters testified that they were eyewitnesses to the shooting inside the café. Following the investigation, Capt. Michael Ryan of the 22nd Street Police District recommended that Jones' license be revoked. The license was held under the name "Ray Campbell," which officials now suspected was a dummy owner. "Duffy the Goat" remained at large.

Most importantly, the police backed Jones' story that Henagow was shot in the street, while eyewitnesses testified that two uniformed policemen and two plain clothes officers carried the body upstairs while they waited for an ambulance. Jones doubtless paid heavily for police protection and, that night, he got it. The mounting, conflicting testimony was grist for State's Attorney Maclay Hoyne's mill, who soon charged the police with protecting criminals.

Hoyne used the case as yet another rallying cry to clean up the Levee, demanding the cooperation of Chief of Police Gleason: "I believe you and I, with the active cooperation of your subordinates, can drive the gunmen and sluggers out of Chicago. Hereafter the assistants in this office will be instructed in the prosecution of all crimes to ask the maximum penalty if the accused when arrested is found to have in his possession a gun, dirk, dagger, slungshot, or other deadly weapon."[19]

When Jones changed his story to avoid perjury, the police turned on him for exposing their complicity in the cover up. Within days, Roy Jones was missing and a threatening sign appeared at the café: "This place is about to be closed because of unjust prosecution. You will hear from me later. Roy Jones."

Before the police could revoke Jones' license, he announced the café was closing and, by April 24, he had sold the business to Joseph Sullivan, August Riley, and Dan Blanco's friend and partner, Bert White. Sullivan was an entertainer and Riley managed several other Chicago cafés.

On May 1, Roy Jones' former place of business reopened. The new owners claimed the café had reformed. Their promised good behavior did not last long. As spring turned to summer along South Wabash Avenue, enthusiastic nightlife continued well beyond 1 a.m., the city's legal closing hour. Electric lights continue to flash in front of saloons, cabaret singers mingled with the guests and automobiles lined the streets in front of busy establishments. The proprietors' excuse? They would go broke if they did not "sneak" or "steal" extra hours, serving liquor between 1 and 5 a.m.—the official off-hours.

In early July of 1914, Bert White, remained the proprietor of Roy Jones' old place, was named along with Cadillac (2138 South Wabash) and Colosimo's (2128 South Wabash), as businesses evading liquor laws. On July 4, John J. Jordan, saloon keeper at 2008 South Wabash, was the first arrested on three charges of selling liquor after hours. Owners were also warned about the illegality of punch board gambling.

In flagrant violation of existing laws and ordinances pertaining to lotteries and gambling, punch boards had become prevalent not only in saloons citywide but also at newsstands, in cigar stores, barbershops, billiard halls, poolrooms, and even candy stores. Each board had between 400 and 800 numbered holes. The player paid ten cents per "punch" (one hole in the board), for the chance of winning a prize. Unsurprisingly, a large portion of the players were children gambling for trinkets.

On July 5, a warrant was issued for the owner of the former Roy Jones' place. It was unclear to the press if the warrant was for that elusive man named Campbell, the presumed owner of the café, or for Bert White, who likely lent only his name to the business, not any capital. Along with the Cadillac and Colosimo's, Bert White's establishment was running all night, selling liquor without the slightest attempt at secrecy. Under White's proprietorship, entertainers outnumbered patrons late into the night. In mid-July, plain clothes policemen found performers singing and shouting in the back room full of empty tables.

It was not long before underworld dominoes began to fall. A detective named Birns was shot and killed. Kingpin Big Jim Colosimo was arrested and grilled for seven hours. Mayor Harrison ordered the revocation of licenses for the Cadillac Hotel Café and for Roy Jones' old place, operated by Bert White. Indictments were ordered for both Roy Jones and Colosimo's lieutenant, Johnny Torrio, along with several witnesses in connection with the shooting of Officer Birns. Another Levee cleanup was in full swing.

Three years later, when Dan Blanco prepared to open his café, the Lower North Side was only slightly more respectable than the South Side Levee had been when Bert White replaced Roy Jones in the South Wabash café. Since 1911, the Lower North Side had been the target of vice and political reform. As with the Levee, efforts to clean up the district were, at best, always temporary. Blanco and McCloskey's investment in one more Lower North Side cabaret, situated at an excellent location, immune from a successfully bribed police force, must have seemed like a shoo-in.

1911: Early Reform On The Lower North Side

During 1911, a citywide cleanup campaign had exposed pervasive police protected vice in the Lower North Side. That year, Mayor Carter Henry Harrison, Jr. took office again, inaugurated to a fifth term on April 17, 1911.

During the first week in April, the city's first Vice Commission had presented its report to exiting Mayor Fred A. Busse, whose tenure in office was noted for city-wide corruption and the rise of organized crime. The Vice Commission's report suggested the establishment of a Morals Commission and a Morals Court, with the primary goal of reducing prostitution. The report targeted the Levee, including the elegant brothel the Everleigh Club. The Vice Commission condemned lax police attitude towards crime of all manner and the ease with which the force accepted payment to look the other way.

The prostitute's arena was the wide-open, ordinance-ignoring saloon. The Commission counted 445 "disorderly houses" situated across Chicago which admitted unescorted women to ply their trade, some of which featured vaudeville shows of an "improper nature" in their back rooms. The report demanded that regulations be established for police behavior and insisted that existing ordinances be enforced, including the abolishment of private and semi-private areas within saloons which had proliferated over the last decade. Booths, as well as screens and curtains around backroom tables, had become ubiquitous. The now illegal, intimate, all-night wine rooms, where sex and thievery took place behind locked doors, must be immediately eliminated. Coupled with these dens of prostitution was the growing social problem of the sale and consumption of illicit drugs, particularly morphine and cocaine.

The report criticized the city's double standard when it came to provocative women appearing in public, a criticism that directly affected saloons. In 1917, the same objections would be raised again against cabarets across the city. In April of 1911, the Commission wrote:

> Unfortunately, there are two standards of morality in Chicago. One standard permits and applauds dances by women almost naked in certain public places under the guise of art and condemns dances no worse before audiences from the less prosperous walks of life. This same hypocritical attitude drives the unfortunate and often poverty stricken prostitute from the street, and at the same time tolerates and often welcomes the silken clad prostitute in the public drinking places of several of the most pretentious hotels and restaurants of the city.[20]

Another seduction to vice was the ragtime music now a popular fixture in the barroom; many moralizing citizens believed this "noise" encouraged immoral behavior. In May of 1911, an order was issued to curtail café music, focusing on the saloons south of Chicago Avenue while ignoring those to the north in the district now dubbed the Clark Street Levee. The order, issued by Lt. John "Sandy" Hanley, was quickly rescinded by Inspector John L. Revere, who stated, "I play no favorites." Yet, it wasn't long before Inspector Revere reissued the ordinance that he rescinded, apparently playing favorites. The affected saloonkeepers prepared to take their complaint to Mayor Harrison. Ragtime brought in business and appealed to the soon-to-be flaming youth of Chicago.

Following Lt. Hanley's no music order, in early June, curious journalists investigated the Lower North Side, finding that ragtime was still liquor's handmaiden. Intrusive in the neighborhood, music and revelry roared out of the cafés lining North Clark Street. Tin Pan pianos banged out ragtime tunes and café entertainers sang syncopated and suggestive hits like "Alamo Rag," inviting listeners to dance the night away.... "Place your arm around your lady's waist. Just to show the folks you've got good taste."

In June of 1911, a reporter for the *Tribune* cruised the district's bars, including McGovern Bros.' (North Clark and Erie streets) and McGovern's (432 North Clark Street) where an electric piano attempted to drown out a competing keyboard next door. Jack Deutches' was a family buffet, complete with a busy piano and singing patrons. Around the corner at Chicago Avenue and Clark Street, Barney Cole's featured a chanteuse. That dive, the reporter noted, was "within a stone's throw from the police station and no one was stopping the music."[21]

By September of 1911, Mayor Harrison took a strong public stand, ordering Chief of Police McWeeny to strictly enforce the city's laws regulating saloons, specifically: abolish all winerooms, enforce the 1 a.m. closing law, and stop vaudeville shows in saloons. In October, to the surprise of many Chicagoans, the long-protected Everleigh Club closed. With a smile and toasts to many lucrative years, the wealthy owners, sisters Minna and Ada Simms, bade farewell to the city.

In November, the North Side found itself in the crosshairs of Attorney W. W. Wheelock and the Civil Service Commissioners. There were eighteen lawless saloons on North Clark and Wells street alone. Lists were made of disreputable resorts and shady hotels. Gambling spots, which fostered dice and poker games, as well as betting on the horses, were exposed. Street walkers and women without escorts were closely watched. Police officers from the Chicago Avenue Station fell under investigation, and by the end of the month seven charges were filed against Inspector Revere, Capt. Bernard P. Baer, and Lt. Hanley, who had instigated the order against café music, stating that these officers had neglected their duty by permitting public gambling in saloons and hotels; for allowing disreputable women to walk the streets; and for sanctioning saloons which were operating after hours.

Official positions varied as to the extent of vice on the Lower North Side. Inspector James A. Quinn defended Capt. Baer saying that, by July, he had stopped all the music in the tough saloons and driven out forty-seven disreputable resorts. During the proceedings Inspector Quinn (a.k.a. "Hot Stove Jimmy") was named as a key member of the city-wide political graft combination controlling the district north of the river to North Avenue. The year ended with the dismissal of Police Inspector John L. Revere, the exoneration of Lt. John "Sandy" Hanley, and the referral of Capt. Bernard Baer's case to Mayor Harrison. A lot of time, money, and breath had been spent on cleaning up the North Side Levee. Very little, however, had changed.

During 1912–1916, details of an elaborate game of cat and mouse between city officials and cabaret owners filled the newspapers, fueling hopes of reform while providing scandalous stories of on-going vice. Gambling establishments, disorderly houses and saloons of every description, shady hotels, and drug dens persisted all over the city, the North Side littered with lawbreakers. James "Hot Stove Jimmy" Quinn's reign appeared unshakable.

Mayor Harrison was sympathetic to Chicago's South Side, where thousands of night workers toiled in factory districts and was not considering a city-wide, all-night saloon closing ordinance. "There are good reasons why some saloons should be kept open all night," he told the press, "but they are not the places were the sports would gather to take a few more drinks."[22]

By October of 1912, Mayor Harrison went on record concerning a successful clean-up of the North Side. The outstanding exception was North Clark Street, future home of Dan Blanco's Grand Café. The notorious McGovern brothers and Joseph Frez were called to the Mayor's office, where they were told the vice must stop.

A year later, a vice report found that there had been no improvement in street soliciting in the Lower North Side. A published list of North Clark Street establishments welcoming prostitutes and their "catches" included: Ontario Hotel; Hotel Metz, operated by Mrs. Metz who also owned a disorderly house on La Salle; Hotel Belleview; German Hotel; Superior Hotel; McGovern's saloon, despite the fact that its license had been revoked sometime prior; 440 North Clark, a saloon and "hangout" for street solicitors; 456 North Clark (the proprietor's name was Hancock), another address welcoming street walkers; and the Belvidere, where women solicited from booths in a rear room.

Capt. John Rehm of the East Chicago Avenue Station argued, "I have six men detailed on that work. When anything is reported to us we go after it at once and I am doing all I can to keep all forms of vice out of my territory." Clearly, the men were far outnumbered by unescorted women.[23]

In early 1914, the situation was, if anything, worse. An investigation of North Clark Street and the southern districts of South Wabash and Cottage Grove avenues found that backrooms in saloons remained ubiquitous and many taverns were attached to pseudo-hotels. The report of an unnamed committee claimed that, on a daily basis, 14,000 girls found their way to the backrooms of 445 saloons in Chicago, most of them not professional prostitutes. The screens, stalls, and booths had not disappeared from the city's barrooms and 80% still had backrooms. So much for reform.

During 1915–1916, the Chicago newspapers continued to print lists of shady hotels and establishments that violated the Sunday closing ordinance which had been established in October of 1915. North Clark Street was well represented. Licenses were revoked, then restored by vice-friendly Mayor William "Big Bill" Hale Thompson, who was inaugurated on November 3, 1915.

By the spring of 1917, Dan Blanco and Ray McCloskey doubtless believed that North Clark Street was beyond the reach of the law thanks to police protection. Its bars, cafés and now burgeoning cabarets, had survived years of clean-up efforts. Why not get a piece of what seemed like guaranteed action?

Beginning in late 1915, a wave of change swept the city's purveyors of liquor and its associated pleasures. Between the establishment of the Sunday closing order on October 4, 1915 and February of 1916, 200 saloons took out licenses to become restaurants. Eateries, of course, could be open on Sundays. If a separate room could be shut off from the bar, a once decadent backroom in a "disgracing dive" could be transformed overnight into something that could technically be termed a restaurant. Sanitary inspectors for the Chicago Health Department scrutinized hastily installed kitchens. Once an establishment passed its inspection, the payment of a highly affordable $15.00 fee turned a former saloonkeeper into a restauranteur.

Saloons, of course, did not go away on the North Side and not all converted to restaurants or cabarets. During 1916, many saloonkeepers simply ignored the ordinance that attempted to close their establishments on Sundays—the so-called "Lid Order." Summer brought hot days and Sunday or not, men and women were thirsty for beer. The lid slipped in nearly every section of the city which was not typically dry. Interestingly, during a city-wide raid on July 16, no Loop District saloons were reported open. The Beldman Festival Harmony and Singing Club was caught selling beer on Sunday, reported by E. J. Davis, superintendent of the Anti-Saloon League. The Illinois (459 North Clark), McGovern Bros.' (North Clark and Erie streets), Windsor Café (1226 North Clark), and others even further north, including the Athenia, were among fifty-three saloons caught in violation of the ordinance. A second offense supposedly resulted in a revoked license. The *Tribune* printed many of the specific violations, some more flagrant than others:

> 1301 Madison Street: "Five men drinking beer from icebox in rear poolroom."
>
> 1050 Fulton Street: "Rear door open and bartender on duty."
>
> 1125 Ohio Street: "Lights all burning; screens obstruct view of bar."
>
> 545 North Paulina Street: "Lights burning and shades violate ordinance."
>
> 2368 Chicago Avenue: "Crowd of men and women in rear. Front and side doors locked."
>
> 1756 South State Street: "Front door open."[24]

In a town filled with fixers, many licenses did not stay revoked. Mayor "Big Bill" Thompson had the power to taketh away and giveth back. During a single week in July of 1916, Mayor Thompson revoked ten saloon licenses, eight of which had violated the Sunday closing law, and announced that he had restored eighteen others. An overall win for saloonkeepers.

The cabaret wars were far from over.

Dan Blanco's Grand Café

By the time Dan Blanco and Ray McCloskey were ready to open Grand Café, North Clark Street and the Lower North Side had been transformed from streets packed with saloons to a cluster of cafés, cabarets, and buffets offering food, entertainment, and, of course, plenty of liquor. This change in the nature of the establishments also attracted a new clientele. Where the saloon once served as the prostitute's parlor, the lively cabaret was a magnet for young adults, servicemen and their lonely young wives, as well as the proverbial traveling salesman out for a night on the town. Some simply offered the old standby, a ragtime piano, but a growing number, like Grand Café, were true cabarets with a legitimate program of entertainment. This atmospheric change to the district brought a new threat—the Juvenile Protective Association. Minors, never before attracted to the Lower North Side in significant numbers, now found cabareting a dazzling temptation. During 1917, underage youth out on the town would become a mounting social concern.[25]

Blanco and McCloskey opened the Grand Café on a Saturday—June 2, 1917. War news filled the daily newspapers. Three U. S. ships had been sunk by a German submarine, one with a Chicago man on board. The previous evening, sixteen women had been arrested for gambling and a saloon on West Division Street had been robbed. The weather was cool. A high of only 52 degrees was expected, accompanied by wind and rain showers. These were not particularly auspicious conditions for a grand opening.

Soon the two men had more to worry about than a distant war or inclement weather. A week later, on June 9, a spectacular Saturday night raid delivered hundreds of persons to the East Chicago Avenue Police Station. Fifty detectives had combed the North Side. All available patrol cars had been put to use. It was a wholesale raid, with detectives ordered to enter every hotel and rooming house, as well as cafés and cabarets. Anyone on the streets after midnight on June 10 had better be ready to provide a good reason to be there.

The next day, the newly opened Grand Café did not make the published lists of raided cabarets and was, apparently, not operating in violation of any law. Among the targets was Grand Café's neighbor, McGovern Bros.', located at 661 North Clark (Erie and Clark streets). One of the district's toughest joints, McGovern Bros.' was a frequent violator of one ordinance or another, yet the brothers managed to stay open, quickly regaining revoked licenses. During this particular raid, forty-five men and thirty-three women were arrested in McGovern's cabaret. Later, it was reported that two Alderman were present in the café shortly before the raid, barely escaping arrest. The McGovern brothers also operated a hotel at the same address. Upstairs, sixty people were arrested while the establishment's much advertised jazz band played on. The raiding force was faster than the hotel's internal buzzer system designed to warn occupants. As a result, scantily dressed men and women were hurried to the East Chicago Avenue station, while bystanders hooted at the indecent parade.

After five days of deliberation, Mayor Thompson revoked the liquor, cabaret/restaurant, and cigarette licenses for McGovern's. Chief of Police Schuettler called the place vile, a menace to the neighborhood and the entire community. Flagrant disregard for the law was the norm at McGovern Bros.'. Schuettler indicated there were always twenty women available to drink with customers. Vulgar entertainment, both song and dance, was the establishment's stock and trade. Police reported hidden financial connections between the cabaret and the hotel upstairs. Sergeant Charles E. Turk, who led the raid, insisted that minors frequented the place.

Remarkably, less than a month later, John McGovern was found not guilty of keeping a disorderly house by a jury in Judge Howard Hayes' court. As a result, McGovern requested that his licenses be restored. Mayor Thompson said he would follow the recommendation of Chief Schuettler. Given the newspaper reports, John McGovern's acquittal seems incredible. Either the police were extremely misled as to the nature of McGovern Bros.' cabaret and hotel or bribes worked. Soon, on August 26, in a routine Saturday night raid, McGovern's was visited by Lt. Schumacher of the Chicago Avenue Station. Since his acquittal, John McGovern had been selling only soft drinks. That night, they must have been spiked by some evildoer or, perhaps, enhanced with unseen hip flasks. Ten men were arrested and the police were seeking John McGovern as the saloonkeeper responsible for the violation.

Nearby, at Wells and West Chestnut streets, Frank "Spiker" Fleming's establishment was also caught in the June raid. There, thirty-five men and seven women were arrested. Fleming had recently been released from the "Bridewell" (probably Cook County Jail). A perfect example of the city's merry-go-round of vice and reform, Fleming's license had been revoked following his previous conviction and was restored a few days prior to the raid.

The day after this spectacular sweep of the North Side, Chief of Police Schuettler made a shocking move towards exposing corruption within the police force. He thoroughly shook up the East Chicago Avenue Police Station, instigating the largest dismissal in the station's history. The district, he maintained, was packed with scores of cafés, cabarets, and questionable hotels, operating in complete disregard of the law. This condition, the Chief believed, was due to long-standing police corruption. The June 9 raid, the newspapers revealed, was carried out by Sergeant Turk, who operated out of Chief Schuettler's office. Capt. Joseph C. Mullin of the East Chicago Avenue Police Station was not consulted and, apparently, was taken by surprise. If the raid had been conducted directly from the local station, presumably, many more buzzers would have sounded across the North Side, clearing out both barrooms and hotel rooms.

Following the raid, Chief Schuettler transferred virtually every officer to other stations, ultimately relocating ninety-three policeman. Three captains, four lieutenants, and twelve desk and patrol sergeants were transferred out of the station, all of whom were believed to be long associated with unscrupulous bondsman, corrupt politicians, and saloonkeepers. Graft, apparently, had completely permeated the East Chicago Avenue Police Station. Capt. Mullin was transferred south to Cottage Grove Station. One of the few men remaining at the East Chicago Avenue station was Lock Keeper O'Gara, who previously expected to be transferred out by the entrenched organization because he refused to accommodate the Hennessey brothers in their bond racquet. Instead, his honesty was rewarded by Chief Schuettler and he remained at his desk.

The Hennessey brothers, Thomas ("Spike") and Maurice, operated a saloon at North Clark Street and Chicago Avenue convenient to the station, and did a booming business on Saturday nights selling liquor and providing bonds for arrested revelers who were drinking after the stroke of midnight. "Spike" Hennessey was on a bond shark blacklist. It was later learned that, during the

June 9 raid, a call went out from the police station to Hennesseys' saloon. That night, the brothers provided twenty-seven individuals with cash for bonds. Some of those caught in the raid were forced to use bondsman. At least three of the men arrested at McGovern Bros.' were carrying enough cash to pay their own bond in Judge Uhlir's Morals Court. The judge refused their cash and made the men wait until a professional bondsman provided them with the amount to cover their bond, complete with fee, giving the appearance that one North Side judge was part of this long chain of corruption.

A War On Cabarets

Virtually overnight, Dan Blanco and Ray McCloskey found their brand new Grand Café in the middle of a serious North Side clean-up, an upheaval they could never have anticipated. Officers long friendly to the neighborhood were suddenly gone. The overlords of the North Side underworld protested to the Mayor, claiming undue police activity in the district. Chief Schuettler promised the cabaret owners more of the same and appointed Capt. James Gleason as the new commander at East Chicago Avenue Station.

Other distressing news concerning the rough neighborhood of North Clark Street found its way into the newspapers. Opposite the Grand Café sat the six-story St. Regis Hotel, long established and, presumably, legitimate. It opened in April of 1873 as the Albany and, in 1914, underwent a $90,000 remodel and was renamed the St. Regis. During 1917, the hotel, situated at 512–522 North Clark Street, advertised in *Variety* announcing new management, with rates beginning at $5.00 per week. The proprietor also operated the hotels Marion and Breslin. The St. Regis claimed to be the "Home of the Profession"—indicating it catered to show people, a special brand of transients who enjoyed the nightlife North Clark Street had to offer. No doubt Dan Blanco and Ray McCloskey hoped that the St. Regis would provide a steady stream of colorful patrons to the Grand Café. A decade later, Dan Blanco's Club Alabam would be a favorite spot for entertainers to gather after they finished performing their vaudeville or nightclub acts.[26]

On September 1, 1917, the St. Regis made chilling national headlines when Miss Rae Wilson, a cabaret singer, jumped to her death from a third floor window. It is quite possible that the alleged suicide was committed in full view of the Grand Café. Photographs printed of Rae Wilson revealed an attractive woman, wearing a jaunty beret, her wide eyes looking deeply into the camera. The cabaret where Miss Wilson worked was not disclosed in the newspapers. Nor did journalists reveal the cabaret(s) she visited that fateful night.

In the midst of a heated affair with a married man, Mr. Gerald Shepard (whom the *Chicago Examiner* dubbed "Lovely Gerald"), the illicit couple had begun drinking early that evening. Shepard told a reporter for the *Tribune*: "We went to a cabaret in North Clark street, and she suggested I get a room at the St. Regis. I did so and she arrived later. We had a few drinks and I fell asleep. That's the last I remember until the bell boy rapped on the door and told me she had jumped out of the window. She must have been brooding over her fancied troubles and decided to end it."[27]

The *Examiner* printed a radically different version of the story in which Shepard claimed he was asleep and was awakened to see Rae Wilson opening the window. She jumped before he could reach her. Contradicting Shepard's story, others in the hotel informed the police that thirty minutes before Miss Wilson fell to her death, they heard a man and woman loudly quarreling in the hotel room, claiming that the man cried, "I'll get even with you if it's the last thing I ever do." Others, standing on the street below, said they saw a man and woman struggling in a window.[28]

A small flask of whiskey and spare change were found in the room. Later, Gerald Shepard admitted that he and Rae Wilson had quarreled, bitterly. They had registered as Mr. and Mrs. C. E. Hall. Shepard's wife, Louise, was already considering divorce and had taken the doubly loved Gerald to court. Rae Wilson, her stage name or alias, was actually Lucille Leonard of Rochester, New York and Mrs. Fred Rolph. She was separated, but not divorced, from Rolph, who was a resident of Los Angeles. Gerald Shepard was booked on the charge of murder. Shortly thereafter, he was exonerated by a coroner's jury and additional charges of disorderly conduct were dismissed. Towards the end of the month, Mrs. Louise Shepard told the newspapers that she loved Gerald, would forgive him, and was ready to take him back. Such were the melodramatic and deadly goings-on along North Clark Street.

◆ ◆ ◆

Cabarets on the Lower North Side remained in the headlines. In September of 1917, a shooting took place at the Ohio Café, located at 601 North Clark. One Friday night, Havalin Racine, a "mulatto" singer, ran screaming from the café, informing a policeman that a man had fired a shot at her and fled. Immediately, the café was raided. Joseph Cavalini, owner of the Ohio Café, and fifteen others, including four jazz bandsman and a waiter, were arrested. Once in court, Judge Barasa concluded that a proprietor was not responsible for the misconduct of his patrons. "A minister cannot be convicted for something unlawful that occurs in his church," the judge concluded, discharging Cavalini and the others.[29]

Mean street, North Clark.

The Case Of Hazel Castle And Other Delinquent Minors

Just south of Grand Café, at Kinzie and North Clark (401 North Clark Street), sat the Casino Café (a.k.a. Casino Gardens). In late September, that café was targeted as police action increasingly focused on minors frequenting cafés. Public outrage at stories such as the downfall of sixteen-year-old Hazel Castle ignited what would become Chicago's war on cabarets.

On September 26, 1917, Hazel Castle, of Cicero, Illinois, was apprehended at the Rogers Hotel, located at 442 North Clark Street, just a block and a half from Dan Blanco's Grand Café. Her testimony resulted in the arrest of eight men (including a lawyer and a clerk of the Municipal Court) and two women, believed to be part of a vice ring. Unstated in the press was that the ring was likely some version of the dreaded "white slavery" movement which brought vulnerable girls from the countryside and small towns, systematically leading them down the Primrose Path.

Miss Castle stated that she was forced to attend parties at Casino Café and that the men she named also took her to Freiberg's Dance Hall (operated by the notorious Ike Bloom) in Chicago's South Side. There, she danced and drank liquor. One of the men, Wallace Rogers, was the owner of Rogers Hotel. John Reeves and Ray Ankenbaur, proprietors of Casino Café, as well as waiter William Fitzpatrick, were also named. One of the two women was Miss Lucille Maxfield, formerly a checker at the Casino Café. Assistant State's Attorney Walter W. L. Mayer found Hazel Castle's case all too typical and stated that similar stories unfolded daily in the Lower North Side neighborhood.[30]

On September 28, Chief of Police Schuettler announced he intended to slam down the lid on Casino Café, calling the situation a "Cabaret War." The Chief's first step was to forbid music at the café where Hazel Castle had been led astray, learning her first lessons in the ways of the city's underworld. If the girl's claims proved true, the Chief promised the citizens of Chicago that Casino Café would be shuttered.

When Capt. James Gleason of the Chicago Avenue Police Station was asked why Casino Café had been allowed to operate so long without interference, Gleason admitted it was probably no worse than a dozen other establishments on the Lower North Side. He categorically announced that all the cabarets were bad and that law-abiding saloonkeepers wanted them shut down.

Albert E. Webster, acting superintendent of the Juvenile Protective Association, stated, "The Casino is an old offender. It is one of the places which seems to specialize in young girls." Webster further condemned the entire district, "The cabarets are worse than the old levee district for the reason that decent girls get inveigled into them because of their semi-respectable appearance."[31]

By early October, not only was the Casino Café *not* shuttered, police gave the proprietors permission to resume playing music and staging cabaret entertainment. They had been acquitted of the charges of contributing to the delinquency of sixteen-year-old Hazel Castle. Despite this good news for the Casino Café, on November 1, 1917, Capt. James Gleason recommended to the City Council's License Committee that the licenses for both Casino Café and Moran's Café be revoked.

On the night of September 28, Chief of Police Schuettler had made an example of Patrick Moran's cabaret, located at 848 North Wells Street, charging Moran with contributing to the delinquency of a fourteen-year-old girl named Anna Sichy. Moran's Café had earned a reputation of serving liquor to underage girls. Frequented by ex-cons and women of the underworld, Police Lieutenant Schoemaker complained that Moran's always beat its cases. When Anna Sichy's case was heard in October, owner Patrick "Pat" Moran insisted that the girl was served brown soda pop by bartender George McKenna, not beer. Miss Sichy was apprehended with a married man named Frank Primrose (his real name?) and testified that Mr. Primrose bought her beer, not soda pop. Described as a Mary Pickford look-alike, her oval face, large gray eyes, and curly locks made a charming picture. She was fortunate. Her first foray into cabaret life resulted in arrest. Caught immediately, it might be her last.

Yet another underage drinker, Ruth Wicher, was arrested at Moran's and told her sad story to the *Chicago Daily Tribune*. Arrested by policewomen Teresa Johnson and Agnes Walsh, Miss Wicher testified that she had been brought to Chicago by a man named Lloyd Raymond of Waukegan, Illinois. She had been cabareting in the North Side bright light district for about six weeks. Once arrested, she begged the police to let her go home. Hers was a familiar story, a country girl who dreamed of "a city's life and gaiety after tiring of the farm and the chickens." It is remarkable that she lasted six weeks without more harm done.[32]

The story of Eva Johnson, another minor served liquor at Moran's Café, was a tragic contrast to the tales of Anna Sichy and Ruth Wicher. Tall, slender, and seventeen, Johnson admitted to becoming addicted to cabaret life at sixteen. Over the course of a depraved year, she had liquor forced on her, was drugged, held prisoner, married, and deserted. In court, she named several cafés that did not hesitate to serve her alcohol, placing them in league with the men who took advantage of her youth. By October of 1917, Eva Johnson languished in the county hospital, ravaged by her year of debauchery.

◆ ◆ ◆

While the press hammered away at sob stories concerning young victims, the police department stayed on the warpath to clean up the cabarets in the area. These establishments, struggling to stay afloat in an increasingly expensive environment, were now fighting among themselves. Concurrently, Chicago's City Council was hard at work crafting what would be referred to as an anti-cabaret ordinance.

At 11:00 a.m. on September 28, 1917, the City Council Committee for Licensing listened to arguments concerning a proposed ordinance supported by the Chicago Brewer's Association, the Chicago Retail Liquor Dealer's Association, the United Societies, the Chicago Hotel Keepers' Association, and the Illinois Liquor Dealer's Protective Agency, as well as societies representing leading restaurant owners, women's clubs, and various civic-minded organizations. Their goal was to forbid cabaret entertainment and dancing any place where liquor was sold. Every form of amusement would be abolished from saloons and cafés, excepting places seating 500 or more persons where, they suggested, orchestras could be permitted. Chicago's newspapers predicted that the twilight of the cabaret was at hand and were filled with anti-cabaret sentiments. Outspoken city leaders included:

William Kramer, The United Societies: "This is Chicago's chance to put the selling of liquor on a legitimate and clean merchandising basis. The cabaret is a parasite and factor for evil and immorality...."

William Legner, Chicago Brewers' Association: "We are going to carry the fight against the cabaret to the finish. Now is the time for the renaissance of the saloon. Chicago should—and I believe it will—take the initial step toward putting the saloon on a better, cleaner basis that will bring it popular approval."

Edward R. Diederich, Chicago Brewers' Association: "The average cabaret to-day is a recruiting place for evil. We must pull out the cabaret business by the roots."

Alderman Stanley H. Kunz: "The cabaret of the dangerous type has broken up more homes and wrecked the lives of more young men and women than any other factor I know of.... Some cabarets are not dangerous, but there are many who abuse the privilege. You can't discriminate, and for that reason I believe the projected law should be a rigid one."[33]

♦ ♦ ♦

The larger, more established cabarets joined forces. Ike Bloom's Freiberg's Dance Hall, on 22nd Street between Wabash and State, and influential gangster Big Jim Colosimo's establishment, Colosimo's Café on Wabash between 21st and 22nd streets, were under direct threat of closure. The Bismark Hotel and Restaurant, Lamb's Café, Congress Café, Green Mill Gardens, and North Clark Street's Athenia all prepared to fight the proposed ordinance.

In early October, the police arrested proprietors of three more Lower North Side cabarets, all charged with contributing to the delinquency of children. Among them was Dan Blanco's partner, Raymond C. McCloskey, who was booked on more than a dozen infringements of the law, specifically contributing to the delinquency of minors. During a raid, the police found three boys and three girls, all reported to be age fifteen, drinking liquor at the Grand Café. All were members of wealthy North Side families and, initially, the police refused to release the names of the minors to the newspapers.[34]

The *Tribune* ran the headline: "Café Man Fined Heavily for Selling to Minors." Ray McCloskey was identified as the owner of the Grand Café and was fined $25.00 and court costs on each of five charges of contributing to the delinquency of minors. The arrests were made on September 29, 1917 and the minors involved were ultimately exposed: Mary O'Neill, Loretta Turner, Eulalia Murray, Frank Springer, Richard Ettleta, and Gerald Murray. So much for protecting the children of Chicago's elite. All, except Frank Springer, were under seventeen. They testified in court that they were served beers and ginger ale highballs. They also admittedly lied to their parents who thought they had gone to the theater. Dan Blanco's name did not appear in the press coverage.[35]

During October alone, further north, numerous raids in the district brought dozens of underage men and women to the Summerdale Police Station, as well as young sailors in uniform. Some of the minors arrested were from the very best Chicago families. Edgewater Dance Hall and Superb Café were, apparently, hot spots for the sons of millionaires. Following one raid, Second Deputy Funkhouser told a reporter that wealthy parents, as well as the government, complained against these dance halls where minors were sold drinks.

Cabarets in Chicago's Loop District also fell under police attack. In the absence of regulations, afternoon tea dances where a host or hostess introduced men to young ladies had become disreputable opportunities for sexual liaisons. In otherwise respectable establishments, potential dangers for naive young women were nearly as pervasive as in the Lower North Side.

In October of 1917, Chicagoans hotly followed the story of pretty, petite Dorothy Crosby, who nearly committed suicide by jumping out of a window of the Bismark Hotel on Randolph Street. The hotel's Berlin Room and Blue Bird Room, where a man called Dresden China facilitated introductions, were the attractive settings for Dorothy Crosby's downfall. Accounts varied wildly as to her age and her marital status, though she might have been as young as sixteen. Five or six weeks of cabareting, living out of hotel rooms, mingling with con men, and nearly becoming part of a blackmail scheme drove her to thoughts of suicide. Once saved from death and arrested, she told reporter Kate J. Adams, "My advice to any girl under twenty-five years of age is to stay away from cabarets. They never should set foot in them. My heart goes out to any girl who gets into that life for even a short time. It is awful."[36]

The police concluded that beyond the availability of liquor, jazz music was the irresistible and addictive attraction of the cabaret. First Deputy Westbrook's solution was to "divorce jazz music, liquor, and dancing." The combination of these three, he said, was the menace. He didn't find the combination of music and eating to be a problem and, importantly, dining out did not attract young people. Dancing did. "Jazz band music is no more music than whisky is a thirst quencher," Westbrook continued. "It is a syncopated form of noise that appeals to the passions. With that kind of music, what kind of dancing can you expect?"[37]

Judge Victor P. Arnold of the Juvenile Court blamed these vicious cabarets for selling liquor to young girls, stating: "A girl is attracted by the lights and the music, and before she knows it she is drinking liquor and doing things which make her ashamed to return home. I have cases like this every day."[38]

Lonely Wives Of Soldiers And Sailors

In addition to this rash of arrests of minors, there was a new problem facing law enforcement in Chicago: young wives left behind by absent husbands who were quickly joining the armed forces. The first draft for World War I began on June 5, 1917 (three days after Dan Blanco opened the Grand Café), registering men between the ages of twenty-one and thirty-one. A significant demographic that enjoyed cabareting was now being syphoned off as young men went to war. They left behind lonely wives and sweethearts who enjoyed an evening on the town.

By the end of October, during a weekend raid on the lower North Side, seventy percent of the women arrested were married. This was a matter for the Federal Court. Letters poured in to newspapers from servicemen complaining about the degrading actions of their young wives. The *Chicago Examiner* printed pathetic and heartbreaking quotes from the correspondence:

"'I married a girl of twenty. She started on cabarets when I was on the Texas border. She was found in a raid with the man—a father of two children.' He obtained a divorce. There were eight co-respondents."

"[My wife's] downfall was due to cabarets. I don't think married men who contribute to these girls' downfall should be let go. I was in the Army on the border last summer while this was going on. If this evidence can be of any use, you are welcome to it. I hope cabarets can be abolished. She was only eighteen years old."

"My wife used to go out at night and get drunk. She would say she got it at her sister's place. Finally I caught her running around and after a row she left. Now my mother is taking care of my three children.... I had a nice home almost paid for and what I have now is my children and I live for them only.... Pearl is only twenty-two, I went into the national army at Rockford two weeks ago. A girlfriend said that she felt 'sorry for her' and introduced her to a man. She spent the evening in a loop cabaret and became intoxicated. She was arrested ... in the Lorraine Apartments at Ellis Avenue."[39]

◆ ◆ ◆

Most of these letters were anonymous and only a sampling were printed. Invoking federal authorities, Judge Uhlir of the Morals Court insisted that this demoralizing trend had to be stopped.

The situation quickly escalated as the police embarked on an intense clean-up effort on the Lower North Side's bright lights district. In late October, Chief of Police Herman F. Schuettler addressed seventeen owners and managers of eleven downtown cabarets and cafés, including the popular College Inn (Hotel Sherman) and Friar's Inn. All appeared as summoned. If these proprietors did not know the law before the chief spoke to them, they were certainly clear afterwards:

> "I have reports on irregularities in your places of business. Children have been served with alcoholic drinks. Women entertainers in tights have mixed with patrons and the dancing has been indiscriminate and indescribable. Women in a number of restrooms have sold women patrons cigarettes at 5 cents each. These things must stop. I will issue no more warnings. My next move will be to revoke the licenses of all who violate the law."[40]

Chief Schuettler was no-nonsense, stressing he wanted no more alcohol sold to young girls or sailors and soldiers in uniform. He concluded that the mayor constantly acted on his recommendations for revocations of licenses and warned against counting on influential friends for protection.

A similar session would take place the next day, with proprietors and managers of seventeen more cabarets called in front of the police, including several establishments located in the even seamier areas of South Wabash and South State streets. Chief Schuettler took another opportunity to speak out strongly to the press: "We know conditions in each place, and these folks cannot evade responsibility. Promiscuous mingling of guests, introductions by [employees] and raw dancing must stop. One warning will be all owners of these places will get. They will respect the law to the letter or be put out of business."[41]

With articles about these notorious cabarets appearing daily in the Chicago newspapers, Dr. E. C. Dudley of Chicago, President of the State Commission of Public Welfare, weighed in on the public scourge cabarets had become, demanding they be put out of business: "They, together with some of the cheap boarding houses, cater to the type of young woman who the state should protect. The lonely ones, who want to have a good time, are rather weak sisters and haven't any social training to fit them for coping with these vicious influences."[42]

At the end of the month, Chief Schuettler called a third session with cabaret owners and read them the now familiar riot act. Among the next twenty-five called in front of the Chief were a cluster located on North Clark Street including Casino Café (a.k.a. Casino Gardens, no. 401), Erie Café (no. 662), Royal Café (no. 701), Belvidere Café (no. 838), and Suburb Café (much further north at 6311 North Clark Street). The scandalous Moran's Café (a.k.a. Moran's Buffet) at 846 Wells Street and the well-known West Side hot spot the Arsonia Café (1654 West Madison) were also in this group.

Chief of Police Schuettler continued to call cabaret proprietors to his office for their final warning, vowing to continue until every tavern keeper in Chicago had been personally informed of the laws and ordinances. Violations now equaled revocations.

Less than a month after Ray McCloskey's appearance in court, the Grand Café was included in another sweep of twenty-five cabarets targeted by the police-driven round up of saloonkeepers. Captain Gleason of the Chicago Avenue Police Station was well aware that this section of Chicago harbored one of the city's worst nests of immoral operations. Proprietors, including an unnamed representative from the Grand Café, were summoned to appear before Chief of Police Schuettler, who threatened to close them down if conditions in their establishments were not corrected. The list revealed that the immediate neighborhood was packed with bars and cabarets. Grand Café's competition on North Clark Street alone included Transfer Buffet, Leader Buffet, Sheerin Brothers, Fireman's Inn, The Bar, Hastings' Saloon and Cabaret, Ohio Café, Troy's Buffet, Pete's Buffet, Windsor Café, International Café, Miller's Café, Athenia Café, Dave's Buffet and Cabaret, and Crystal Café. Establishments lining West North Avenue and Wells Street were also in this group. Many were well-established cabarets that had been targeted six years earlier.[43]

Where did Dan Blanco stand on vice in his establishment? In his days performing at White City, he presented a clean show and had no responsibility when it came to who or what was served. During the off-season, when Blanco worked in saloons like O'Bryne's, he was witness to much more open vice and a multitude of illegalities. As an entertainer, he did not directly contribute to crimes. Now he was an impresario, even though Ray McCloskey was apparently the financially responsible party at the Grand Café and likely the owner of the cabaret license. Who was pouring the drinks for the minors? With strong, legitimate talent like Bert White, Bernie Adler, and Flo Kennedy, were there girls in tights walking among the tables or hawking cigarettes in the powder room?

Unquestionably, Dan Blanco and his Rathskellerians had given Midwesterners a taste of intimate entertainment when they popularized European cabaret at Chicago's White City. Whether or not liquor or hours laws were broken at the Grand Café and other North Side establishments, the reformers of the early 20th century would fight to abolish what they viewed as immoral contact between performers and patrons.

Café Owners Fight Back

Concurrent with the police crackdown on the Lower North Side, as the autumn of 1917 progressed, the cabaret license committee of Chicago's City Council hotly debated the proposed anti-cabaret ordinance, designed to prohibit the intimate mingling of entertainers and customers, and particularly the sale of alcoholic beverages where there was dancing. Cabaret players rubbing shoulders (and possibly other body parts) with a dining room full of inebriated customers was filled with immoral potential. This attempt to close cabarets and bring back the comparatively clean saloon may have been designed to appease reformers, however, it ran parallel to an equally severe national movement—the climaxing fight between wets and drys battling their way to legislating morality with the Eighteenth Amendment to the U.S. Constitution. Proposed in the Senate in August of 1917, the amendment would ultimately be imposed on Americans beginning on January 17, 1920.

The cabarets' fight to survive got nasty. Large cabarets turned on smaller establishments like Grand Café. Hoping to avoid extinction, the large cafés suggested setting high license fees that would drive smaller places out of business. Despite a public hearing, the license committee took no immediate action on the proposed ordinance. In mid-October, the suggested measures to solve the cabaret problem would strictly forbid any form of entertainment, except instrumental music, in any place where liquor was sold. This had the backing of Chicago brewers and liquor dealers. Those representing the brewing interests insisted that 95% of the city's saloonkeepers were in favor of the abolition of cabarets, their lively atmosphere providing stiff competition to the straightforward bar.

In response, a Café Owners' Association was hastily organized, taking out large advertisements in daily newspapers, supporting regulation and condemning the abolishment of café entertainment. In a public statement, café owners asked to be heard, argued for wholesome entertainment (whether in a theater or restaurant), and agreed that the public should be protected by regulatory laws. The café owners acknowledged that some evils had developed and that they favored the abolition of afternoon dancing in public eating establishments, including the elimination of the professional hosts and hostesses who facilitated those dances. Under all circumstances the association supported the strict enforcement of the laws regarding all-night dances and the serving of liquor to minors. They argued in favor of satisfying their clientele, which included "the best people" of Chicago:

> The members of the Café Owners Association do not believe that clean, wholesome entertainment should be prohibited in restaurants, as is contemplated by some interests. At the dinner hour and during the evening people seek recreation, and it is their right that it should be provided. In these times of stress, national governments find it the best policy to increase opportunities of amusement, rather than curtail them. The policy of our local government should be to regulate the people's amusements—not to destroy them.[44]

In late October, the City Council's license committee continued to discuss the drastic ordinance proposed by the Chicago Brewers' Association, et al., to abolish all cabarets. Alfred S. Austrian, attorney for the association, argued that the City Council had complete authority to regulate the conditions pertaining to where and when liquor was sold. By the end of November, the city's license committee had recommended that dancing would be prohibited where alcohol was available. Only instrumental music would be permitted, with a special annual license priced at $300.00. After intense argument, a compromise was reached. Cafés and restaurants could apply for a license permitting vocal and instrumental entertainment. The cost would be $250 to $1,000 annually, depending on the size of the venue. For the small cabarets that dotted the Lower North Side, this would be a direct and likely fatal blow. There was a loophole, if the business' space was big enough. A bar could be sectioned off from a full-fledged dry cabaret in an adjoining room.

During the fall of 1917, the cafés that lined North Clark Street suffered under rising prices and increased taxation on liquor, putting additional pressure on the smaller operations. Tile Bar (551 North Clark), for example, accommodated 150 patrons and closed in the first week in October. M. Frank, Tile's proprietor, explained to reporters: "Everything is high; liquor, food—all! Tomorrow night at midnight I close my cabaret. Ten entertainers will go. The boys are all gone to war. We can't sell to anyone under draft age, and the fellows over thirty-one don't go cabareting. Only the bar here will run. The Café will become a quiet restaurant. I'm closing voluntarily."[45]

John Reeves, manager of the Casino, blamed rising taxes as a serious squeeze on profits. "In thirty days these drinks [now $.25] will be three for a dollar," he told reporters. "In another year there won't be more than five saloons in twenty blocks from the river to North Avenue." He continued explaining that smaller establishments that had not laid in stocks of whiskey, anticipating the rising price of liquor, would all close their doors. Reeves stated that the current government tax was eighty cents a quart, $3.20 on a gallon. Casino had $10,000 worth of whiskey in bond and would owe $32,000 in tax. Of the 7,000 saloons in Chicago, 6,500 would close if they had to pay all their bills. "The saloon business is wrecked," he bemoaned. "We made $20,000 last year. They took our music away last week and the place is dead. If we can't get our music back...."[46]

Like Dan Blanco and Ray McCloskey, Isadore Rothschild of the Erie Café at 660 North Clark Street had been open just eight months. At that time, North Clark was "wild and woolly." The street accommodated all kinds of women, some would say the wrong kind, who attracted men into saloons. Rothschild argued that the old crowd had been chased away by police pressure and was replaced by men who brought their wives to sit around and listen to music. Rothschild liked his new clientele and credited Lieut. Shoemaker, who was known for saying, "Bring 'em in. Take 'im down cellar," for the change. The cleanup was apparently working, however, without music, North Clark Street would lose the couples they now depended on.

In early November, Capt. James Gleason of the Chicago Avenue Police Station proved he was serious about changing the atmosphere on North Clark Street. Mayor Thompson had received recommendations to revoke the licenses of both Casino Café (owned by Raymond "Ray" A. Ankenbauer & John C. Reeves) and Pat Moran's Café. The Casino held two licenses, one for the upstairs bar and one for the basement cabaret. By November 1, Moran's was closed. Chief of Police Schuettler and Mayor Thompson directed City Collector Forsberg to deny applications for ten new saloon licenses. A dozen additional resorts were designated for further investigation, including Casino Café and Peter Morrelli's at 537 North Clark. Citywide, an estimated 500 to 700 saloons closed their doors on October 31, 1917.

Yet on Friday night, November 9, Casino Café was operating. It was raided and, once again, Chief Schuettler ordered the lid clamped down on the cabaret—at least temporarily. A reporter for the *Tribune* described this den of vice: "Sylphlike and unadorned ladies, painted upon the walls of the Casino café looked mutely down last night upon a scene that was strange to them. It was a liquorless cabaret that they beheld and the jazzing was done to lemonade and soda pop. Chief of Police Schuettler had cut off the drinks."[47]

The bartender was selling ginger ale; however, at least one patron also received a stiff shot of whiskey in his soda pop. Three policemen observed the act, arrested proprietor Ray Ankenbauer, and whisked him off to the Chicago Avenue Station. A Saturday night raid on November 10 resulted in the closure of the Belvedere Café at Clark and Chestnut streets, a few blocks north of Dan Blanco's Grand Café.

While the police did their best to keep a lid on vice in the Lower North Side, the City Council continued to debate the specifics of the proposed anti-cabaret ordinance. A sliding scale of licenses based on seating capacity was discussed, beginning at $250 per year for a café seating up to 100 persons. Establishments seating 500 persons or more would pay a maximum fee of $500. Beyond the matter of fees, the committee sought to legislate the morals of the cabaret in numerous ways. On November 11, the following points were up for consideration:

- No suggestive songs.
- No women in tights. Thighs must be covered with skirts, at least to the knees.
- No transparent materials in costumes.
- Runways extending the stage area into the seating would be forbidden.
- Entertainers would be forbidden to mingle with customers.
- Soliciting women would be barred.
- Hosts could not facilitate "promiscuous introductions" to a patron.
- Performers must not drink intoxicating beverages at any time while on the job.
- No boisterous behavior on the part of either patrons or performers.
- No cigarette smoking by women patrons.

In other words, many of the elements that defined cabaret would be subject to fines—specifically anything that brought the performer and audience together in close contact. This was Dan Blanco's specialty, his gift to Chicago that had been so widely imitated. Could the unique pleasures of cabaret be confined to a more traditional stage and still delight audiences? Would Dan Blanco create a successful adaptation?

◆ ◆ ◆

The debate continued into the new year and, at the end of March, the cabaret owners made one last desperate attempt to stop the anti-cabaret ordinance, threatening to make Chicago "bone dry." Their plan was to introduce a substitute ordinance which would prohibit the delivery of intoxicants to homes as well as businesses for the duration of the war. It was a hollow threat. On March 26, 1918, the Chicago City Council finally passed the long anticipated ordinance. Beginning May 1, there would be no dancing, live music, or cabarets where liquor was sold. Mechanical music, such as a pianola or gramophone, was exempted. A license for an orchestra would require the consent of the police. The vote was sixty-three to two in favor of the ordinance which, temporarily, staved off Federal interference to clean up Chicago's saloons. The loophole of separate rooms or floors for a bar and a cabaret still existed, allowing the larger establishments to get around the new ordinance. If Dan Blanco's Grand Café managed to stay open until May 1, 1918, its days were numbered.

Reformers. Politicians. Tavern keepers—large and small. The daily press. All played a part in the cabaret wars, which once the music was stripped away, was a veiled war on vice. Reformers were civic-minded groups and individuals, though, their desire to legislate morality was met head on with resistance. Politicians waffled on applying the law, lining their own pockets with graft, mostly interested in the preservation of power. Tavern keepers, naturally, wanted their establishments to thrive or, at the very least, stay in business. And while some journalists may have backed reform with sterling social consciousness, they consistently fueled the cabaret war with dramatic stories of suicide, wealthy minors on a spree, and innocent farm girls led down the primrose path with a single goal in mind—to sell newspapers.

Prohibition On The Horizon

In 1918, Dan Blanco described himself as a self-employed restauranteur, a business that would soon dramatically change across America. The challenges of dodging Chicago's reform movement would soon pale in comparison to the looming threat of a Federal war on booze. In January of 1919, the passage of the 18th Amendment to the U. S. Constitution would ban the selling and public consumption of alcohol beginning at midnight on January 17, 1920. Chicago's bars, cafés, saloons, and taverns would then be under a brand new kind of pressure to compete and survive. Soon, there would be no more pouring of complementary drinks by Dan Blanco. In fact, Chicago went dry on August 1, 1919, months before the rest of the nation. If the Grand Café wasn't already closed, the inability to legally sell liquor would further cripple business and lead to its demise.

Chicago's war on cabarets was a personal battle for Dan Blanco. Over a dozen years, he evolved from the founder of The Rathskellerians (clean cabaret-style entertainment—four men and a piano—no girls in tights), to a solo performer in cafés and vaudeville, to a partner in the Grand Café. His willingness to bend the law was evident based on the charges brought against the café's owner Ray McCloskey, who was found guilty of serving liquor to minors. Of course, they functioned like most (if not all) of the cabarets on North Clark Street—competing for business in a crowded market increasingly scrutinized by the law and city officials.

Grand Café likely had closed before September of 1918, when Dan Blanco was playing a two-night engagement in a vaudeville show at the Orpheum Theatre in Hammond, Indiana. A postcard from the era claims: "Hammond's Most Beautiful Playhouse! High-Class Vaudeville and Musical Attractions!" Surviving images of both the interior and the exterior of the playhouse support the claim; it was indeed beautiful. The quality of the attractions may have varied. During September 26–27, 1918, Blanco's act was at the bottom of the bill, just ahead of *Hands Up*, a movie serial featuring action-adventure star Ruth Roland.

Preceding Dan Blanco were: The Two Milmars, Hill's Society Circus (Ponies, Dogs, Monkeys and a Bucking Mule), George Clark & Co. (Comedy), and Ball and Sinclair (Songs and Music). Billed as a Singing Comedian, Blanco may have fallen back on a musty repertoire. A review of the program praised The Two Milmars and Hills' Society Circus. One line concerning Blanco's performance indicates he wasn't giving the act his all: "Good time to step out to the manager's office and have a chat or smoke a cigarette."[48]

Not discouraged, in January of 1919, Dan Blanco was on the road with a musical skit, "Birds of a Feather," playing a week's engagement at Indianapolis' Lyric Theater where seats sold for 10, 20 and 30 cents. Positive reviews in the *Indianapolis Star* erased Blanco's sour reception in Hammond. Described as a nautical musical comedy, Dan Blanco portrayed Capt. Kidd, who is discovered on his treasure island by members of a twelve person company. Inez Bellaire, whose dimpled cheeks and blonde curls were featured on the sheet music for "The Girl You Can't Forget" (1916), played the ingénue and the act was said to be one of the costliest then touring the vaudeville circuits. The costumes and scenery were particularly lavish and Blanco was called "a funmaker well known to devotees of musical farce." One review noted that Blanco's "piratical mustaches" and Bellaire's "graceful dancing" were received with "hearty and impartial applause." Business was looking up![49]

By January of 1920, Dan Blanco was living in central Chicago, sharing a house with fellow Rathskellerian Slayter Brockman, his widowed mother and her family. On the national census, Blanco gave his occupation as songwriter, disassociating himself, at least for the immediate future, from the world of saloons, cabarets, and restaurants. During the early 1910s, his original tunes written for the Rathskellerians were "song hits" and he may indeed have been writing music and lyrics that sold.

One of his songs became the subject of a copyright infringement suit. In 1923, contralto Emma Carus (1879–1927), filed an injunction against Redline Publishing Company of Mitchell, South Dakota and H. Pres Porter, author of "Has Anybody Seen My Kitty, Come Pussy, Pussy, Pussy" (1922). Mrs. Carus, an alumna of the Zigfeld's *Follies* and popularizer of Irving Berlin's "Alexander's Ragtime Band," claimed that Porter's tune infringed on Dan Blanco's "Has Anybody Seen My Cat" (1916). Sheet music for the tune calls it "Emma Carus' Big Song Hit" and credits her, Dan Blanco, and Walter Leopold as the songwriters. Newspaper reports of the suit described Blanco as a "Spanish music composer of Chicago." A reporter for Sioux Falls' *Argus-Leader* mentioned that the clerk had filed sample copies which were strikingly similar.

For about three years, Dan Blanco's name fell out of the popular press. Then, in early 1923, he was performing at The New Drexel Café, located at 39th and Cottage Grove, touted to be "Chicago's Newest and Finest Pleasure Spot." Advertisements encouraged readers to dine and dance to the impelling syncopated music of Randolph's Famous Drexel Orchestra. A fixed menu was priced at $1.00, raised to $1.50 on Sundays. With a capacity for 1,000 diners and dancers, the Drexel also offered entertainment. Dan Blanco was featured with six other acts.[50]

His association with the Drexel Café may have been brief, for before March of 1923, Albert "Papa" Bouche, a well-established Chicago restauranteur, presented Blanco with a plum opportunity, offering to put him in charge of entertainment at Bouche's newest restaurant in the Loop District, a top drawer establishment—Moulin Rouge Café.

CHAPTER THREE

Albert Bouche's Moulin Rouge Café

In October of 1921, Albert "Papa" Bouche, former proprietor of the highly successful summer resort Moulin Rouge Gardens (4812-36 North Clark Street) and a recently established summer-only café called House That Jack Built (located on the Milwaukee Road), announced plans to open a new Moulin Rouge Café and restaurant at 416 South Wabash Avenue. Bouche claimed it would be the most luxurious restaurant in Chicago's Loop. Located at the site of the former Mandarin Inn, the building would be completely remodeled and lavishly redecorated at an impressive cost of $30,000. The interior would be plush—rose-colored velvet covering the walls, with accents of gold and ivory. The menu would feature French and Italian cuisine. Bouche, confident in his new project (despite Prohibition), took out a five-year lease, costing him $16,000 annually.

Bouche's advertisements announced—in superlative style typical of the day—that Moulin Rouge Café was poised to become "The Leading Café and Restaurant in Chicago." Spaghetti and Ravioli were the house specialties. In the long run, cuisine was not the draw. Dance bands and cabaret talent would attract the crowds.

The restaurant opened on December 2, 1921, in plenty of time to take advantage of the New Year's Eve rush. Bouche ran combined advertisements for House That Jack Built and Moulin Rouge Café, wishing his customers a "Merry Xmas and a Happy New Year." And, in January of 1922, *Variety* gave the new venue a positive review:

> The Moulin Rouge Café, Chicago, is the latest restaurant to be turned into a cabaret. Albert Bouche manages it....The new café is a novelty. The color scheme is red, and is offset with a low and colored lighting scheme. The place has a soothing air about it. The main floor has a dance floor as

well as the balcony. Two orchestras supply the music; in the early part of the evening a four-piece band entertains, and the better part of the time Jack Sharpe's eight-piece band offers the syncopation.[51]

This new Moulin Rouge Café would be a class act. The only thing cramping its style was the national prohibition of intoxicating beverages. The café offered its clientele appetizing food in a pleasant atmosphere. More restaurant than cabaret, Bouche presented a smattering of good talent, along with dance music. He could not, however, legally sell his patrons liquor. Like many establishments in Chicago, the staff at the Moulin Rouge Café looked the other way when customers arrived with a hip flask or a discreetly concealed bottle. They likely sold set ups—chipped ice and ginger ale—at stiff prices. If so, they did at increasingly high risk as attempts to clean up Chicago's Loop grew more frequent.

From the inception of his newest venture, Bouche was targeted by Chief of Police Fitzmorris, who protested the opening of the cabaret and restaurant. Rather than look for a violation of the National Prohibition Act (commonly called the Volstead Act) to shutter the café, Fitzmorris attempted to enforce the 1 o'clock closing ordinance. Moulin Rouge manager, Nick Sebastian, immediately pushed back, asking for an injunction to stop the police from harassing him.

By early February 1922, there was a case pending against Bouche. Chief Fitzmorris' campaign, however, met with resistance from the city's First Assistant Corporation Counsel, James W. Breen, whose opinion read, in part:

> If you suspect that the said Albert Bouche is engaging in the illegal sale of intoxicating liquor, it is your duty to diligently investigate and secure evidence of the same, and this you can do by having investigators enter his place of business and endeavor to purchase intoxicating liquors.
>
> If successful in purchasing the same, the most effective way for you to permanently abate the unlawful sale of intoxicating liquors by the said Bouche is for you to obtain a search warrant, together with a warrant for the arrest of Bouche.
>
> The search warrant will authorize you to enter the premises of the said Bouche and seize all intoxicating liquors found therein.[52]

With or without search warrants, city-wide raids were frequent and the Loop was constantly on the police radar. Moulin Rouge Café would be no exception. In June of 1922, Albert Bouche's establishment and seven other nightspots throughout the city were placed under a federal injunction for the sale of liquor. If these restraining orders were violated, the proprietors were liable for a fine of $10,000 and a one-year sentence in the penitentiary.

Under this order, the management at the Moulin Rouge needed to build a dry reputation. Bouche struggled to compete with clubs that allowed customers to pour their own booze and promoted his restaurant as a refined establishment. In January of 1923, he ran an advertisement appealing to high tone types with a sense of humor:

> **Moulin Rouge**
> **Café**
> **and Restaurant**
> **416 So. Wabash**
> Where class meets class.
> Where cabaret artists are classic.
> Service with class.
> Surroundings with class.
> Management with class.
> Cuisine with class.
> Dinner with class.
> 7:15 show with class.
> Dance music with class.
> Vaudeville acts with class.
> Everything with class.
> What a classy place!
> Come and meet the class at the
> **Moulin Rouge**
> **Café**

Inevitably, liquor found its way into the Moulin Rouge Café. In early 1923, Albert Bouche was one of sixty-five owners of Chicago summer gardens, cafés, restaurants, and clubs charged with infractions of the Volstead Act. All of the cases were based on evidence gathered the previous summer by ace prohibition agent William D. "Count" Yaselli. His covert methods struck fear in owners of taverns throughout Chicago and in the surrounding roadhouse zone, which included Bouche's House That Jack Built. Ironically, Yaselli proved indiscreet when it came to liquor and found himself entrapped by "girl detective" Miss Betty Johnson. Yaselli and Johnson were caught with a pint of booze under their table at a North Side restaurant. Yaselli claimed the liquor was planted. Washington D. C. officials were not convinced and Yaselli was dismissed as a prohibition agent. The charges were dropped against the Chicago sixty-five, though the truce between the law and some of the city's nightlife impresarios proved to be temporary.

Dan Blanco: Stage Manager

Moulin Rouge's year-long restraining order was nearly over when Albert Bouche beefed up his entertainment, advertising stellar talent under the direction of his new stage manager—Dan Blanco. During March of 1923, Bouche ran a series of advertisements touting Blanco's work, announcing: "This is the first time that musical comedy has been presented in an eating place." Technically, this was not the first time Bouche had attempted to introduce dining plus cabaret to Chicago. In 1917, he opened his first Moulin Rouge—a summer garden resort at Clark Street and Lawrence Avenue—modeled after the famous Parisian home of gaiety. Manager and cuisine supervisor, Albert Bouche claimed to be a former chef of the Parisian Moulin Rouge. (This biographical detail was likely a complete fabrication and not believed even in 1917.) Within six months, Moulin Rouge Gardens managed to violate the Sunday liquor laws and in short order closed its doors. By September of 1918, the property was renamed Rainbo Gardens and the new owner Fred Mann was applying for a dry cabaret license.[53]

Now, partnered with cabaret expert Dan Blanco, Bouche had high hopes for the new Moulin Rouge Café. Early in March of 1923, the restaurant's musical comedy featured seventeen artists, including Baroness Olga Baklanoff who performed the Tut Ankh Amen dance, the latest sensation from Paris, Vienna, and New York, never before seen in a Chicago café. The entertainment included an Apache dance and Fannie Albright, a "brilliant" South Sea Island dancer.

Chef Mozzie, discovered by Bouche, prepared only the finest food, properly flavored. Dinner was served from 6:30 to 9:00 p.m. The first show began at 7:15 p.m., with a second show starting at midnight. Vaudeville acts filled in between and there was dancing until nearly dawn. By March 29, the program had changed and Dan Blanco, Stage Manager, engaged six new vaudeville acts to supplement the "Moulin Rouge Musical Comedy," including a return engagement of Olive Hill.

Unfortunately, Dan Blanco's deservedly prestigious position at the swanky Moulin Rouge Café would be short-lived. On April 11, 1923, several minor raids had been made during the day, including the arrest of the manager and a waiter at the Moulin Rouge by a police squad led by John E. Earley.

Within days, *Variety* noted that the United States attorney sought an injunction to close the Moulin Rouge. Were its violations of the Volstead Act really so egregious? Or, had the café become a magnet for underworld activity?

Other news depicted the café as a potentially dangerous place to dine and relax. While these stories might attract some thrill-seeking customers, they could just as easily repulse the toney diners Bouche desired. Months later, he would claim that during this period he received death threats if he refused to meet blackmail demands. Moulin Rouge Café, like other Loop nightclubs, lay in territory controlled by the criminal organization known as the Chicago Outfit. Johnny Torrio and his partner, Alphonso "Al" Capone, provided the liquor that was bought and sold in this part of the city. Was Bouche not buying enough liquor for his dry café?

On April 30, a disturbing incident took place in the back rooms of the Moulin Rouge, which put Miss Silvia Chaulsea, a dancer at the restaurant, in St. Luke's Hospital with a severe bullet wound. Police investigated. Witnesses said the shooting was an accident. Manager Nick Sebastian proved to be the owner of the gun that fired the shot. Sebastian offered the police an incredible story, claiming that Miss Chaulsea came into his office looking for a silk neck scarf. Accommodating her, he opened his safe, found the scarf wrapped around his revolver, and, as Sebastian unwrapped the gun, it accidently discharged. The police had some burning questions. How did the scarf get into the safe? Why was it wrapped around Sebastian's revolver? And, perhaps, most importantly, why had Sebastian not reported the shooting?

Reform Mayor William Emmett Dever and his Chief of Police were on the war path and, by May of 1923, newspapers printed rumors that Moulin Rouge Café might voluntarily close its doors. At this juncture, underworld characters were not Bouche's sole concern. On June 12, 1923, Judge Adam C. Cliffe officially closed the café with a federal injunction for violation of the Volstead Act. An undercover prohibition agent, Al Johnson, had joined the restaurant's orchestra, easily obtaining the necessary evidence that liquor was being consumed (though not sold) at the restaurant. This time there was no grace period for the café, the padlock went on the door for a year and Dan Blanco was once again looking for a job.

Someone in Chicago was making a nice living selling padlocks.

CHAPTER FOUR

Northern Lights: Shootout At The Roadhouse

It wasn't long before Dan Blanco was hired at a new roadhouse, Northern Lights, located barely within the city limits at 6342 North Broadway. When the club opened in December of 1923, it was touted as "Chicago's Coziest Café," despite a seating capacity for 400. Preparing for its initial New Year's Eve celebration, manager Al Von Albert presented a prima donna singer, a premiere danseuse, a tenor, and Hutton's Dixie Orchestra. Like the urbane Moulin Rouge Café, Northern Lights featured French and Italian cuisine. Dinner was priced at $1.25, slightly undercutting the former Moulin Rouge menu set at $1.50.

In June of 1924, Northern Lights advertised "Dancing & Entertainment, As Only DAN BLANCO Can Dispense." Entertainers were not mentioned in the advertisement, however, song titles were, indicating that popular music was a strong draw, along with Dan Blanco's showmanship. Readers of the advertisement were asked to request such "Big Song Hits" as: "You'll Always Be the Same Sweet Baby," "Underneath the Stars," "Pretty Baby," "Way Down Honolulu Way," and "They Didn't Believe Me" by Jerome Kern. Dan Blanco was back on top in the world of dining, dancing, and cabaret.

New Moulin Rouge: Bomb Threat

Simultaneously, the Moulin Rouge was about to reopen at 416 South Wabash, without Dan Blanco's talents as stage manager and, apparently, without Albert Bouche as proprietor. During the year the restaurant was padlocked, Bouche told *Tribune* reporters that he had sold it to his former assistant manager, Jack Spangler. In the spring of 1924, Bouche had decided to transform his House That Jack Built into Villa Venice—reconceiving the road house on Milwaukee Avenue. He planned to spend $25,000 remodeling the building and an additional $15,000 on the grounds—an expensive proposition. It was rumored in the local newspapers that the Moulin Rouge Café was being remodeled as well. By whom? Bouche or Spangler, or someone else behind the scenes, out of the public eye?

The injunction which closed the cabaret expired on Wednesday, June 11, 1924. Talent and staff were hired. A new show went into rehearsal. Meanwhile, someone, some group, or some organization was determined to at least slow down the christening of the "new" Moulin Rouge Café.

On Monday, June 16th, at about 4:00 p.m., Richard Dillon, an African-American porter employed by Richards Furniture at 410 South Wabash, noticed two men loitering near the café entrance. Suddenly, a bomb exploded just inside the front door at no. 416. Nearby businesses and cafés on Van Buren and Wabash shook with the blast, including a Fanny May candy store. Windows broke. China and glassware shattered in the dining room of the New Richmond hotel, situated above the Moulin Rouge. Employees and hotel guests evacuated to the street, unsure what might happen next.

Headwaiter Harry McKelvey was standing a few feet from the front doorway when the bomb exploded in the café's entryway. He was knocked unconscious and early reports suggested that he might lose his sight or even die from his wounds. Minutes before, McKelvey had summoned electrician Rollin Williams to fix some fuses near the front of the building. Luckily, Williams was only grazed by flying glass.[54]

The new floor show was in rehearsal at the time of the explosion. Most of the performers, some thirty men and women, were standing near the stage in the rear of the restaurant. With the exception of McKelvey, the majority present were saved from serious injury, though a few may have been superficially cut by glass. Needless to say, in Chicago, the story was front page news. The *Evening News*, published in faraway Harrisburg, Pennsylvania, printed a thrilling version of the incident, sent to the newspaper "hot" from Chicago.

The headline read: "Bomb Exploding In Chicago Café Stops Jazzers." The article oozed with tabloid-style prose.... "While the tom-toms pulsed, the jazz whistles shrieked, the saxophone emitted yearning notes and the trombone registered amazing flights up and down the scale, a black powder bomb went off late yesterday in the Moulin Rouge Café...."

The article conjured a "bevy of beauties" surrounded in "clouds of smoke and talcum powder dust." Dramatically, the "colored" orchestra stopped playing and a frightened drummer stepped through his instrument. Harry McKelvey, Maître de Hotel attempted to reach the bomb before it exploded. "Not being a ten-second man," the reporter observed, "his spring was poorly timed as he found himself enveloped in a flare of fire and smoke." Burned on the face and shoulders, McKelvey was taken to St. Luke's Hospital. The vestibule and twenty boxes of cigars were also caught in the blaze. The vestibule would be repaired. The cigars were trashed.

Cynical about the work habits of Chicago's finest, the article continued, "Several squads of firemen and all the policemen who were not busy visiting friends in soft drink parlors, cigar stands and movie shows in the neighborhood rushed to the place." On a more serious note, the reporter commented that an argument with a labor union might have resulted in the bombing.[55]

Immediate reports noted that Albert Bouche was present at the time of the blast and that he suggested to journalists that the bomb had been special ordered by other café proprietors in the neighborhood who objected to the reopening. An article circulated by the Universal Service, quoted the owner and manager of the Moulin Rouge Café, identified as "John Bouchet," saying that Bouchet told authorities: "I had some electrical work done by a union faction that is at odds with another union organization. I have been warned the place would be blown up." Who actually gave the statement to the police? Albert Bouche? Jack Spangler? Was Bouche sometimes called "Jack" or "John"? After all, he created the House That Jack Built.[56]

◆ ◆ ◆

All across Chicago, restaurant, café, and cabaret proprietors paid high prices to the city's crime bosses for protection against bombs coming through their plate glass windows. It was widely known that Chicago gangsters had infiltrated union operations. Was the electricians' union one of them and did the current owner of the Moulin Rouge Café pick the "wrong" union? Or was Bouche and/or Spangler trying to operate outside the gangster-connected sphere of construction? Was the bomb meant for Bouche himself, who months earlier had not submitted to blackmail? Perhaps, Bouche's initial reference to other club owners was a red herring, designed to direct attention away from a criminal connection to the bombing. Whatever the intent of this extremely unfriendly calling card, a tense atmosphere engulfed the reopening of the Moulin Rouge. In time, the establishment recovered. Anticipating New Year's Eve 1924/1925, the café prepared to entertain 1,500 guests in Chicago's festive Loop.

Northern Lights: A Gangster-friendly Roadhouse

Dan Blanco must have been relieved to be miles away from the Loop, focusing on entertainment at Northern Lights. Once again, however, calm was short-lived in gangster-ridden Chicago. Open just a few months, Northern Lights already had a reputation for a tough atmosphere. Police at the local Summerdale Station received numerous disturbance complaints. The owner, Andy Craig, was a familiar figure in Chicago's old red light district, the notorious saloonkeeper of Village Inn on South State Street, and the one-time political lieutenant of gangster-friendly Michael "Hinky Dink" Kenna, former First Ward Alderman. It was Dan Blanco, however, who held the cabaret license for the Northern Lights.

As the summer of 1924 progressed, August was filled with thunder storms and hot, muggy days, fueling smoldering tempers. Outside the oppressive city, the suburban roadhouses attracted a wide variety of pleasure seekers. It was 2:00 a.m. on the morning of August 27 when violence exploded at Northern Lights. Johnny Phillips, known criminal and habitué of north side cabarets, was shot and killed on the sidewalk in front of the establishment. Earlier, Phillips and three or four others had arrived at the roadhouse in a Cadillac touring car.

Flashing a diamond ring valued at $4,500, Johnny Phillips was a classic punk, with a police record for burglary. Far from handsome, his protruding ears gave him a comical look. One of his companions was believed to be either Louis Alterie or his cousin, Thomas Alterie, both alleged beer runners connected to bootlegger Dion O'Banion's mob, which controlled the flow of liquor on Chicago's North Side. Intoxicated, the group was boisterous and demanding when they joined owner Andy Craig and manager Dan Blanco in a back room.

The serious trouble started when Phillips slapped one of the café's entertainers, Dorothy Kester, who rebuffed his advances. Kester's youth was accentuated by her girlish Dutch bob and doe-like eyes. While she may not have been an innocent victim, she fully looked the part when her photo appeared in the back page gallery of the *Chicago Daily Tribune*.[57]

A riot call went out to nearby Summerdale Station. Two police officers went into the club to investigate. A third, Officer Frank Sobel, remained outside. When the policemen began to question Phillips, the thugs pulled their guns and headed for their touring car, using the law men as a shield. The attempt to kidnap the two policemen failed when Sobel shot Phillips three times in the head. Phillips' companions fired at Sobel, who lost part of a finger when a bullet grazed him. The gunmen quickly dispersed, leaving their Cadillac behind on the now crowded street. When photographers arrived, Johnny Phillips lay face up on the concrete and the majority of the several dozen onlookers glared at the camera rather than the corpse. By then, Phillips' death was old news.

An unflattering report in the *Tribune* stated that Andy Craig and Dan Blanco watched as Phillips insulted Miss Kester and applauded loudly when he fired several shots into the café ceiling, intimidating patrons who might interfere with his "fun." During the confusion of the altercation and aftermath, owner and manager conveniently disappeared.

Indeed, Craig and Blanco may have enjoyed themselves at Dorothy Kester's expense, at least up to the point when the police walked in. Generally speaking, riots were not good for business, nor were gangland shootouts. The next day, Capt. Martin O'Malley of Summerdale Station recommended that the license for Northern Lights be revoked by Chicago's Mayor William Emmett Dever.

The investigation which followed the shooting of Johnny Phillips revealed extensive violations of the Volstead Act at the roadhouse, which led Federal Judge James H. Wilkerson to forego the usual temporary injunction like the one placed on Moulin Rouge the year before. On September 6, the judge issued a permanent injunction, closing Northern Lights. As an added precaution, he ordered Chief Deputy Marshal Sam Howard to seal the place, making sure the café did not enjoy its usual weekend business before the order was executed.

While Andy Craig, Dan Blanco, Dorothy Kester, and Louis Alterie anticipated summons for a court date, Blanco announced his willingness (perhaps eagerness) to get out of his lease for the Northern Lights' building, which had four years to run. Chances were good that the roadhouse would not reopen following the investigation, leaving him responsible for a costly commitment. In late September, a surprising offer was announced, deepening civic tension over the Northern Lights' property. An unnamed group might assume the lease at the modest rent of $400 per month for a proposed boarding school for African-American girls, doubling as a "colored" church on Sundays. In response to this news, locals, including the Loyola Sheridan Business Association, sprang into action to stop this transfer of the lease, fearing a negative effect on real estate values. Apparently, the offer was dropped or was never actually made. Just how Dan Blanco was released from the lease is unknown.

◆ ◆ ◆

The cooler temperatures of autumn did not slow down Chicago's gangsters. On November 10, the murder of Dion O'Banion, the North Side rival of Johnny Torrio and Al Capone, became national news. The result was a war on crime. Authorities recruited fearless detectives. Forty-two highway police were told to make the drinking and gambling palaces surrounding Chicago think an earthquake had hit them. Nightly raids kept policemen busy and jails full.

Coincidentally, there was a link between O'Banion's murder and the shooting at Northern Lights—Louis Alterie, O'Banion's top lieutenant and confident. Superior Court Judge Joseph B. David was furious when he discovered that Alterie was connected with the death of Johnny Phillips, stating: "Three gunmen kidnap and try to kill two policemen, and because one of the gunmen, instead of the brave police officers, was killed, for some mysterious reason no one is prosecuted. Here is the place for Mayor Dever to begin his war against gangsters. Let him dig into this rottenness!"[58]

Incensed that Louis Alterie was at large, Judge David called his escape "a woeful miscarriage of justice," ordering the gangster's arrest and insisting that the investigation of the gun battle at the Northern Lights be reopened.[59] He vehemently denied the charge of rubber stamp judges saying, "Alterie is the man who said he would shoot things out with the slayer of Dion O'Banion. Perhaps he'll be allowed to shoot things out in the penitentiary."[60]

During the red hot investigation of O'Banion's murder, a writ was presented to Judge David requesting that Mayor William Emmett Dever issue a new café license to Daniel Leblang, alias Dan Blanco. "Bring them all in next Saturday," the judge commanded. This included Blanco and Andy Craig, whom Judge David believed might know the whereabouts of Louis Alterie. Addressing the Assistant Corporation Counselor for the City of Chicago, Joseph J. Thompson, the judge continued, "If you, Mr. Thompson, can prove your charge that Leblang is an intimate of gunmen, that his cabaret is a hangout for notorious denizens of the criminal world, he will not get a license in this court."[61]

The judge's orders failed to produce most of the individuals concerned with the Northern Lights' shooting. Louis Alterie had fled Chicago. Neither Andy Craig nor Miss Kester could be located. A conservatively dressed (complete with bow tie), bespectacled Dan Blanco appeared in court but refused to talk on advice of his attorney. Whether Blanco was innocent or guilty of intimate dealings with gangsters, Judge David decided that Counselor Joseph J. Thompson had failed to present sufficient evidence to substantiate the charge. The judge issued a writ of *mandamus* directing Mayor Dever to issue Daniel Leblang his cabaret license. The judge also took the opportunity to admonish the state's attorney's office for its failure to indict Louis Alterie in connection with the incident at the Northern Lights.

Judge David called Dan Blanco's case a farce. In his opinion, a man couldn't be blamed for a crime committed in the street in front of his establishment. The judge noted: "Leblang further is charged with conducting an immoral resort. The city proved that women entertainers went among the patrons, singing to them and chucking them under the chin. That is no crime. Mayor Dever attended a banquet at which women singers came into the audience. He ordered nobody arrested. The city can't discriminate."[62]

Dan Blanco was cleared. Contrasted with 1917, now cabaret-style entertainment was not tantamount to vice, however, Blanco's career at the Northern Lights had come to an end.[63]

♦ ♦ ♦

The Moulin Rouge Café was once again operating at full capacity, prepared to entertain 1,500 patrons celebrating New Year's Eve 1924/1925. Chicago's underworld was as busy as ever. The *Chicago Daily Tribune* ran articles with headlines like "Guns Edit Gangland's Who's Who," featuring a checklist of men "In Cemeteries" and those "In Jails." Dion O'Banion, leader of the North Side Gang, and George Morgan, alias Johnny Phillips, were both six feet under. Bootlegger John Torrio, Al Capone's mentor and head of the criminal empire the Chicago Outfit, which controlled the Loop and much of the South Side, was behind bars, along with other less familiar names. Louis Alterie was neither dead nor imprisoned, but "temporarily unclassified," continuing to frustrate the law and elude justice.[64]

During 1925, impresario Albert Bouche expanded his sphere, trying his luck with a liquorless café in Manhattan, Café Bal Masque, located at the corner of Broadway and 44th Street. He spent a small fortune on entertainment and decoration. The food was outstanding. The couvert charge low. The no-drinks rule strictly enforced. Advertised as "The Most Beautiful and Unique Café-Restaurant in America," Bouche offered the "Biggest and Best Broadway Show ever presented in any Broadway Restaurant."

Bouche promoted the new venue with gusto and linked it to his Villa Venice in Chicago. In November, he moved his Chicago production to Manhattan, reminding potential patrons, "The Bal Masque is not a supper club, but is the only Theatre Café Restaurant in America. If you do not visit this famous place you do not see New York."[65]

Despite the novelty of dinner theater, Bal Masque failed. Both New Yorkers and tourists wanted booze with their dinner and their entertainment. By December, Bouche gave up on the enterprise, focusing on properties in Chicago. Having abandoned Moulin Rouge, he purchased Little Club Café at 151 East Chicago Avenue. In January of 1925, he ran an eye-catching advertisement for his newest venture—"The Persian Room" at Little Club Café—describing it as "One of the most beautiful rooms in the country! The only café decorated in Persian style. Colors and lighting effects unsurpassed." Clearly, Bouche placed a high value on the atmosphere.

The intimate room sat 200 persons and the kitchen was under the supervision of Bouche's discovery, Chef Mozzi. In the restaurant business, retaining a popular chef was a key to success. Again, Bouche offered Chicagoans a Theater Restaurant, competing with his former establishment, Moulin Rouge. The Persian Room's Table d'Hotel Dinner was priced at $2.00. Top talent, of course, was equally crucial. Bouche had sold "class" at his Moulin Rouge Café and now invited Chicago's smart set to The Persian Room. Comedian Sir Harry Glynn, who had worked for Bouche at the Bal Masque, acted as the cabaret's Master of Ceremonies. Specialty numbers filled in between shows. Concurrently, Bouche's Villa Venice flourished, despite a run-in with the law over an illegal roulette wheel.

Bouche's competition would be stiff. William R. "Bill" Rothstein, proprietor of the "new" Moulin Rouge, soon had his eye on Dan Blanco.

Dan Blanco and His Four Rathskellerians, 1913. (AUTHOR COLLECTION)

White City. (AUTHOR COLLECTION)

White City at night. (AUTHOR COLLECTION)

On May 27, 1905, White City opened in the center of Chicago. Founded by Hungarian immigrant Morris Beifeld and touted as "Chicago's Brightest Spot" and the "World's Finest Amusement Resort," the $1,000,000 amusement park was the city's answer to New York's Coney Island. Its Rathskeller was a perfect venue for Dan Blanco and his troupe.

Dan Blanco, 1913. (AUTHOR COLLECTION)

"King of the Mafia," by Dan Blanco. 1910. (Author Collection)

"Has Anybody Seen My Cat," by Dan Blanco ©1916, copyright Emma Carus, 1922. (Author Collection)

Moulin Rouge Café Advertisement, 1921.
(AUTHOR COLLECTION)

Mandarin Inn, 414-416 South Wabash Avenue. Chicago, Illinois.
(AUTHOR COLLECTION)

In 1921, entertainment entrepreneur Albert Bouche spent a reported $30,000 transforming the Mandarin Inn into a high-class cabaret and restaurant, the Moulin Rouge Café. Located in Chicago's Loop District, the new establishment would feature French and Italian cuisine.

Karyl Norman, c. 1922. (AUTHOR COLLECTION)

The extraordinarily popular female impersonator Karyl Norman, known as "The Creole Fashion Plate," typically appeared in vaudeville. In 1926, Norman was billed as "Vaudeville's Highest Priced Star," when he graced the stage at Bill Rothstein's Moulin Rouge Café. Rothstein advertised his intimate cabaret show as … "The Most Talked About Revue In Chicago."

Mike & Ike. (Author Collection)

Popular twin midgets "Mike & Ike," were born Bela (Mike) and Matyus (Ike) Matina. In 1926, they worked at Bill Rothstein's Moulin Rouge Café alongside Evelyn Nesbit.

Northern Lights Cafe

6342 N. Broadway
Near Devon

The Road House Beautiful
Within the City Limits

Unexcelled French - Italian
Table d'Hote Dinner $1.25
6:00 to 9:00 P. M.
No Cover Charge During Dinner

Dancing & Entertainment
As Only DAN BLANCO
Can Dispense

Ask Us to Sing These Big Song Hits:
"You'll Always Be the Same Sweet Baby," "Underneath the Stars," "Pretty Baby," "They Didn't Believe Me," "Way Down Honolulu Way."

Northern Lights Advertisement, c. 1924. (AUTHOR COLLECTION)

"A Bud." Evelyn Nesbit, 1901.
(Photo by Otto Sarony. Courtesy Library of Congress)

Following her father's death, Evelyn Nesbit, her mother, and her younger brother, Howard, moved from Pennsylvania to New York City. By 1900, Nesbit was supporting her family, modeling for respected artists. Beautiful and cooperative, she quickly became a favorite of photographers, appearing in a wide variety of periodicals from the old-fashioned <u>Police Gazette</u> to the up-to-date <u>Collier's Weekly</u>, posing for Charles Dana Gibson's famous sketch, "Woman: The Eternal Question." A Gilded Age celebrity, postcards of her lovely face and figure flooded the market. Her talents extended to the legitimate stage, where she performed as a specialty dancer and was admired by wealthy men, including the influential architect, Stanford White. Following a protracted affair with White, Nesbit married millionaire Harry K. Thaw in 1905.

Evelyn Nesbit and son, Russell W. Thaw, 1913.
(PHOTO BY ARNOLD GENTHE. COURTESY LIBRARY OF CONGRESS)

In 1913, German-born photographer Arnold Genthe (1869–1942) captured a wistful Evelyn Nesbit with her young son, Russell W. Thaw. In 1917, mother and son appeared in the silent film "Redemption," presented by Viennese actor-director-producer Julius Steger.

Murderer Harry K. Thaw was spared execution, many believed due to Evelyn Nesbit's candid testimony concerning her adolescent love affair with Stanford White, who after giving her alcohol, raped her. Thaw was committed to Matteawan State Hospital for the Criminally Insane in Beacon, New York. The couple remained married and were permitted conjugal visits. According to Nesbit, her son, Russell William Thaw, was conceived during one of these trips to Matteawan. Russell was born in Germany on October 25, 1910. Harry Thaw never acknowledged the boy as his son and provided only spotty financial support for Nesbit, though she received a lump sum from the Thaw family at the conclusion of the trials. The couple was divorced in 1915 and, the following year, Nesbit married her dance partner, Jack Clifford.

Evelyn Nesbit's Specialty Food Shop, 1921.
(Photo by Underwood & Underwood Photographers. Courtesy Library of Congress)

Evelyn Nesbit and Russell W. Thaw, 1923.
(Photo by Underwood & Underwood Photographers. Courtesy Billy Rose Theatre Collection, The New York Public Library for the Performing Arts)

In 1923, Evelyn Nesbit, son Russell W. Thaw, and three of Nesbit's Belgian Griffons posed for the camera while taking a chariot ride on Atlantic City's Boardwalk. Beginning in the 1920s, Nesbit was one of Atlantic City's most celebrated citizens.

Ed Lowry, c. 1925. (AUTHOR COLLECTION)

In 1925, singer and monologist Ed Lowry went to work for Bill Rothstein at the Moulin Rouge Café. Enhancing a successful career in vaudeville, Lowry added cabaret work to his resume, working for Rothstein until the café was padlocked in early 1927.

Edward C. Yellowley, 1937. (Author Collection)

In September of 1925, Edward C. Yellowley arrived in Chicago, taking over as Prohibition Administrator. The greatly feared "still smasher" died in 1964, at the advanced age of eighty-eight.

CHAPTER FIVE

Dan Blanco, Evelyn Nesbit & Bill Rothstein's Moulin Rouge

Sometime during 1924, William R. "Bill" Rothstein took over as the proprietor of the renewed Moulin Rouge—"Chicago's Playground of Beauty." Located in the Loop near the theater district, the café gained a reputation as a hangout for show folk. Known as "a sweet guy," Rothstein was a cordial proprietor, who warmly welcomed his patrons and was sorry to see them leave. In the world of cabaret, a genial personality was definitely a business asset.

In early 1925, advertisements in *Variety* announced Moulin Rouge's "entire new ownership," prominently displaying "William R. Rothstein Presents," with Bernard Franklin as his manager. The New Year's entertainment opened with Ernie Young's "Winter Frolics of 1925," featuring five revue-style shows nightly. "Eddie Richmond and His Moulin Rouge Orchestra," entertained patrons and dancers between performances. Dinner was a deal. A "Roman Banquet" priced at only $1.50.

Variety was positive about the show, singling out showgirls Beth Miller and Margo Raffaro as "two bright shining stars" in Young's Winter Frolics: "Miss Miller, a striking brunette and brimful of personality, new to Chicago night life sector from New York. She sings, dances and does some astonishing splits. Miss Raffaro, who makes her appearance with Pat Conway and his Ten Girls, is a dancer of vim and verve. She is one of the speediest in cabaret. In the course of her act, she does some excellent high kicks."[66]

Ernie Young was a somewhat shady, though popular, producer in Chicago's theater world. A broker, booking agent, ticket scalper, and tax dodger, in 1922, Young was rising to fame as an impresario of beauty. That year, he was the talent behind a richly costumed, flashy pageant entitled "Arabian Nights." The following year, he would be charged with perjury. He made a name for himself at the North Side café Marigold Gardens. By 1925, Young managed Picture Theaters Attraction Company, specializing in booking acts in movie houses—anything from a singer to a fifty person revue. No doubt, Young could quickly fill a bill for any club in Chicago. Bill Rothstein must have liked the package that Young put together in "Winter Frolics" and featured it at the Moulin Rouge through February of 1925.[67]

In addition to manager Bernard Franklin and showman Eddie Young, Bill Rothstein had a shadowy financial partner named Frankel who was seldom seen at the nightclub. On a day-to-day basis, Rothstein relied on his gray-haired maître d'hotel, Harry "Mack" McKelvey, the headwaiter who was knocked unconscious when the bomb went off during the Moulin Rouge renovations in June of 1924. McKelvey kept order among the waiters and made sure his guests were properly served. A man named Leo doubled as Rothstein's bouncer and liquor procurer. Importantly, in case of a raid, liquor was never stored on the premises. When a fresh supply was required, Leo would slip out the back door and quickly reappear with more illegal booze. The cache may have been stashed next door in a Chinese laundry.

Typical of cabarets throughout the city, Moulin Rouge supplemented its showgirls with hostesses who worked on commission, paid by the number of drinks they sold to customers seeking company. The young women drank tea or ginger ale while their companions were served liquor and were charged for two cocktails instead of one. In theory, hostesses consumed only nonalcoholic beverages, though frequently they ended the evening as inebriated as the paying customers.

From time to time, all cabaret shows need refreshing. The entertainment at Moulin Rouge was no exception. After a couple of months, "Winter Frolics" was wearing thin and the coming of Spring would also make the program obsolete. In early March, Ernie Young presented a new show entitled "Parisian Nights," appropriate to a café named after the famous French cabaret, if rather obvious. By mid-April, the revue had grown stale and Young opened two other shows in town, one at the Pershing Palace and one at the Rendezvous, where his picture, housed in a large frame, was featured outside the club. The show at the Rendezvous was another predictable, flashy Ernie Young revue with ten choristers, some of whom contributed specialty numbers. These revues were particularly well-suited to the hotter months to come, and would grace the stages of the summer garden venues on the outskirts of Chicago. Bill Rothstein was in search of something different, something less generic, more exciting, for his next offering.

In April, Moulin Rouge's manager Bernard A. Franklin advertised in *Variety*, informing readers that the club was on the lookout for top talent: "Can Use Good Sister Teams—Blues Singers and A-1 Dancing Acts at All Times." Though not mentioned in the papers, the café was also in need of a new producer of entertainment to replace Eddie Young. Someone with taste and fresh ideas. Someone like Dan Blanco.

Blanco's Back And Rothstein's Got Him

When Blanco received his new cabaret license in late 1924/early 1925, where did he turn for employment? The Northern Lights was padlocked. His former stage, Moulin Rouge, had reopened and was now owned by Bill Rothstein, who wanted something more than another Eddie Young revue.[68]

In May of 1925, Rothstein dumped the revue, switching to a star booking. The change reflects the Dan Blanco touch. In a sensational move, the Moulin Rouge announced the Chicago comeback of the scandal-tainted showgirl and vaudevillian Evelyn Nesbit.[69]

In May of 1925, Evelyn Nesbit's forthcoming appearance at the Moulin Rouge was national news. Almost twenty years earlier, Nesbit was the catalysis behind "the crime of the century"—the murder of architect Stanford White by her then husband, Harry K. Thaw. Reviews of her 1925 cabaret show claim that, despite her advancing age, at forty she maintained her youthful beauty. Her famous Gibson Girl curls had long been bobbed, adding to her pert appearance. Wearing striking black and white gowns, Nesbit no longer danced professionally. Instead, songs filled her act. "No more musical comedy for me," she admitted. "The cafés are more profitable."[70] Midwesterners stood ready to warmly embrace the mature performer. Her songs were simple and, as the years passed, she would ease into the role of cabaret entertainer and hostess.

She also confided to reporters that she needed the money, primarily to educate her only son, Russell Thaw. With a puppy tucked under each arm and a twinkle in her eye, Evelyn Nesbit was once again the journalist's darling.

On this trip to Chicago, Evelyn was accompanied by four Belgian Griffons. "They are so much more companionable than men," she told the press. "Dogs are honest and faithful and never deceitful. That's more than you can say for some men."[71]

Enthusiastic newspaper advertisements, featuring a charming sketch of a windmill representing the red mill of the club's name, warned that this engagement was "Positively Miss Nesbit's Last Public Appearance." Bill Rothstein had a potential hit on his hands.

The publicity savvy Nesbit knew she was a curiosity—a once beautiful young woman who drove her husband to murder. She had a practical attitude towards her artistic limitations. She told reporters that she enjoyed her work. She liked Chicago, too—well enough to consider opening her own café on the city's Gold Coast. This, though, turned out to be a pipe dream. Strapped for funds and rumored to be drinking heavily, Evelyn Nesbit was closer to the end of her rope than she was to revitalized stardom.

Evelyn Nesbit: A Star Is Reborn

Following Harry K. Thaw's trial in 1906 for the murder of Stanford White and his eventual commitment in Matteawan State Hospital for the criminally insane, Mrs. Harry K. Thaw reinvented herself as "Miss Evelyn Nesbit," returning to the stage with dance partner Jack Clifford. Their 1913 tour was nothing short of a sensation. Nesbit recalled that theatrical producer Morris Gest went to great lengths protect her from crowds at railway stations, hotels, and stage entrances. A private railroad car, "The Magnet," served as her living quarters. It was a demanding tour. They gave two shows daily, Sundays included, except for a few states where lingering "blue laws" kept theaters closed on the Sabbath. Box office receipts were impressive across the country. Despite what one reviewer called an "indifferent vaudeville exhibition," she packed the house. Chicago came out to see her in its Auditorium, where operas were performed, drawing an audience of 7,400. Hundreds were turned away.[72]

In 1916, Nesbit married Jack Clifford. Born Virgil James Montani, Clifford was the son of the late Brigadier General Joseph Montani of the Royal Battalion of Italy and nephew of Comte Esmeraldo Enrico Milo, Italian Minister of Marine. The newspapers portrayed their union as the perfect happy ending to their love affair. The announcement was front page news. Nesbit and Clifford had been dancing partners for three seasons and it was generally understood that they would marry when her divorce from Harry Thaw was finalized. At the time, they both gave their ages as thirty-one and Nesbit firmly believed that she had married for love.

Their marriage quickly failed, though it took many years to end in divorce. On her own, she tried her hand at sculpting, made a handful of well-received silent motion pictures, but concluded that the movies were not a permanent solution for her failing career.

Her brief resume, though, was impressive, international in scope. In 1919, her entry in the *Motion Picture Directory* read as follows:

NESBIT, Evelyn; b. Tarentum, Pa.; educ. Shakespeare School at Pittsburgh and private tutors; stage career 4 yrs. vaud., in Follies, Marigny Theatre, Paris; London Hippodrome; screen career, Jos Schenck ("Her Mistake," "Redemption"), Fox ("The Woman Who Gave," "I Want to Forget," "Thou Shalt Not"). Hght. 5, 3½; wght., 122; brown hair, hazel eyes. Ad., 201 W. 54th st., N. Y. C.[73]

In the fall of 1920, she toured in a play, "Open Book," which was met with harsh criticism. It was time for Evelyn Nesbit to take a break from show business and find a less public means of supporting herself. She conceived of opening a tearoom and specialty shop and, in the spring of 1921, returned to New York City where she rented a property in Manhattan's theater district at 235 West 52nd Street, within sight of Broadway. The four-story building included an apartment over the shop which would serve as her home.

Nesbit needed capital to achieve her dream and went to the unscrupulous, mob-connected jeweler and antique dealer Sam Schepps to secure a loan. As collateral, she offered several pieces of jewelry, including a Tiffany marquis diamond ring worth $6,000 and a diamond lavaliere valued in excess of $3,000. The resulting loan, she recalled, was far below their worth, about $1,500, only enough to purchase half the equipment necessary for the tearoom.[74]

Next, Nesbit approached prominent fashion and costume designer Madame Frances. A loyal customer over many years, she owed Madame Frances a balance of nearly $3,000, plus interest. In the fall of 1920, the designer had sued her client for the debt with little hope of recouping her money.

Together, the women devised a plan to zero the balance, get the jewels away from Schepps, and raise a bit more money for the proposed tearoom. Madame Frances redeemed the jewels, advancing Nesbit the remaining cash she needed to equip her business.[75]

Preparations for the shop got off to a rocky start. In April of 1921, Evelyn Nesbit's estranged husband Jack Clifford broke into her apartment, accompanied by private detectives and a friend serving as a witness. Clifford hoped to catch his wife with a gentleman friend, giving him solid grounds for adultery to continue pursuing a divorce. To his satisfaction, Clifford found a man named James "Jimmy" Johnson, dressed in pajamas and dressing gown, in Nesbit's front room.

The compromising situation was quickly explained. Nesbit had been afraid to stay alone in the top-floor apartment on West 52nd Street. The entire building was empty, except for her quarters. As the tea shop was prepared for the May 1st opening, there were numerous workman in the building. Mr. Johnson was her secretary, also overseeing some carpentry work in the shop. He had been seen walking her dogs. Importantly, Nesbit stated that he would remain with her every night, until she found other protection. Thirty-five years old, tall, and slender, Johnson spoke with a slight English accent. Reportedly a homosexual, his presence in Evelyn Nesbit's apartment was ultimately useless to Jack Clifford in court. The episode was unsettling, though just the beginning of intrusions into Evelyn Nesbit's life as she embarked on her new enterprise.[76]

News of Nesbit's soon-to-open, Oriental-themed tearoom confirmed that she sought relief from the grind of performing. She nestled in near friends and theater folk. Gilt lettering on a multi-paned glass door announced "Evelyn Nesbit Specialty Food Shop" and on the French plate windows was written: "deep, home-made apple pie, old-fashioned southern ice cream, and individual coffee can be had within." A cheerful, striped awning hung under a jutting marquee-style sign, which could be seen from Broadway, boldly read EVELYN NESBIT.

And Evelyn Nesbit is what customers got—close up and personal.

The venture was announced across the country, accompanied by drawings depicting a modest proprietress, sitting behind the cash register. The tearoom's interior was a testament to Nesbit's refined aesthetic sensibility. A life-size sketch of her head, sporting a jaunty tam, sat atop the register. As hostess, she surveyed the room, perched on a high teak-wood stool. The color scheme mixed terra cotta, blue and yellow, reflecting her ever optimistic outlook. Pink tables, with delicate stenciled chairs, filled a long, narrow room, which Nesbit claimed provided seating for 100 guests. Comfortable lounges lined the walls, sitting under a freeze of life-size Japanese dancers. Soft carpets, Oriental tapestries, exotic plants, and Persian incense completed her Eastern atmosphere. Was Nesbit's motif a nod to the infamous photograph dubbed "Beauty and the Beast," picturing her adolescent self, wrapped in a kimono, asleep on a bear rug, which caused a sensation in the murder trial of Harry K. Thaw?

On display was a bookshelf of Nesbit's current reading, including the Koran; "Salomé," a play by Oscar Wilde; *The Private Memoirs of Marie Antoinette*; *Democracy and Social Ethics* by Jane Addams, founder of Chicago's Hull House; current political volumes, *Mirrors of Downing Street* (1921) by Edward Harold Begbie and *Mirrors of Washington* (1921) by Clinton W. Gilbert; and a complete set of the writings of Richard Harding Davis (1864–1916), the prolific American journalist, author, and dramatist. Not exactly the typical reading list of a flighty vaudeville dancer.[77]

Her wedding silver, complete with the Thaw crest, was put to use in the café. Most importantly, patrons would enjoy intimate time with Evelyn Nesbit, who offered them black or green tea, with lemon or cream, as well as individually made coffees. She told journalist R. H. Whitney, "My whole heart is in this.... I am going to sell an apple pie that hasn't been duplicated since 1861. It will be very deep, very thin crust and very much homemade. And I am going to sell an ice cream that no firm in the world has ever made. There will be no cornstarch, no eggs in it. Just pure, thick cream. And I am going to sell the best coffee in the world."[78]

Nesbit explained, "Yes, I'm serious about it. I've taken the place and I'm getting my supplies. I've always wanted to be a businesswoman, and this is my chance. The stage is much harder than people think. And, besides, I want a place where I'm the boss."[79]

Photos of Nesbit dressed in a gingham frock, hair bobbed with bangs, looking young and fresh, appeared in newspapers across America. Flashing a big smile for the camera, she appeared attending two fashionably dressed women holding delicate, china tea cups.

Advertisements were simple.

THE EVELYN NESBIT
SPECIALTY FOOD SHOP
235 West 52nd St.
Telephone 9117 Circle.
SPECIAL LUNCH, $1.00
SPECIAL DINNER, $2.00
Best Food in New York. Deep dish apple pies a specialty.

Over the years, New York City had been kind to Evelyn Nesbit, more tolerant of her notoriety than other locales. The tearoom was initially successful, frequented by her supportive theatrical friends. A steady cash flow helped Nesbit meet her debts and establish an independent income. Nesbit called the fare "distinctive and superior." While living in Germany, Nesbit had studied cooking, though business was never her forte.

At every turn, Evelyn Nesbit presented a confident persona to the public, a key ingredient in her enduring charm and fascination. Yet, there were indications she was uneasy about her new venture. Pointedly, she installed two burglar alarm systems. Above the shop, her apartment was roomy enough for a Steinway baby grand piano. Filled with fresh flowers, the space easily accommodated her toy-size Belgium Griffons. Originally bred as rodent killers, the Griffons served as Nesbit's tiny watchdogs. She would need them.[80]

By July, even Canadian newspapers ran articles about Nesbit's successful establishment:

> …To watch her wandering about the tea shop, chatting in a carefree manner with the lunching or tea-drinking folk, it is difficult to conjure up a picture of her as "a woman with a past," as she is so often pictured.
>
> The salads are really the best things on the menu today, she advises, and the strawberry shortcake—she really can recommend it because she sampled it herself and found it necessary to demand a second helping! Wandering to a far corner, she finds two girls intent on consommé. "Do you like it—it is good, isn't it?" she says as she passes. And so on—an

individual interest in the whim and fancies of tea shop habitues, and a charming freedom of manner.[81]

On the surface, the tearoom was a success. Nesbit made money, her patrons a constant stream of old friends and new. At least in the beginning, she attracted the cream of Broadway. It was not long before deepening trouble plagued the popular establishment. In August, the shop was robbed of $200 worth of silverware, chicken meat, and $40 worth of cigarettes. Her vulnerable safe was broken into not once, but twice. Initially, the thieves got $400. Two weeks later, another $700 was stolen. The robberies threatened to devastate the small business.

Later, Nesbit remembered that except for a few faithful waitresses, her employees were to blame, aiding the thieves by leaving the place unlocked. They stole cash and emptied the larder. Dozens of broilers, racks of lamb, and expensive Delmonico roasted beef all disappeared. Additionally, and somewhat curiously, several cases of rich Burgundy were also stolen. What was a significant amount of Burgundy doing in a tea shop at the height of national Prohibition? Were some of Nesbit's dinner specials accompanied by wine-filled tea cups?

♦ ♦ ♦

On September 19, 1921, Evelyn Nesbit was once again front page news when it was reported that kidnappers entered her building. She was alone in the apartment, her ten-year-old son Russell visiting Fanny Brice and husband Nicky Arnstein at their Long Island home. At 3:00 a.m., Nesbit became aware that men were loitering on the sidewalk below her window. Fearing burglary, she threw a fur-trimmed evening cape over her negligée and ran into the street, clutching her dogs and her jewels. She yelled "Fire!" and successfully frightened the intruders. Nearby, a policeman apprehended four men on charges of disorderly conduct; bail was fixed at $1,000 each. Later, they were found guilty and sent to the workhouse. The men included twenty-four-year-old Joseph "Spot" Leahy, a known assailant, previously arrested for possession of a revolver when gangster "Red" Murray was murdered. These were criminals with impressive records.[82]

At the time, local police stated that there had been other robberies in the neighborhood, suggesting the assault on Evelyn Nesbit was not personal. Was the notion of kidnapping farfetched? Not in Nesbit's mind. She remained closely associated with the Thaw family's millions. Who knew how much the madman Harry Thaw might forfeit to save the woman he once dubbed "the dearest girl in the world."

The incarceration of these men was a short-lived victory as it became increasingly clear that both Nesbit and her business were being targeted by criminals. She owed money to multiple sources, including legitimate creditors like Mrs. Hannah E. Watt, who sold Nesbit $450 worth of merchandise and remained unpaid. Having struggled to raise capital to open her specialty shop, Nesbit relied heavily on her precious cash flow, which was being syphoned off by thieves and, possibly, her own lavish spending, invested in gourmet foods and Burgundy wine.

It seems unlikely that her landlords, the Trebuhs Realty Company, controlled by Lee and Jake Shubert (the company name was Shubert spelled backwards), had sent the "kidnapping" thugs. By strange coincidence, though, two days following her narrow escape, City Marshalls appeared at the tearoom to dispossess Nesbit for back rent.[83] Reading the headlines, had her landlords concluded that their tenant also owed money to persons who employed unsavory characters?

In a public response, Nesbit was photographed in front of the tearoom, wearing a cheery polka dot dress and matching jacket, laughing hardily, waving a fist full of cash, proving she had plenty on hand to pay her rent. Despite this bravado, the burglaries sent business into a tail spin. She continued to fall behind in her rent. An auction of some of her most valuable possessions, held on October 26, was designed to raise enough money to pay creditors and keep the tearoom open. The announcement read:

>Preliminary announcement of the Public Sale of Sumptuous
>Furniture, Works of Art and Personal Effects.
>**BROADWAY ART GALLERIES**
>Auctioneers—Broadway and 36th St.
>Commencing
>Wednesday Oct. 26th, at 2 O'Clock
>Rich and costly Furniture, Bronzes, Persian Carpets and Art Works,
>Fine China, Linens, Glassware, Silver, Gold, Diamond Jewelry,

Paintings, Prints, etc., etc.
Formerly Property of
EVELYN NESBIT
(Formerly Evelyn Nesbit Thaw)
For inspection entire week with Catalogues.

The auction raised $16,000, however, news reached Nesbit too late.

On October 28, Nesbit's landlords once again ordered eviction. Her response, according to news reports, was to consume fifteen grains of morphine. While City Marshal William Kelly was in the process of moving the furnishings of the shop to the sidewalk, the telephone rang and he answered. Evelyn Nesbit was calling from upstairs and informed Kelly, "I've just taken enough poison to kill a truck horse. I don't care what you do now."[84] He ran upstairs, found Nesbit was telling the truth, and summoned an ambulance from Flower Hospital. Later, she credited her private physician with saving her life.

On October 30, the *Daily News*, "New York's Picture Newspaper," carried a provocative story about a mystery man who sent ten, crisp $20.00 bills to help Nesbit pay the Schuberts and buy some time. She may have received as much as $300 from friends. Her three pups—Raffy, Gaminette, and, ironically, Morphine, who had just been gifted to Nesbit—were blissfully unaware of their owner's hardships.

If Evelyn Nesbit indeed wanted to end her struggles, it was both convenient and unfortunate that she had so much morphine at her disposal. At the time, neither the press nor the public knew that she was addicted to the drug and, undoubtedly, indebted to criminals who supplied her habit. Years later, Nesbit's version of the demise of the tearoom and the reported suicide attempt differed dramatically from contemporary newspaper accounts. Pieces of what had become an increasingly cockeyed story finally fell into place.

In 1921, Evelyn Nesbit's dependence on morphine placed her just steps away from Manhattan's most powerful gangsters. The men she identified as "parasites, vultures, and leeches" who distracted her from her business were actually criminals selling, buying, and using illegal drugs. If she owed these undesirable characters a significant amount of money, it was no wonder her shop was burglarized and her livelihood threatened. Looking back from 1934, Nesbit revealed that, on October 28, 1921, she did not voluntarily take a lethal dose of morphine in a suicide attempt. It had been accidentally administered by her supplier. The revised story went like this....

One afternoon, the woman who routinely brought Nesbit her "medicine" unintentionally prepared what had the potential to become a lethal injection. Not wanting to bother with sterilizing multiple needles, the woman prepared one with at least six doses. That evening, when it came time to give Nesbit her shot, the woman forgot how much was in the needle and gave her the full load. It wasn't long before Nesbit felt ill and frightened. Doing her best to keep a level head, Nesbit told the woman to leave, explaining that if she died it could be considered murder.

Once the woman was safely away from the apartment, Nesbit called a doctor, who gave her a powerful stimulant. He kept her awake, walking the floor with cup after cup of strong black coffee. She told the doctor, and ultimately the reporters, that she had attempted suicide. Her mother came from Pittsburgh, insisted that she close the tea shop, and moved her daughter to a furnished apartment nearby. Nesbit remained in the care of a physician, who brought her down gradually to a minimum dose of morphine.

This was not the first time, nor would it be the last, that Evelyn Nesbit's version of her life's events conflicted with the public record. As time went on, numerous stories would be generated to cover up her years of addiction to morphine.

◆ ◆ ◆

On October 30, 1921, photos of Nesbit, son Russell, and her Belgium Griffons filled the nation's newspapers accompanied by the shocking statement, "I'm not saying that I wish I'd have lived differently. I just wish I hadn't lived at all."[85]

The next morning, Evelyn Nesbit greeted the press in the tearoom. Dressed in signature black and white, her velveteen gown needed brushing. Her bobbed hair was covered in a black velvet toque, her eyes swollen and red, cigarette smoke ringed her exhausted body.

Widely-read journalist Winifred Van Duzer interviewed Nesbit, describing her hazel eyes still dull from the lingering effects of a nearly lethal dose of morphine. The day after Nesbit's escape from death, Van Duzer found the pink tearoom "garish"—"a queer little restaurant." Sold on the suicide attempt story, the newspaper woman explored reasons for Nesbit's apparent despair, noting a "Long List of Failures," most recently, the lukewarm reception (by both the public and the critics) of her vaudeville and acting career, as well as her miscalculated marriage to dance partner Jack Clifford.

Despite her mother's advice, Nesbit was determined to keep her enterprise going. The Shuberts gave her a three-day grace period to pay the back rent. Friends provided her with cash. Presumably, proceeds from the auction also helped Nesbit meet her obligation to the Shuberts, clear some debt, and keep the tearoom doors open. The shocking news story brought curious patrons to the establishment. By mid-November, she was fully recovered and ready to soldier on.

Nesbit's name and reputation had been dragged through all-to-familiar journalistic mud. Her life story was employed as a cautionary tale. Headlines evoked the wages of sin, linking her to other women who had fallen as they trod the Primrose Path. Mothers were warned to protect their daughters who might be cursed with too much beauty.

One damning editorial found Nesbit's impasse to be the logical ending to a sordid life: "It is a pitiable finish that humiliates this aging woman, once a butterfly toy of wealth and luxury." Initially introduced to the public eye as an innocent flower destroyed by lechery and madness, this disgusted writer blamed Nesbit for capitalizing on "the notoriety attaching to her disgrace," which justified her downfall, ending in a "jazz tea room" and morphine. Little did this unsympathetic critic know, Evelyn Nesbit's melodramatic story was far from over.[86]

Kinder commentaries noted that Nesbit's life had been a series of misfortunes, suggesting she suffered under seven years of bad luck or the spell of hoodoo. What mirror she had broken or witchdoctor offended went unstated.

Conversely, Alice Rohe's widely-printed article featured a determined, forward-thinking Evelyn Nesbit. Rohe, like Nesbit, was an exceptional woman. In 1914, she lived in Rome, working as United Press staff correspondent, as well as a correspondent for London's *Exchange Telegraph*. Through World War I, until 1919, she managed the Rome office, making her the first woman to head an overseas bureau for a large news agency. Her portrait of Nesbit was no fluffy, woman's interest article. Rather, it captured a conversation between two worldly women.

When Rohe interviewed Nesbit in her tearoom, she still was recovering from the effects of the morphine overdose. In one hand, the proprietress held a volume written by Rabindrath Tagore; in the other a butcher's bill. The shop was packed, not a table to be had. Rohe studied Nesbit's face, recalling her tragic life story: "Sitting opposite this young woman with the strained and strange eyes, I couldn't help recalling the slim young girl, a child in fact, from whose eyes the wonder look had not yet vanished before she was plunged into the vortex of life."

Nesbit declined to discuss the overdose. It was past. Her mind was on the future. "I'm still feeling ill—but mentally I feel strong to face and fight life anew," she told the journalist.

"Why did I do it? Surely you know that we all get moments when we feel we just can't go on." But she had her son Russell to consider. Still a school boy, he was currently living with his grandmother in Pittsburgh. Nesbit envisioned a wonderful future ahead of him, reminding Rohe that Russell had already appeared in motion pictures.

Nesbit's self-perception, at least the one she shared that day, included a persona as "an artistic nut." She saw the tearoom as an attempt to balance her aesthetic nature, grounding her in the business world. As always, Nesbit's humor shown through even the darkest times. "Why did I choose a restaurant? I was sick of everything pertaining to the stage. A specialty shop—well you'll admit good food is certainly a specialty in New York."

Nesbit could be a surprisingly deep and thoughtful individual. Self-educated, she read broadly, especially in philosophy and religion. "All my experiences must help," she explained. "I've got to have courage—you'll admit I've had courage in my life." She picked up her copy of Tagore's "Personality," saying, "This expresses it better than I." Reading a few passages to the reporter, Nesbit reflected on woman's position in the world. The journalist made a mental note: "Who better then Evelyn Nesbit has a right to philosophize on those lines?"

In the bustling shop, a Japanese artist hired to sketch patrons sought Nesbit's attention. Next, the two women were interrupted by an Indian tea merchant. Nesbit introduced him as a scholar, a gentleman of the Orient, intellectually superior to Westerners in his philosophies. Quickly, Nesbit jumped to discussing Shopenhauer, a favorite philosopher, despite his views on women.

As the interview concluded, Alice Rohe stepped out into a refreshing rain. Her thoughts turned to "tragic waste in life's endless circle." Nesbit's Oriental atmosphere had successfully permeated the conversation, yet, her eternal optimism was lost on her afternoon companion.[87]

◆ ◆ ◆

As 1921 became 1922, Evelyn Nesbit was permanently evicted from the Shubert-owned property, two months behind in her rent. Carelessly, her lovely pink tables were set on the sidewalk. Nesbit moved her now meager belongings, reportedly consisting of a trunk and a small handbag, to a modest room at Broadway and 52nd Street. Mental depression may have set in. Only her friends knew her state of mind. For once, journalists fell silent.

Then on February 8, 1922, her death by drowning in the Potomac River was falsely reported. In classic Nesbit style, she laughed off the sensational press. She was very much alive, about to flee Manhattan and head to Atlantic City. The tearoom had lasted longer than many critics predicted. Her morphine habit remained a secret and would plague her for many years to come.

Evelyn Nesbit: The Comeback Cabaret Girl

By mid-February, 1922, Evelyn Nesbit was appearing at Atlantic City's Café Bal Tabarin (located at New York Avenue and Boardwalk), delivering her signature song, "I'm a Broad-minded Broad from Broadway." Having failed with her tea shop and (at least temporarily) turned her back on vaudeville, Nesbit settled into her next career—playing cabarets throughout the East, South, and Midwest. Well into her thirties, her international experience and innate charm was an excellent match for nightclubs. Her easy manner meshed well with the intimacy of the cabaret's environment, where she interacted with customers and doubled as hostess or Mistress of Ceremonies.[88]

With Prohibition in full swing, the Boardwalk was filled not only with its famous wicker chariots but also with strolling, celebrated criminals. Despite the national ban on alcohol, or maybe because of it, the town was wide open, offering Nesbit temptations of liquor and narcotics, difficult to resist.

Try as she might to the contrary, trouble just followed Evelyn Nesbit. In the coming months, the *Trenton Evening Times* found numerous opportunities to report her activities, typically with unflattering headlines such as "Taxi-Driver's Wife Names Evelyn Thaw" (as co-respondent in divorce), "Evelyn Nesbit Faces Suit For Contempt," "Evelyn Nesbit Arrested For Fight With Doctor," and "Evelyn Nesbit May Wed Poolroom Aide" (a purposely degrading headline that proved not quite as sordid as it sounded).

In mid-May, a nationally syndicated news release announced that Nesbit was considering a proposal of marriage from a Hungarian Baron named Sandor De Windt. They first met in New York, where he worked as a bond salesman. The Baron followed Nesbit to Atlantic City, lived luxuriously for several weeks, then his cash (or his credit) ran out. In reduced circumstances, he took a job as an assistant manager of the billiard room at the Ambassador Hotel. Nesbit was quoted in newspapers, saying that his gracious manner outweighed his empty wallet and admitting, "He has the almost irresistible charm of the cultured European." Of course, she was married to Jack Clifford and, in early June, would tell journalists that she had no intention of marrying anyone. A charming photo of her circulated, dressed in a modest bathing costume, sitting on the Atlantic shore, and holding her "Japanese Poodle" (one of her Belgian Griffons). Her health regained, she had happily gained fifteen pounds, and, presumably, was ready to go back to work. In 1929, she would once again fall for continental charm, still legally married to Clifford.[89]

On August 2, 1922, capitalizing on Nesbit's recent notoriety, Henri Martin of Martin's Café, located at Atlantic City's New York Avenue and the Boardwalk, contracted her to perform at Martin's Jazz Palace. By October, Nesbit was desperate to get out of her contract, launching a public and dangerous quarrel with her employer. Fearing arrest in the workplace, she claimed that Martin conducted a disorderly house, flagrantly breaking wine and liquor laws. Nesbit railed publically against Martin, seeking shelter with Max Williams, owner of Palais Royal, a rival Atlantic City café. Martin demanded a restraining order, stating that Nesbit was under exclusive contract to him. She countered, maintaining that she acted as hostess for Williams and was not performing.

Behind this squabble lurked a much bigger story and possible explanation for Evelyn Nesbit's desperate and erratic behavior—a return to dependence on morphine.

In December of 1922, Nesbit's press went from bad to worse when a Greenwich Village-based drug ring was busted. $50,000 worth of drugs were seized, along with roughly 500 letters and telegrams concerning the purchasing of narcotics. The correspondence, some of it written by notable people in show business, was now in the hands of Special Deputy Police Commissioner Dr. Carleton Simon. One of the men arrested was William Williams, who dealt in Atlantic City. News reports revealed that drugs and paraphernalia were delivered to Nesbit at the Palais Royal. Was he connected to Max Williams, Nesbit's protector and proprietor of the club?

The confiscated collection included numerous items signed—"Evelyn Nesbit Thaw," "Evelyn Nesbit," "E. Nesbit," and "E. N." In them, she specified her drug needs and preferences:

"German, but not Swiss stock."
"Next time please bring one dozen Luer spikes."
"P.S. If you cannot come down send package to Abdul Kader (Mrs.), 126 South Kentucky Avenue—and inside put my name. Always use candy box. E. N."[90]

A few days after the news broke, Evelyn Nesbit gave a shocking, impromptu interview, admitting her struggles with morphine. She confessed that she had been through "Hollywood dope hell." She sympathized with the demise of silent picture stars such as Wallace Reid, who had become addicted to morphine originally prescribed for pain. The *Washington Post* published Nesbit's lengthy statement, which opened: "I've fought the grimmest, most heart breaking fight any woman or man could fight, and I've won.... I've beaten the drug habit which had me going, almost gone, for nearly a year."

Nesbit explained that she was introduced to morphine in Hollywood, calling it a Hades for men and women who did not have the knowledge and fortitude to stay away from narcotics. "The dope peddlers and their victims are waiting there at every corner, in every home, at every party, for a chance to trap another victim." She recalled one soirée were cocaine was passed around in a sugar bowl. Every few minutes someone would say, "Pass the sugar." Not yet hooked, Nesbit marveled at their casual air.

According to this version, a terrible toothache was the basis of Nesbit's "fall." A Follies girl offered a solution to her pain in the form of a shot of morphine in the leg, plus a cotton ball stuffed with cocaine in the tooth cavity. Almost immediately, Nesbit was feeling no pain. "How I blessed that girl. And how I've cursed her ever since," she recalled.

From that point on, Nesbit paid for the girl's dope, as well as her own. The habit, she stated, cost her $100,000 in cash alone. There was an even higher, personal price—the loss of friends, of her self-respect. Her mother insisted she take the cure, threatening to take Russell away from her. An Atlantic City doctor put Nesbit under a grueling treatment, slowly weaning her off the morphine. It worked. She had been clean for eight months when Dr. Simon revealed some of the letters she had written to William Williams, a gesture she found deeply unjust. The correspondence was over a year old and no one had bothered to investigate if Nesbit remained an addict. Her name alone was too valuable. Her suffering, not to mention her involvement in criminal activities, sold newspapers.[91]

A tough gal, Nesbit weathered the negative press concerning her drug addiction and, on New Year's Eve of 1922/1923, she stood for two days, greeting customers at the Palais Royal Café and Cabaret in Atlantic City, accompanied by manager and friend Max Williams. Exhausted, she contracted a cold which deepened into pleuropneumonia. On January 5, 1923, reports were that she was dying in an undisclosed hospital. The ever rebounding Miss Nesbit did not die. Instead, she told (or, more likely, sold) her sordid story of morphine addiction to be serialized and syndicated in the newspapers. The series highlighted the fact that she was a rare example of someone who had successfully kicked the habit.[92]

By the time the tale was published, Nesbit had perfected her story, which differed somewhat from her original reaction to seeing her name smeared in the newspapers. Openly admitting that she had hoped never to disclose these details of her life, she now conceded she had been an addict. By her own admission, during 1922, her habit had escalated to a shot every hour or so.

In this revised version, Nesbit painted herself as a naïve victim, who fell prey to drugs not in Hollywood but in New York City. Performing in vaudeville, on Broadway, and saving money, she was prosperous and believed that her steady income made her a target for the local drug rings. Additionally, her popularity in show business and wide circle of friends put her in a position to encourage more users. It all began, she told her readers, with an extremely painful toothache. Nesbit spent a night pacing the floor in agony. At last, a blonde showgirl named Marie offered her pain relief in the form of a syringe filled with morphine.

From the first injection, Nesbit went on to describe her dependence on both Marie and the drug. Through Marie she met other drug peddlers across New York City and soon her addiction became common knowledge. She was hounded by strangers likely connected to the underworld, some of whom were undoubtedly the degenerates who plagued Nesbit at her tearoom during the spring and summer of 1921. Over time, her need for higher doses steadily increased. She admittedly lost everything—her money, her furs, her jewels.

Nesbit related the tortures of addiction, including hallucinations of spiders nesting in her hair and of her house engulfed in flames. Consumed by delirium, she would finally collapse into unconsciousness. She cautioned readers how easy morphine was to acquire and to administer. She carried daily doses of the narcotic in her handbag. In Manhattan, the drug was never difficult to find when her supply ran low. She was introduced to one man who operated an uptown "dairy lunch." According to Nesbit, he supplied narcotics to hundreds of users. A patron would come into the lunchroom, order a bowl of milk, and the waiter would serve it with a little package of morphine.

In the end, Nesbit was unable to perform, her stage career ruined. She successfully took a cure and opened her tearoom, hoping for a new lease on life. Probably in debt to drug dealers and living under their constant pressure, she may or may not have attempted suicide when the enterprise failed. By 1922, her health and her normal body weight restored, Evelyn Nesbit believed she was ready to face yet another new chapter in her life. Her constitution, though, may have been more compromised than she realized.

In January of 1923, it is likely few readers of her serialized confession could rectify this terrifying story and the optimistic Evelyn Nesbit who had opened an off-Broadway speciality shop in the spring of 1921. Now the world knew that Nesbit had left vaudeville, at least in part, because of her addiction to morphine. It is also possible, that a toothache or neuralgia, whichever pain plagued her, might have been connected to her psychological state—her disappointment over a mediocre theatrical career.[93]

◆ ◆ ◆

How Evelyn Nesbit recovered financially, if indeed she did, is unknown. In mid-March of 1923, she was dealt another blow when her New Jersey farm house, located between Kingston and Rocky Hill, was destroyed by a fire of unknown origin. She had purchased the property, known as the old Darlington Farm, in 1919. The quaint stone house, which dated to 1749, was completely destroyed. Prior to the fire, the interior was remarkably preserved and local legend maintained that General George Washington had stopped there with his men, who drank from the spring near the entrance. Was the fire accidental? Or was it another act of menace?

In Atlantic City, she found work at Martin's and at Palais Royal Café, where she believed that proprietor Max Williams, previously her friend, cheated her out of thousands of dollars. Then, in the summer of 1923, she was approached by yet another Atlantic City investor, who had purchased a rundown club on New York Avenue. Nesbit offered to go to work for him and personally supervise a complete renovation of the establishment. She chose black and silver for the interior color scheme, accented with rose-hued lamps. Tired of the trend in French names—"Palais D'Or," "Palais Royal," and "Palais du Dance"—Nesbit suggested they call the place "El Prinkipo," after a popular club in Constantinople. A double sign, visible from the Boardwalk as well as from the business section of town, was erected and El Prinkipo became an immediate success, angering rival nightclub owners on Cabaret Row who, according to Nesbit, planted liquor behind the cashier's desk and notified the police of illegal booze on the premises. On a Saturday night in July of 1923, a raid ensued. The next morning, headlines screamed: "EVELYN NESBIT JAILED IN RAID ON HER CABARET."

Nesbit and manager, Al McDonald, were arrested in the crowded café. Four quarts of whiskey and choice wines were seized. That night, Atlantic City political boss Enoch L. "Nucky" Johnson was in the audience, as was a Senator and his wife. "Alleged proprietors" Nesbit and McDonald were taken to City Hall. Johnson arranged for their release and Nesbit was back on the cabaret floor at 12:30 a.m., announcing the review as though nothing had happened. Having Nucky Johnson as an ally was critical to success in Atlantic City. Evelyn Nesbit's immediate release from the police station certainly demonstrated that.[94]

Shortly, it became clear that her partner was not a good businessman and Nesbit disliked his underworld companions.[95] Severing their relationship, she went to work for Harry Katz, owner of the old Palais Royal and the Silver Slipper, who offered her a salary of $750 a week. She spent the summer working for Katz and, in the fall, replaced Evan-Burrows Fontaine at the Silver Slipper. This merry-go-round of engagements, which frequently ended in disappointment, arguments, and broken promises, would continue for many years. Prohibition guaranteed that the criminal element was firmly entrenched in the café and cabaret business, making for unstable and unreliable partnerships.[96]

◆ ◆ ◆

The pressures of cabaret work may have pushed Evelyn Nesbit to the edge of a nervous breakdown. Less than a year after she had so openly confessed her addiction to narcotics and claimed herself cured, Nesbit was again headline fodder with newspapers across the country announcing that she had lapsed back to the grip of morphine, and was being treated in the small, rural town of Coshocton, Ohio. In November of 1923, journalists whipped the story into a series of front page assertions and denials. Nesbit was indignant concerning statements that she was a patient at French V. Mizer's Coshocton sanitarium and insisted she was visiting a friend there. After Nesbit was recognized in town, walking her dogs, Mizer contradicted her statement, saying she had received a ten-day cure for a morphine habit.

A Complicated Personal Life

Police raids and arrests had become routine for Evelyn Nesbit—tiresome at best, financially threatening at worst. As if professional, Prohibition-based problems were not enough, 1924–1925 was filled with stressful personal challenges for the world-weary Nesbit. She struggled to stay off morphine and, in her sphere, booze was always available to drown her sorrows and frustrations. Eventually, liquor would prove the more dangerous for Nesbit's wellbeing.

Her home base became the Hotel Martinique in Atlantic City. During April and May of 1924, Nesbit was consumed with the on-going sanity hearings of her ex-husband, Harry K. Thaw. If proved sane, he would be released from Kirkbride Asylum in Philadelphia where he had been institutionalized since 1917, following another scandalous trial for kidnaping, beating, and sexually assaulting a nineteen-year-old named Frederick Gump, who was said to resemble a young Evelyn Nesbit.

In April, Nesbit filed a petition opposing Thaw's release, arguing he remained a lunatic and, if released, would undoubtedly dissipate his own estate (valued at $1,000,000), as well as his life interest in his father's estate. She didn't expect a settlement, though she hoped that her thirteen-year-old son, Russell, might benefit from the Thaw fortune despite the fact that Harry Thaw persisted in denying paternity.

When Nesbit appeared in court, reporter Julia Harpman wrote an emotional account of Nesbit's first encounter with Harry Thaw since 1910. Those in the courtroom saw "a woman whose youth is gone but who still looks young, her pretty brown eyes darting about like a bird's; her scarlet lips pursed in a pouting expression." Harpman went on to quote Nesbit's attitude towards her former husband: "I feel only pity for him. He is insane and I am sorry for him. I would have recognized him, though he has changed greatly."[97]

Incredibly (at least to Miss Nesbit), Thaw was found sane and other family members who had an interest in preserving and benefitting from his personal fortune declined to continue a court battle. In early May, the exhausted Nesbit announced that she would drop any further litigation against Thaw. Fighting millions proved pointless. While she didn't believe Thaw was mentally fit to be at large, her personal fears that he might visit Atlantic City were alleviated once she decided to stop legal action against him.

Later in May, Nesbit's son, Russell, was injured in a car accident. The driver, fifteen-year-old William English, son of Dr. L. H. English, broke both ankles in the incident. Their car was sideswiped by Dr. Edward H. Coward, an Atlantic City physician, who apparently left the scene. A warrant was issued for Coward's arrest.

In June of 1924, Evelyn Nesbit's second husband, Jack Clifford (born Virgil James Montani), was granted a divorce in his suit against Nesbit (a.k.a. Florence Montani, Florence being Evelyn's first name) when she failed to contest his charges of infidelity the previous April. Long separated, they began their legal battle in 1920 when Nesbit discovered that Clifford held the deed to their "camp" on New York's Upper Chateaugay Lake. She maintained that she purchased the property (250 acres) with over $20,000 of her own money. Grounds for divorce were based in charges of adultery. Clifford named motion picture actor Eugene Strong as co-respondent. Nesbit eventually countersued, naming actress Ann Luther and others.

Following the decision in June of 1924, a discontented Nesbit petitioned the court stating that she was unable to attend Clifford's hearing because she became ill following the pressures of Harry Thaw's sanity trial during April and May of 1924. She denied Clifford's allegation of misconduct with Eugene Strong at Murray's restaurant. At the time Clifford claimed she was with Strong, Nesbit said she could prove she was on a vaudeville tour. In October, Justice O'Malley decreed that the case must be tried again, ordering Miss Nesbit to pay the costs of Jack Clifford's case, as well as costs incurred by actress Ann Luther. This domestic issue further distressed Evelyn Nesbit during most of 1924 and was destined to drag on until July of 1933 when the couple was finally divorced.

Despite these courtroom dramas, Evelyn Nesbit continued singing and dancing at the Atlantic City's Palais Royal Café, working for the reliable Harry Katz. On May 8, 1924, at 1:00 in the afternoon, city authorities surprised the occupants of that café with a raid—a well-organized, well-executed assault on Atlantic City's clubs. Fifty-five federal prohibition agents, some from as far west as Detroit, raided twenty-five cabarets and other establishments. They seized significant amounts of liquor and issued warrants for the arrest of fifty-one proprietors and employees of the seaside resort's nightspots. Officials declared this was the first step to clamp down on the lawless conditions in Atlantic City.

Meanwhile, Evelyn Nesbit attempted to prop up her theatrical career by performing in, of all things, a Yiddish play entitled "The Dance of Death," which opened in June of 1924 at the Arch Street Theatre in Philadelphia. Nesbit was featured in a cabaret scene, written especially for her, singing several songs in Yiddish.

In December of 1924, in an attempt to perform at a roadhouse in Miami, Florida, Nesbit was threatened by the Ku Klux Klan. Proprietor Emanuel Katz told the press that a group of Klansman approached him explaining that if Evelyn Nesbit appeared, they would make her stay in Miami very unpleasant. Katz replaced her with Evan-Burrows Fontaine. When asked for an opinion about the incident, Nesbit thought the action incredible, refusing to discuss the matter.

Dan Blanco Takes A Chance

Thus when Bill Rothstein, proprietor of Chicago's Moulin Rouge, agreed to sign Evelyn Nesbit for her Chicago "comeback," he was taking a calculated risk. Was she really off the morphine? Was she sober? Would her behavior be erratic? Could she perform multiple shows per day? Nesbit was playing Detroit in a $1,000 a week engagement when she was asked to come to the Moulin Rouge Café. Years later, she recalled that her Chicago comeback was an instant hit. The velvet ropes were up at Moulin Rouge, controlling the crowd at the door, even on the usually slow Monday nights.

Who contacted Nesbit to come to Chicago? Her eventual long-term association with Dan Blanco, already in charge of entertainment at Moulin Rouge, points to him. While the club may not have been as close to collapse as Nesbit later suggested, during the spring of 1925, there were strong indications the establishment was undergoing significant changes, possibly due to waning patronage. Ernie Young's reviews had grown stale. Bill Rothstein remained the owner/proprietor. Bernard Franklin was acting as manager. The new management mentioned in the April, 1925 advertisement in *Variety* was likely Dan Blanco, who actively read the trade papers and knew that Nesbit was mounting a successful act in Detroit.

◆ ◆ ◆

Did Dan Blanco already have a professional relationship with Evelyn Nesbit? Her spectacular 1913 performance at Chicago's Auditorium, with acrobatic dance partner Jack Clifford, may have lingered long in local memory. At that time, Dan Blanco was a hit at White City, "King of the Mafia" and King of Cabaret in Chicago. Since her separation from Clifford, Nesbit had eased her way towards a less physically strenuous single act. Initially, she stayed in vaudeville, making her home in Atlantic City.

Over the intervening years, both Blanco and Nesbit worked for the Orpheum Vaudeville Circuit. In January of 1920, she played Orpheum venues in Tulsa, Oklahoma and Kansas City, Missouri, warming up for her much anticipated arrival in Chicago. In February, Nesbit opened at Chicago's luxurious Palace Music Hall—known for "Superb Vaudeville"—where she offered a "New and Exclusive Song Revue," with Jimmy Dunn as her comic partner. Eddie Moran accompanied her at the piano. *Variety* noted that Nesbit had simplified her act, which played better as a result. As usual, she wore gorgeous and expensive costumes, receiving both gasps and applause from eager audiences. In 1920, America thrilled to see the woman who had driven Harry K. Thaw to murder Stanford White.

In March of 1920, Nesbit headlined a second Chicago engagement at Orpheum's new State-Lake Theater, located at 190 North State Street, which featured both vaudeville and photoplays. Chicago adored her. While the theater had been nearly filled to capacity since its opening on St. Patrick's Day 1919, box-office receipts during Nesbit's engagement set a fifty-week record, resulting in a happy, one-year anniversary for the Orpheum management.

With this kind of reception over the years, no wonder Evelyn Nesbit loved Chicago. And no wonder Dan Blanco and Bill Rothstein thought she might be a sensation at the even more intimate Moulin Rouge.

◆ ◆ ◆

Whoever beckoned the cabaret star to Chicago, on May 6, 1925, an excited, perhaps nervous, Evelyn Nesbit arrived in the Windy City apparently ready to fulfill a limited engagement at Moulin Rouge. Her first return to Chicago in several years, newspapers across the country carried the story. Advertisements called her "America's Most Celebrated Artist," claiming this was "Positively Miss Nesbit's Last Public Appearance." This was ultimately not the case, however, the way her luck had been heading, it might have been.

Immersed in the club's atmosphere—"A Dash of Paris in the Heart of Chicago"—Nesbit sang her own songs at Moulin Rouge, breaking all records for attendance. A favorite was her speciality, "I'm a Broad-Minded Broad from Broadway." Supported by ten other "star acts," African American Jimmy Wade's Moulin Rouge Syncopators provided the dance music. Dinner remained affordable at $1.50. The cover charge didn't apply until 9:30 p.m. The air inside the club was cooled to a pleasant 70 degrees.

All night long, James Wade and his dance band sizzled. *Variety* observed that they were "the hottest band the Chicago cabarets have to offer." An enthusiastic review continued, "It's a colored aggregation headed by James Wade. When you dance at Moulin Rouge you have to be in condition. It's serious business keeping afloat. But a joy for the dance-fiends." The review concluded, "A snappy place, this Moulin Rouge."[98]

On a stranger note, one of the acts supporting Evelyn Nesbit was "Mike & Ike," popular twin midgets. They were born Bela (Mike) and Matyus (Ike) Matina, in 1903. Playing carnivals and circuses, the twins developed a boxing routine. In 1933–1934, they appeared at The Midget Village at the Chicago World's Fair and, in 1939, were cast as Munchkins in *The Wizard of Oz*. Some years later, their equally diminutive brother, Lajos (Leo), joined them in a family act.

Nesbit performed at Moulin Rouge for a month, apparently without incident. At least the newspapers were quiet about her presence on Wabash Avenue. Supported by "10—STAR ACTS—10," at the end of May, the club devised a publicity stunt, advertising that Evelyn Nesbit would pay $500 for a comedy song to be "tried out" during the last two weeks of her "final" engagement. The ad encouraged readers to "Mail your song to MISS NESBIT at the Moulin Rouge Café Today." Monday, May 25, was "Souvenir Night." A photograph of Miss Nesbit went home with every lady who attended the show. Did this boost business on a typically slow Monday night or was business slacking?

On June 8 and 9, Nesbit's closing nights, every lady in the audience received an *autographed* photo of the once-scandalous entertainer—a clever piece of promotion to pack the house. Bill Rothstein and Dan Blanco had taken a chance on a fading celebrity and succeeded. No doubt grateful for their confidence, Nesbit returned to Atlantic City. Within a few months, she would be back in Chicago.

◆ ◆ ◆

During the weeks that Evelyn Nesbit worked at the Moulin Rouge in May of 1925, vaudevillian Ed Lowry was playing Chicago's Palace Theater. At the end of a three-year contract with the Orpheum Circuit, Lowry was spotted by Bill Rothstein, who accosted him in the alley outside the theater. In a husky voice, Rothstein praised Lowry's performance, adding that his "joint" on Wabash Avenue was a perfect room for the singer and monologist. Lowry, who had been hoping for a raise when he renegotiated his contract with the preeminent vaudeville organization, was open to Rothstein's offer. Apparently reading his mind, Rothstein offered Lowry his current pay plus a "C note"—a "century note" or a $100 bill. His eventual salary to act as "Master of Ceremonies" at the Moulin Rouge Café started at a handsome $750 per week.

When Lowry visited the Moulin Rouge, he found the room "quite attractive," feeling that the designer had successfully created a Parisian atmosphere, if a slightly garish version. The intimacy of the room appealed to him and, concurring with Rothstein, Lowry concluded it was "made to order" for his act, remembering: "The first night I walked into the place, Paulette LaPierre was standing against a post and singing 'My Man' in French. It was quite impressive. Every table was occupied. After hearing Eddie South, fronting for a fine Negro orchestra [James Wade], and then watching Evelyn Nesbit Thaw make one of her infrequent personal appearances, I was sold."[99]

That very night, Lowry struck a deal with the impresario of a "Little Dash of Paris in the Heart of Chicago," later admitting that he never had a finer boss. Rothstein assured the vaudevillian that he was welcome to stay at Moulin Rouge as long as he liked. Enlisting the aid of a widely-known Chicago publicity agent called "Rasputin" (Victor Weinshenker), Lowry received a gala opening. Rasputin's promotion packed the house with celebrities and, in a city-wide tradition, competing café owners patronized the new show, hosting lavish parties. Despite Prohibition, wine flowed freely. Lowry was an unqualified success and his tenure at the Moulin Rouge launched a career in cabaret for the vaudevillian.

Like many entertainers, including Evelyn Nesbit, when Lowry wasn't on the floor performing, he was table hopping. Plenty of action on a nightly basis was guaranteed at the Moulin Rouge, where the colorful clientele included bootleggers, bookmakers, a smattering of socialites, out-of-town businessmen, young couples out on the town, misunderstood husbands, and scions of wealthy families out on a spree.

In step with its neighboring competition, Mike Fritzel's Friar's Inn, Moulin Rouge attracted toney clientele, men dressed in tails and women in gowns. Appearances could be deceiving, though. A "gentleman" wearing a tux could easily also be carrying a gun in his pocket or have a sawed-off shotgun tucked in his touring car. Ed Lowery, like Evelyn Nesbit before him, quickly learned there was a downside to cabaret life—intimate association with too many gangsters.

During the Roaring Twenties, wealthy criminals as well as garden-variety scofflaws threw big parties and Bill Rothstein's business relied on their carefree spending. Lowry observed that Rothstein knew how to handle his mob-connected clientele and successfully insisted that their guns were checked at the door. Still, from time to time, the café had its share of tense encounters. Regulars at the Moulin Rouge included Jack "Machine Gun" McGurn, a known killer, a key member of Al Capone's Outfit, and a part-owner of the Green Mill. In 1927, he would order the attack on Joe E. Lewis when the singer/comedian refused to renew his contract with that cabaret. In 1929, McGurn was linked to the St. Valentine's Day Massacre. By 1936, he was murdered by three gunmen, dead at thirty-three.

◆ ◆ ◆

Where was Gene Harris, future partner of Dan Blanco and friend to Evelyn Nesbit during her Chicago come back? By 1925, Harris had lived in Chicago for at least two years and may have been working as waiter under Blanco's tutelage. Beginning in the late 1950s, newspaper articles reported that Harris had been the proprietor of Chicago's Club Alabam since 1925. This story would stick until his death in 1964. Since Club Alabam did not open until 1927, Harris may have begun working with Blanco at Moulin Rouge in 1925, learning the ins and outs of cabaret management. It is possible that the dawn of Harris' career as a headwaiter merged with the founding of Club Alabam, boosting the legend of Gene Harris' longevity as a local nightclub icon.

◆ ◆ ◆

Following Nesbit's successful booking at Chicago's Moulin Rouge, she returned to Atlantic City for the remainder of the summer season. Always in demand, she had no trouble landing a lucrative contract at the Boardwalk nightclub, Follies Bergere. Soon, she left, returning to Martin's and continuing her ping-pong of engagements on Cabaret Row.

While in Chicago, Nesbit may have been nostalgic for Atlantic City, however, her misfortunes during the coming months were constant. In July of 1925, her apartment was burglarized. She was robbed of $1,000 worth of jewelry and costumes. Did she remain in debt to drug dealers who simply stole her property when payments were not forthcoming?

In September, Evelyn Nesbit was once again in the wrong place at the wrong time, playing at Atlantic City's Embassy Café when it was raided. The club had been open only a few months, with Nesbit as the star attraction. It had quickly become a popular spot for wealthy vacationers, who were taken by surprise when federal dry agents entered the establishment. Tumblers were quickly drained of their contents. No liquor was found, yet the proprietor and two bartenders were arrested. Charges were based on past offences. The defendants gave their names as M. W. Katz, William Dunn, and Joseph de Meo.

As with the report of the raid on El Prinkipo Café in the summer of 1923, Katz was called the "alleged proprietor." Did this indicate an invisible owner—as with the Northern Lights case when Dan Blanco held the license for the criminally-connected owner Andy Craig? Was the same true of El Prinkipo, where Al MacDonald and Evelyn Nesbit were the visible proprietors, but not the owners, of the café?

By the end of September of 1925, most Atlantic City cabarets were closed for the season, with a few operating on weekends and others hoping to cash in on convention crowds. Evelyn Nesbit had to search elsewhere for work. In October, she moved on to New York City, where she appeared at Stauch's, located at her old stomping grounds, 52nd and Broadway, earning a comfortable $1,000 per week. The Ray Miller Orchestra, the first jazz band to play at the White House, provided the dance music.

Back in Chicago, Moulin Rouge opened its fall season, with Dan Blanco now identified in the trade papers as the club's manager. James Wade's syncopated orchestra remained in place. Moulin Rouge was the only white café in Chicago to feature "colored" musicians, another Dan Blanco coupe. *Variety* credited a steady improvement in the caliber of Moulin Rouge's clientele to smart management, who paid attention to details many other cafés neglected. This was a nice nod to Dan Blanco, despite the fact that his name was not mentioned.

The bill was a typical mix of comics, dancers and singers, featuring The Kauffman Brothers (Irving and Jack), "comics-in-chief," one of whom acted as Master of Ceremonies. A rift between Dan Blanco and the Irwin Sisters, who specialized in Egyptian dancing, resulted in them leaving the fall show. Because of their youth, the girls had agreed to appear between 7:30 p.m. and 2 a.m. Blanco wanted them working into the wee hours of the morning. So, either they quit or he let them go. *Variety* printed both versions. Despite this hiccup with the talent, the trade paper concluded that Moulin Rouge could look forward to a prosperous season.

In September, Moulin Rouge announced that the management had re-engaged Evelyn Nesbit for a return booking. She was to play six weeks, beginning in early December, at a guaranteed salary of $1,500 per week. Dan Blanco was unquestionably behind this booking. Since summer, she had performed successfully in New York City and Detroit. Still, hiring Miss Nesbit remained a calculated risk.

Once in Chicago, Nesbit settled into a townhouse at 56 East Walton Place, located between Michigan Avenue and Rush Street. Beginning in late November, she shared the bill with the Kaufman Brothers and a half-dozen other vaudeville acts, including the ever-popular twin midgets, Mike & Ike, and Sherman, Van and Hyman, who offered a wholesome vaudeville comedy, specializing in "Fifteen minutes of musical foolishness." This engagement was not without the typical rumors that swirled around Nesbit. New Yorkers wondered why she was not scheduled to open the new, well-appointed Frivolity at 52nd and Broadway. Trade papers whispered that New York City police may have influenced Nesbit's decision; reportedly, the precinct chief did not want a repeat of the tearoom debacle, still fresh in the city's memory. Whatever the reason, Dan Blanco was happy to have Evelyn Nesbit back in Chicago for the holidays and working as his headliner for the all-important, hopefully lucrative, New Year's Eve.

December 16–25, advertisements ran in Chicago newspapers announcing "The Talk of the Town—Evelyn Nesbit—The Incomparable." *Variety* applauded Moulin Rouge, Dan Blanco, and Miss Nesbit, highlighting the management's personal attention to their customers and its successful employment of strong headliners who were suitable to the café audience. Nesbit worked hard, appearing on stage several times during the evening and, when not in the spotlight, acted as hostess. Additionally, Moulin Rouge's central location was especially convenient to patrons of the Auditorium Theater during the opera season, providing a late-night crowd.

New York City's loss was Chicago's gain. Evelyn Nesbit was behaving herself and Dan Blanco's reputation was soaring. Nesbit's salary was an impressive $1,500 per week, however, Moulin Rouge was getting its money's worth.

CHAPTER SIX

E. C. Yellowley & The War On Booze

Concurrent with Evelyn Nesbit's anticipated return to Moulin Rouge, a new Prohibition Administrator, Edward C. Yellowley, arrived in Chicago, ready and able to mop up what had become a city full of blatant (and to a shocking degree sanctioned) violations of the Volstead Act. On October 1, 1925, a blanket dismissal of Chicago's previous prohibition agents was scheduled. Yellowley and his assistant, W. H. Kennedy, would assemble a new department.

Cleaning Up Chicago

Initially, Yellowley planned to strike at big operations, the sources of the booze supply—the rings and gangs and so-called syndicates. The *Chicago Daily Tribune* printed a colorful list—"larger moonshiners, bootleggers, alky cookers, smugglers, beer needlers and grog runners"—targets in Yellowley's crosshairs. Eliminate the producers, and bootleggers are automatically out of a job. In his policy statement, Yellowley admitted, "I fully appreciate the difficulties and I know the extent of the warfare to be waged, but we'll be able to put it over, all right, and close them down with a slam."[100]

A bespectacled, mild-looking man, Yellowley's high brow and soft smile gave him a benign air. For this Prohibition Administrator, the law was the law. Within the United States, no liquor was to be bought, transported, or produced, except for medicinal or religious purposes. What about the average guy with a bottle in the glove compartment of his automobile? What about the tourist who brought a couple of quarts back from Canada? What about the working stiff making "gin" in his bathtub? What about putting padlocks on the doors of offending taverns? Yellowley boldly claimed, "No violator is going to be safe in violating the law."[101] If a police officer encountered a man walking down the street, carrying a bottle of liquor, he would be obliged to enforce the law. On the other hand, to systematically target little offenders would require ten times Chicago's law enforcement team. Yellowley also noted that, on occasion, padlocks had worked well in New York. He would not hesitate to use them in Chicago, however, the search warrant process would always be observed whether he was targeting a nightclub, or a home suspected of small-batch brewing. If Yellowley succeeded, the winter of 1925–1926 might find some bootleggers lining up at pawn shops ready to hock their diamond stickpins and gold watches.

On October 9, following a trip to Washington D. C., Yellowley announced his plan to clean up Chicago's most respectable venues—supper clubs, cabarets, and semi-public hotel sipping centers—the prime locations where patrons brought their own liquor in hip flasks or concealed bottles. These so-called "hippos" were the more affluent members of society, confident to hide a pint behind a menu at a cabaret table. Or the golfer who tucked a bottle in his locker for a nip at the nineteenth hole.

Yellowley appointed R. Q. Merrick, former division chief in New York, in charge of enforcement. Chicago took notice. Merrick came complete with a tough reputation, going to any extreme to catch a violator in action. Once, disguised as a millionaire golf enthusiast, he penetrated several New York and New Jersey golf clubs, as well as nearby fashionable roadhouses. Chicago impresarios, who previously felt safe because they had carefully refrained from *selling* drinks, had cause for concern with Merrick on the job. A recent federal ruling decreed that a restaurant or a club could be considered a tippling house if alcohol was merely consumed there.

Yellowley was no-nonsense. He named names. He singled out Frolics, which charged $1.10 for admission and $1.00 for a bottle of ginger ale; Hotel Crillon on Michigan Avenue where nightly glasses of ginger ale resulted in hundreds of "happy" patrons; and Moulin Rouge's neighbor, Friar's Inn, known as "a gay spot of the subdued, moaning saxophone type." Also on Yellowley's hit list were Chez Pierre, Little Club, Deauville, Silver Slipper, Samovar, College Inn, Rendezvous, and Rainbo Gardens. Moulin Rouge, a café on par with these establishments, was not singled out. Were Bill Rothstein and Dan Blanco doing an exceptionally good job of stopping "hippos" at the door? Or did they have better connections than the proprietors of the other clubs, keeping them off the hit list? Yellowley's goal was to hammer Chicago's favorite nightspots. He bemoaned that cabarets remained far too popular with drinkers. If necessary, he would launch nightly raids on the largest establishments, arresting patrons who were caught with liquor in their possession.

Town was tense. In the early hours of December 24, 300 dancers and diners panicked in Frolics Café when a jeweler named Fremont Zenkere accidentally discharged a revolver concealed in his pocket. Zenkere was quarreling with his fiancée, Miss O'Brien, when the gun went off. The bullet cut his own leg and lodged in the heel of headwaiter Harry Devine. A fist-fight ensued. These were dangerous times, even for headwaiters.[102]

As yearend approached, the challenge of maintaining a dry New Year's Eve was front page news in Chicago. Rumors ran wild as to Yellowley's plans. Would he really padlock 150 cabarets and clubs before New Year's Eve 1925? He advocated equality for women, announcing that ladies would not receive deferential treatment and would be arrested along with their male escorts. Throughout the city, over 16,000 reservations had been made at restaurants, clubs, and cabarets to see in the new year. Fifty-two regular agents and a dozen undercover agents would be spread throughout Chicago's most popular destinations. There would also be uniformed policemen at the principle hotels and cafes. Yellowley announced that his operatives had reservations at the largest venues. Anyone caught drinking would be arrested and, if the bond set at $1,000 was not immediately paid, prisoners—men and <u>women</u>—would be transported to the South Clark Street police station, where they would remain until arraignment on Saturday.

The café managers and proprietors took defensive action. Collectively, they contributed to an "identity fund," retaining private detectives who collected enough information to put the finger on every one of Ed Yellowley's prohibition agents. The Administration responded by creating an intensive course for cabaret managers, headwaiters, and captains. Matriculation took place on December 26, with instruction to begin the following Monday, in preparation for New Year's Eve. The so-called Corridor School was held in the hallways outside Prohibition headquarters on the third floor of the Transportation Building. The exact content of the instruction was not disclosed. Were the authorities letting club owners know that they were aware that the private detectives had identified prohibition agents? Were they telling proprietors precisely how to conduct themselves on New Year's Eve when a manager or headwaiter spotted a patron with a flask? And importantly ... did Dan Blanco or Gene Harris attend school that Monday?

A civil agreement was reached between tavern managers and the federal authorities. Patrons would not be searched at the door. Bottles spotted on a table, though, would be met with more than a frown. Those with reservations at Pershing Palace, for example, were told in advance that boisterous parties would be unwelcome.

Then Yellowley took the agreement a step further—exacting a pledge from the managers of Chicago's nightspots to report drinkers, issuing them a little white card, which carried the telephone number of Prohibition headquarters. On December 30, ten compliant managers of establishments located in Chicago's Loop took the oath. Bernard Franklin or Dan Blanco was likely among them. While the men gathered in Yellowley's office, the administrator impressed upon the proprietors that they were taking a permanent pledge, not simply making an agreement for the holiday.

Because Yellowley's agents had been identified, on New Year's Eve they didn't bother to disguise themselves by renting tuxedos (an expensive proposition for dozens of men) and simply sat in Chicago's nightspots in their civilian clothes. The club managers knew they were being observed and the detectives knew they were recognized. Yellowley's campaign worked. Chicago's New Year's Eve 1925/1926 was surprisingly law-abiding. Proprietors claimed receipts were high. Police reported arrests were low.

Evelyn Nesbit's Brush With Death

New Year's Eve may have gone well for the city, but it was a disaster for Evelyn Nesbit. At the conclusion of her six-week engagement at the Moulin Rouge, Nesbit was scheduled to move on to commitments in Miami and Miami Beach, Florida on Saturday, January 2. Instead, she went on a bender. One reporter described it as "a hysteric fling at death." Miss Nesbit was quoted as saying that she wanted to die—"because I'm tired of life."[103]

Beginning on Tuesday, January 5, 1926 and persisting for days, headlines across the country once again turned Nesbit's tragic life into front page news.

"Evelyn's Suicide Attempt." "Evelyn Thaw Saved By Son After Taking Lethal Dose." "Wild New Year Debauch Ends in Second Attempt to End Her Life." "Evelyn Thaw May Not Survive Suicide Attempt. Dancer Drinks 8 Ounces of Poison."

Reports of her suicide capitalized on her past notoriety and the inherent high drama of her actions. At the conclusion of what may have been a multi-day binge, Evelyn Nesbit swallowed eight ounces of Lysol in an attempt to kill herself. Her fifteen-year-old son, Russell, visiting from Atlantic City for the Christmas holidays, possibly helped save his mother's life by forcing her to drink a combination of olive oil and milk. Her personal maid, Gussie Accoo, also witnessed the act, confirming it was not an accident. When Miss Accoo tried to give her employer some milk, Nesbit knocked the glass out of her hand.[104]

For several weeks, Gussie Accoo had been concerned about Nesbit's mental state, wondering if she was worried about finances or deeper problems she did not share with her maid. Accoo told reporters that Nesbit's energy began to wane shortly before Christmas. The performer had even been advised to cancel the remainder of her engagement at Moulin Rouge and rest. Concerned that Nesbit might have returned to her drug habit, Accoo admitted to journalists that her employer had taken another cure in the fall of 1925, spending three weeks in a sanitarium in Atlanta, Georgia. Apparently, the maid's fears concerning Nesbit's return to morphine use were unfounded. Physicians who examined Nesbit at the hospital ruled out any recent use of narcotics.

Russell Thaw told reporters that this was the third time his mother had attempted to kill herself and that he had administered the antidote as soon as he saw her condition. This statement likely came as a surprise to both reporters and newspaper readers who were only aware of Nesbit's highly publicized morphine overdose in October of 1921, when she was evicted from her Manhattan apartment and tearoom. (Russell was living in Pittsburgh at the time and too young to help his mother even if he had been present.) Later, the doctors stated that Nesbit probably would have died after swallowing the Lysol if her stomach had not been full of gin, which acted as an effective antidote even before her son gave her the olive oil.

Both Russell Thaw and Miss Accoo denied that there had been a party in the apartment on the night of January 4. Neighbors reported otherwise, commenting that a man was ordered out of Nesbit's apartment about an hour before she drank the poison. Accoo admitted that when Nesbit finally came home from her extended New Year's Eve party, she was in "bad shape." Her nose was broken and she had been drinking heavily. All day Sunday, Nesbit continued to drink. Miss Accoo described the scene. "It must have been more than a dozen bottles of beer I went out to get as well as the stuff in the house. About 4 o'clock in the morning she became hysterical and asked me to get some more beer. I told her the place was not open yet." At 5:00 a.m., Nesbit swallowed the Lysol.[105]

While most of the newspaper reports focused on the basic facts of the attempted suicide, an article written by noted journalist Genevieve Forbes Herrick offered several enticing behind the scenes details. On Monday night, after Nesbit was admitted to the Ashland Boulevard hospital, a telegram arrived addressed to "Mrs. Thaw." It said "the other chap is being taken care of" and was signed "Tom." Herrick added, "No explanation was made of the message." Was this in reference to Nesbit's broken nose?

Herrick emphasized that friends believed Nesbit had serious financial troubles and that she was no longer working at Moulin Rouge. Apparently, Nesbit either quit or was fired when she started drinking hard on New Year's Eve and, as a result, quarreled with the management. When she chose to go on a bender rather than work through New Year's Eve, Dan Blanco and Bill Rothstein could have considered her action a breach of contract, thus terminating her services, at least for the immediate future.

Herrick also quoted a peculiar letter found in Nesbit's room. It was dated 2:20 a.m., New Year's Day.

Dear Eve.

Did something day before Christmas that I regret exceedingly, and I know when I explain you will understand.

Damn narcotic gang were pushing me for $150, but could not connect up with friends here or in Pittsburgh. Only have a limited time to send on cash.

Now, pal, I will be much disappointed and chagrined if within a few days I do not hear from you.

Doc R.[106]

A Brownsville, Pennsylvania physician named Dr. W. Calvin Roller claimed he met Nesbit when she was at a sanitarium being treated for her morphine habit, explaining he referred to a payment of a fine. The *Tribune* printed the explanation in spite of its implausibility.

Concurrent with the stories in major national newspapers, *Variety* published an especially thorough and deeply unflattering report on Evelyn Nesbit's condition. One of her Chicago drinking buddies worked for the showbiz trade paper, providing salient and shocking details. The front page headline read: "EVELYN NESBIT, 'ON THE LOOSE,' TRIES SUICIDE IN CHICAGO."

With a dateline of January 5, the account of Nesbit's near-fatal act was written in the paper's typical, colorful prose. It opened describing Nesbit's departure from Detroit, a lucrative engagement, curtailed without notice. This abrupt cancellation of contracts was becoming a pattern in Evelyn Nesbit's career. The article added that she came to Chicago to obtain drugs, doubting that she had been cured of her morphine habit and pointing to her erratic actions as proof of addiction. Stating further that Nesbit was drinking heavily for weeks before she attempted suicide, an unnamed *Variety* correspondent claimed to have been with her during the New Year's Eve binge. He reported her plans to soon go on the wagon, however, for the holidays she was "hitting it up like a sailor on shore leave." The article continued that Nesbit was unconscious when she was carried out of an undisclosed Loop District café.

Additionally, the piece reviewed Nesbit's 1921 "suicide attempt," adding that a newspaper friend, probably Jack Lait, lent her $100 and arranged a deal with Hearst Syndicate to buy her life story for $1,000, with the proviso that it was not to be published until after her death. She used the advance to return to Atlantic City, undergo a sheep-gland cure, and publish her series on the horrors of the drug habit. Then, according to *Variety*, about six months prior to the New Year's Eve near-tragedy, Nesbit had returned to narcotics and alcohol, reminding readers that it was a glass of wine that led to her "downfall" with Stanford White. The report was unclear as to exactly how her engagement at

Moulin Rouge ended. When sober, she told friends that she planned to return to Atlantic City, and then accept a winter engagement in Miami, Florida.[107]

Despite the lack of sources, this was a surprisingly sensible account of the events leading up to Evelyn Nesbit's suicide attempt.

By Tuesday evening, January 6, Nesbit was pronounced out of danger, though newspapers suggested that her vocal chords might have been permanently damaged by the poison. Photos showed her lying in a hospital bed, resembling a prize fighter with a plaster over her nose. At that time she stated, "I was nervous and blue, life just didn't seem worthwhile." Once on the road to recovery, she added, "Now life seems colorful and bright and I want to live."[108]

Nesbit's ability to bounce back was phenomenal. By the end of the month, she and her son had returned to her apartment on Vermont Avenue in Atlantic City. In late January of 1926, an incredible explanation for her recent suicide attempt became low-key national news, in buried blurbs she stated: "I was feeling slightly blue on New Year's eve. For a little diversion, I picked up Schopenhauer's 'Essays' and became interested in the essay on 'Suicide'. You know what happened. It was on an impulse. I regret the incident."[109]

Schopenhauer? Rather dense reading for New Year's Eve, especially for someone already well into a bender.

In her 1934 memoir, *Prodigal Days*, Evelyn Nesbit contradicted much of what had been printed in early 1926. In "I Try Suicide," she freely admitted that nightclub work was increasingly stressful. The thrill of working in cabarets had long ago worn off, becoming exceedingly monotonous. Working from 11 o'clock at night until as late as 8 o'clock the next morning was exhausting. She could no longer muster forced gaiety for her public persona. Perhaps most importantly, she consistently spent more than she earned. Unstated was the fact that her narcotic habit had devastated her finances.

Nesbit went on to relate a confusing story about unnamed, feuding partners at the Moulin Rouge, one of whom planned to open a club in Florida. She made the mistake of volunteering the opinion that a Florida club might be successful, igniting a quarrel. One went down to Florida. The other, who remained in Chicago, took a dislike to Nesbit, constantly provoking her to misbehave. If she reacted, exploding temperament could become an excuse to fire her.[110]

One night, dressed in a lightweight Greek boy's costume, she shivered offstage while the manager delayed the show. When Nesbit complained, he encouraged her to quit. Taking his cue, she left the club and embarked on a spree with two newspapermen. They had a "grand time," club hopping in the Loop District. She reached her apartment at dawn and prepared for bed. Then, completely exhausted (and perhaps still drunk), she fell into a dark mood and swallowed the Lysol.

In 1934, Nesbit blamed journalists for exaggerating the story and for planting "evidence" to support their fabricated reports of her suicide attempt. She claimed they photographed her wastebasket stuffed with empty beer bottles; reproduced a letter from her mother complaining that she didn't write; and inappropriately published the mysterious letter from a doctor recently cured of a drug habit.

Evelyn Nesbit was down but not out! While in the hospital, she received an invitation to return to Atlantic City for an engagement at the Follies Bergere. Fleeing Chicago, Nesbit returned to the Atlantic coast where she admitted that the salt air "made my heart sing."[111]

Evelyn Nesbit's version of New Year's Eve 1925/1926 raises intriguing questions. Who were the two owners of Moulin Rouge? Was Bill Rothstein an owner or the proprietor? Had Dan Blanco become a part owner? Could it have been Rothstein's seldom seen partner, a man named Frankel or another financial backer of dubious repute? Was it manager Bernard Franklin who held something against Nesbit? (Within weeks, he would be publicly accused of antagonizing the talent by a disgruntled patron.) During the winter and spring of 1926, all three men appear to be actively involved at the Moulin Rouge. Were there invisible partners, whose names Nesbit discreetly left out of the tale? Whoever wanted Nesbit off the stage at the café, it was not Dan Blanco, who would hire her again as soon as he owned his own club.

Chicago's Notorious Moulin Rouge

Whatever the precise facts of Evelyn Nesbit's dismissal from her contract at Moulin Rouge, January of 1926 began with a bump for the café and its owners. The sudden need to replace Nesbit was filled with a personal appearance by dancer Fawn Gray, ironically (or purposefully) another woman associated with Harry K. Thaw. Her Charleston may have been above average but it was likely her scant costume that brought in patrons. *Variety* commented, "Her act consists of a generous exhibition of a figure that would show up better after a spell of lamb chops and pineapples. The flimsy costume accentuates it. That costume, however, created a world of excitement among several groups of stags who made noises indicative of high blood pressure."[112]

It seems probable, given the limits of Fawn Gray's talents, her connection with Thaw (who had recently given her a $10,000 bracelet) was the inspiration for her job at the Moulin Rouge and Dan Blanco ingeniously cashed in on the millionaire's scandalous life.

Blanco rolled into the new year with a solid plan for the café's entertainment. His approach was to offer a Whitman's Sampler of talent, showcasing ten different acts each night. Every week or two, one was dropped and a fresh one brought in. If an attraction was a hit, Blanco kept it on the bill until crowds thinned. In January of 1926, Mike & Ike, the twin midgets, were closing an exceptionally long engagement. Jimmy Wade's Orchestra kept patrons happy with the latest hot jazz. Advertisements touted the café as "one of the gayest spots along South Wabash Avenue."

It wasn't long before Moulin Rouge was, once again, in the newspapers when Mrs. Clara Harcq claimed she was struck by the café manager, presumably Bernard Franklin, though the press referred to him as "Ben" Franklin. Heated discussions and café fights were common occurrences and the story might not have made the paper, except that Mrs. Harcq had recently been acquitted of murdering her mother, making her name and reputation on-going newspaper fodder.

In early March of 1926, Judge Francis Borrelli of the South Clark Street Court heard conflicting versions of what happen to Mrs. Harcq at the Moulin Rouge. She admitted that she visited the café with her friend Miss Darlene Begerny, who wanted to see "her sweetheart, a waiter there." The ensuing fight had nothing to do with Miss Begerny. Mrs. Harcq became upset when manager "Ben" Franklin roughly reprimanded one of the entertainers, Yvette Troy. Mrs. Harcq intervened and Franklin allegedly struck her. In May, the case for assault and battery was dismissed when Dan Blanco testified that Miss Troy was in his hotel room when the beating supposedly occurred on the dance floor. How Mrs. Harcq got her black eye would remain a mystery. And what of Darlene Begerny's unnamed sweetheart waiter? Could it have been Gene Harris?

◆ ◆ ◆

In mid-March, a practical joke (or possibly a malicious act) set Bill Rothstein's Moulin Rouge on the path towards its eventual demise. On March 13th, radio station WBBM, while broadcasting dance music from the café, announced that State's Attorney Robert E. Crowe and his good friend, Judge Charles V. Barrett of the Board of Reviews, were enjoying ringside seats next to the dance floor.

In fact, Crowe was not at the Moulin Rouge. He was home with his family listening to the radio. Infuriated, at 1:00 a.m. he headed a raid on the club, accompanied by Chicago police and plain clothes detectives. Officers from the South Clark Street Station blocked the exit doors. The orchestra stopped playing mid-foxtrot, bottles crashed to the floor. A woman screamed as Sergeant O'Malley ripped a stage microphone from its stand. Someone yelled, "Hide the stuff!" Crowe's primary goal, he stated later, was to find out who was slandering him on the radio.

Manager Bernard Franklin and proprietor Bill Rothstein denied any connection to the radio broadcast. Franklin blamed Philip L. Friedlander, announcer for the North Side Realty Company, for the prank. A few days earlier, five officials of that company had been arrested for brutally attacking a young girl in a North Side hotel. Friedlander claimed the radio announcement was a mistake. Franklin, Friedlander, and three patrons were arrested. Franklin was charged with being the keeper of a disorderly house, Friedlander with disorderly conduct, and the patrons with possession of liquor. Unsatisfied with the results of the raid, Crowe sued, launching Chicago's first radio slander case.

Two months later, Moulin Rouge and two other Loop District cafés— Friar's Inn and Al Tearney's Town Club—received injunctions for "pour your own" liquor law violations. A recent decision in Milwaukee by Federal Judge Geiger made it possible to close establishments based on the actions of patrons. Customers carrying a hip flask and consuming liquor on the premises could cost a café owner his business. Charged with violating the nuisance clause of the Volstead Act, the three managers planned to unite to test the right of

Federal Judge Adam C. Cliffe to serve them with injunctions without proof that the liquor had been purchased on the premises. If necessary, the owners were prepared the take their case to the United States Supreme Court.

In June, former prohibition prosecutor Edwin L. Weisl took on the cases of Mike Fritzel's Friar's Inn and Bill Rothstein's Moulin Rouge. The attorney argued that clubs should not be made responsible for patrons who bring in hip flasks and spike legally sold ginger ale.

In August, the proprietors of the three loop cafés had their day in court, appearing before Judge Adam C. Cliffe only days after the Avalon Café and forty other Volstead Act violators were padlocked across Chicago. Within days, 110 additional establishments were scheduled for closure. The *Tribune* reported: "Padlock petitions hit every class of alleged booze selling joint, from private homes selling a tub of brew a week to places where the take ran into thousands of dollars each month. It is estimated that property rentals totaling nearly a million will be erased for a year through the court orders during the week."[113]

Throughout the long legal process, Moulin Rouge remained open and, in October, advertised itself as "The New Moulin Rouge," featuring a revue show with Karyl Norman, "Vaudeville's Highest Priced Star," as the headliner. For a Loop café, Norman's show edged on the scandalous. It may indeed have been "The Most Talked About Revue In Chicago." Known as "The Creole Fashion Plate," Norman was a popular female impersonator who typically played Chicago on a vaudeville bill. His specialty was not simply a quick change of costume but a quick change of gender. The chance to see the performance in an intimate cabaret setting was a shrewd ploy to attract diners and dancers to the currently very "dry" Moulin Rouge.[114]

December arrived and with it the promise of extra cash to be made during the holidays in clubs all over Chicago. Federal Judge Cliffe envisioned otherwise. On December 7, he ordered padlocks for Moulin Rouge, along with Friar's Inn and Al Tearney's Town Club. Only a stay of execution could keep the clubs open until a final decree was entered and, on December 13, Judge Evan A. Evans of the United States Circuit Court of Appeals did just that, granting the three owners writs of *supersedeas* and giving the club owners until January 18 to prepare appeals. Rothstein and Blanco breathed a sigh of relief; regulars would be able to ring in the new year, as usual, at the Moulin Rouge.

Prohibition Administrator E. C. Yellowley, who watched over an enormous district stretching from Milwaukee to Indianapolis, prepared to spread his agents across Chicago. Again, Yellowley discussed the situation with the club owners. The proprietor of Chez Pierre told reporters that owners had met with Yellowley and intended to follow his instructions, strictly obeying the law.

On December 30, 1926, representatives from Rainbo Gardens, Green Mill, Vanity Fair, the Kit Kat Club, L'Aigion Café, and the Hollywood Barn dropped by Yellowley's office. The following morning, men from Rendezvous, the Deauville, Pershing Palace, Frolics and others, paid calls on the administrator. The owners of Chicago's most popular nightspots were making a public demonstration of their allegiance to the law. Clearly, they were concerned about the power of the decision that had brought injunctions to Al Tearney's Town Club, Friar's Inn, and Moulin Rouge. Yellowley delivered a friendly statement to the café owners, stating that he desired to enforce the law in a sane and constructive way. He had no intention of interfering with legitimate operations or preventing clubs from serving their guests. He was relying on the honor of proprietors to keep their establishments dry.

Town was booked for the New Year celebration. Hotels reported 17,000 guests had reservations in the Loop District alone. Ballrooms and restaurants were ready to take on thousands of revelers. Imported booze was flooding the city. The *Tribune* reported that Canadian bourbon was selling at $6 a pint and alcohol was $6 a gallon. Top Scotch was $90 a case. Lower grades, priced from $75 to $50, were bootleg mixtures. Despite the fact that the ever-popular bourbon was being doctored with red pepper, prices ranged from $120 to $150 a case.

Where did the authorities stand on journalists publishing market reports on illegal liquor in the daily newspapers? Strange law, this Prohibition.

Then, on New Year's Eve, Moulin Rouge voluntarily closed for the holiday. No explanation. No details. Likely, Bill Rothstein and his backers wanted to avoid the padlock and the sure fire way was to keep the doors closed.

New Year's Eve came and went. E. C. Yellowley's men were planted around town, as they had been the previous year. Arrests were low. Shootings, reckless driving, and other accidents on December 31 kept police busier than café raids. Yellowley believed that ennui may have finally set in with citizens who continued to drink alcohol. Poor quality booze, high prices, and—lest we forget—the risk of arrest stripped revelry on the town of its fun.

On February 8, 1927, Friar's Inn, Al Tearney's Town Club, and Moulin Rouge lost their appeal and Federal Judge Adam C. Cliffe ordered the clubs padlocked for a year for allowing customers to drink on the premises. Attorney Edwin L. Weisl, who represented both Friar's Inn and Moulin Rouge, made an eloquent argument against the decision. In his brief, Weisl asked: "Where in the Volstead act is there provision that anyone conducting a restaurant or other public places is charged with the duty of suppressing and prohibiting the violation of that law by customers or patrons?" He argued that the federal courts had been largely transformed into police courts.

Attorney Weisl warned against this judgment which turned every restaurant keeper in the country into an auxiliary prohibition agent, creating a veritable army, conscripted without compensation, in support of the Volstead Act. He asked, "Was it the intention of congress to make a policeman out of every citizen?"

If the Court's decision was upheld, Weisl insisted that owners of all kinds of businesses would be responsible for the actions of their patrons. Even lunchrooms and railroad trains would be threatened by the hidden hip flask or by the exuberant patron. The attorney was adamant in his argument. "Let it be known that any bank, department store, office building, hotel, club, or other business structure can be closed for a year upon the uncontroverted word of a prohibition agent and no business will be safe from blackmail."[115]

On March 23, the original order against the clubs was upheld by the Circuit Court of Appeals and Moulin Rouge was closed. In June, a plea for a review of the decision went to the United States Supreme Court. In September, the Court refused to review the case. E. C. Yellowley was satisfied and promised to make good use of the ruling.[116]

Dan Blanco's Club Alabam

Once again, Dan Blanco was out of a job. (And, likely, so was Gene Harris.) Blanco couldn't afford to wait a full year for Moulin Rouge to reopen. Rather than look for another job, he decided to open his own club, choosing to renovate a three-story building at 747 Rush Street, transforming it into the Club

Alabam. The move from South Wabash to Rush Street was significant. Real estate and ongoing overhead would be less expensive. Clientele would be less refined, looking for a good time in a relaxed environment. There, the affable Gene Harris joined Blanco as the establishment's headwaiter, taking the first step toward a lifelong career at the Club Alabam.

747 Rush Street had long been an apartment building. In June of 1911, the property was described as a rooming house catering to businessmen. The management promised the apartments were well-furnished, complete with all modern conveniences. Light, cool, and airy, the building was located two blocks from Lake Michigan. Board was optional and reasonable. Phone: North 5186. By July, the building was for sale. A classified ad read: "**FOR SALE**—10 ROOM, EXCEPTIONALLY FURNISHED; rent $65; income $165; bargain, no agents. 747 Rush-st."[117]

In 1915, when Dan Blanco headed a hit show at White City, Miss Bessie Arbor, of South Bend, Indiana, was hiding out at 747 Rush Street. One of the tenants in the building reported the eighteen-year-old violinist to local detectives. She had shortened her skirts, disguising herself as a child, and denied that she had come to Chicago accompanied by a man.

Occasionally, over the years, classified ads were placed in local newspapers by individuals living at 747 Rush. In 1919, a single man at that address identified as "J. L. C." was looking for a comfortable room to rent, with the use of a private garage if possible, in Windsor Park or Cheltenham. In 1924, someone at the address was eager to sell a new ermine jacket and a Persian lamb coat. Was a furrier living in the building, or someone whose fortunes had turned downward? And, in 1925, a bespectacled and serious looking art student named Ralph Hilson, who lived there, was picked at random on the street by a *Tribune* reporter and asked his opinion on Life. His philosophical answer that modern man was too influenced by superficial, day-to-day events may have represented the growing Bohemian contingent living on the Near North Side.

In 1920, the lodgers at 747 Rush Street were a mixed bag of apartment dwellers. R. Lee Radford, who worked in a paint store, and his wife, Elizabeth, were listed as the head of the household at 747 Rush, though they were renting their rooms. Lodger John M. Keyes was forty, from New York, and an actor. "Union Leaders" was given as his employer. His wife, Christine Keyes, was a much younger twenty-one, an actress on the legitimate stage. Charles and Anna St. Clarie were janitors in an office building. Faith D. Prindle, age twenty-three, was a telegraph operator. A woman named Madlyn Bourchelll; a meter reader for the electric company, a German-born porter; and two factory workers completed the tenants.

Next door, at 749 Rush (which would eventually house show people connected with Club Alabam), Roy L. Davis and his wife, Tillie, were listed as the heads of the household. Roy's occupation was given as the keeper of the lodging house. He may have managed the apartments at both 747 and 749 Rush. There were five additional lodgers living at 749 Rush: an electrician, a hotel clerk, a clerk at a boiler company, a manager whose employer is illegible, and a piano tuner. There was another rooming house at 751 Rush. Among those tenants there was a theater stagehand and a French-speaking waiter who worked in an unnamed hotel.

Except for the actors, these apartments were rented by a variety of working class men and women. This would change dramatically when Dan Blanco created the Club Alabam. Over the coming decade, during the roaring years of Prohibition, this area of the Near North Side emerged as the late night place to be. Before the Federal Census was taken again in 1930, 747 Rush Street would become the entrance to the Club Alabam while 749 Rush was the front door to the apartments attached to the club, housing a colorful group of entertainers.

◆ ◆ ◆

By September of 1927, Dan Blanco was open for business, calling his establishment "Chicago's Novelty Night Club." Transforming 747 Rush into a nightclub must have involved considerable remodeling. Surely Blanco had investors. Who were they? At its inception, Blanco's place may have had a direct connection with Manhattan's Club Alabam, a popular "black and tan" cabaret located in the 44th Street Theatre Building, just west of Broadway.

Eddie South's Club Alabamians, the orchestra which opened Blanco's nightclub, came directly from New York City. Eddie South, a classical violin prodigy who had turned to jazz, began his career playing with, among others, Jimmy Wade, who was featured at the Moulin Rouge. As always, Blanco strove to offer his customers something different.

The interior of the Club Alabam reflected its downhome name. Red and white checkered tablecloths created a casual atmosphere and waitresses stood ready to serve up your meal—Southern style. Advertisements announced that, after hours at the Club Alabam, you could "watch the modern Aunt Jemima making waffles in the wee hours of the morning."

The club received positive press and was featured in articles alongside familiar names like Merry Garden, Samovar, Frolics, and Club Ansonia. Dan Blanco's Club Alabam was called—a "distinctive song and supper shop."

◆ ◆ ◆

Dan Blanco had been wise to move on from Moulin Rouge. Judge Cliffe's decision had been upheld. Hence forth, consumption of liquor by a patron could result in an injunction and, eventually, a padlock. On November 1, 1927, government locks went on the doors of both Moulin Rouge and Friar's Inn, featured in the backpage gallery of the *Chicago Daily Tribune*. Moulin Rouge never reopened.

New Year's Eve 1927/1928 approached—the first of many for Chicago's Club Alabam. Prohibition Administrator E. C. Yellowley was now a seasoned expert in controlling the city on the wildest night of the year. Four hundred prohibition agents stood ready to spread through cabarets and clubs. In the swankier places, agents would be dressed in tuxedos. Yellowley encouraged Chicagoans to enjoy themselves while abstaining from alcohol.

Described as "Loud, Gay and Orderly," Yellowley's New Year's Eve operation was successful. There was not a single arrest due to a violation of the Volstead Act. Amazing. The Administrator once again told reporters that he had witnessed the driest New Year's Eve to date. There was no trouble anywhere his agents were stationed. Proprietors cooperated and guests in hotels and cabarets were observed to be law-abiding. That was the official stance.

In fact, Chicagoans drank on the sly. In the city's hotels, in private rooms, there was many a hip flask. It was later reported that hotel elevators reeked of alcohol. The crowds in the larger places were late in gathering, perhaps, because they had done their drinking at home, away from the prying eyes of the police. Chez Pierre, for example, had booked 350 reservations. There, the headwaiter told the early arrivals that he hoped they would be orderly and dry. At the Drake Hotel, where 800 guests were expected, the management refused to serve setups. No chipped ice or ginger ale—at any price.

Despite Yellowley's call for abstinence, deaths from tainted alcohol were climbing. On New Year's Eve, the city's coroner, Oscar Wolff, damned the Volstead Act as a failure and menace to the American people. Most Prohibition victims, he claimed, were respectable, hardworking, honorable citizens. Encouraging temperance would save lives. He tentatively advocated legalizing light wines and beer.

CHAPTER SEVEN

Chicago's Club Alabam: Presenting Evelyn Nesbit

In early 1928, Gene Harris' name appeared in the *Tribune* column "Our Town: Neighborly Bits of News and Gossip from All Sides of Chicago." Identified as an "affable headwaiter," Harris commented on his customers at the Club Alabam: "There's been a great falling off in cotton stockings among lady nightclub patrons. In fact, I have not seen a cotton sock in fifteen years."[118]

Cotton stockings had long ago given way to silk or rayon rolled down hose, particularly with the smart set. As the end of the 1920s approached, flappers, according to Gene Harris, had been rouging their bare knees for some time. Having just turned twenty-eight at the time of the interview, Harris apparently had been observing women's legs since he was in short pants!

Gene Harris: From Iowa To Chicago

Gene Harris had traveled a long and indirect road to Chicago, arriving sometime before 1923. His personality was established early—adventuresome, friendly, curious, and a bit daring. Born in a small town in southern Iowa, he was not destined to remain there long.

On October 26, 1897, his Virginian-born father, Clayton Eugene Harris, married for the third time in Leon, Iowa. His bride was Ruth Belle Wales, a native Iowan almost twenty years his junior. Ruth grew up in Appanoose County, due east of Leon. Clay and his only daughter, Minnie, were part of a large, multi-generational Harris clan which had left central Virginia after the Civil War and settled in southern Iowa, near the Missouri boarder. Clay's brothers owned and operated a thriving monument business, catering not only to the roughly 2,000 citizens of Leon, but also to the surrounding states. Clay did not join his brothers in business, choosing to operate a grocery store as he had in Virginia.

On July 12, 1899, Ruth gave birth to a son, Eugene Alexander "Gene" Harris. By April 18, 1900, Clay Harris was dead and Ruth did not return to her family in Appanoose County. In Leon, the extended Harris family gave Ruth financial support and they would remain close to Gene throughout his life. Clay's married sister, Willie Allen, took responsibility for raising Gene's half-sister, Minnie. Eventually, Ruth and young Gene moved to Colorado, where she married a hotelkeeper named Kindred "Wesley" Rose. In 1910, Gene was living in Rocky Ford, Colorado and had a half-sister named Pauline.

Slimly built, with gray, narrow set eyes and light hair, Gene resembled his mother. Educational opportunities in Colorado were limited, especially as he was ready to transition into high school. On this pretext Gene returned to Leon, where he completed the eighth grade. There, he also had opportunities for employment with the successful Harris-owned monument business. It is also entirely possible that by age fourteen, Gene Harris had become a handful.

On June 19, 1913, the *Leon Reporter* noted: "Eugene Harris, who has been living with his mother, Mrs. Ruth Rose at Rocky Ford, Colorado for several years, came last Saturday and will make his home in this city with his uncle, J. T. Harris."[119] Julian Thomas Harris and his brother, John Alexander Harris, served as Gene's guardians and managed his finances, which included $100 and "a contingent interest" in property in Virginia.[120]

Uncle Julian and his wife, Mollie, had no children of their own. Their commodious house, complete with wraparound porch, had plenty of room to accommodate their nephew. Despite their generosity, Gene's rebellious ways quickly made themselves known. In March of 1914, he ran away from home and the local sheriff was engaged to return him to Leon. Expenses to collect him totaled $11.40.

Gene was not a scholar and needed an occupation. In the summer of 1918, he worked steadily at the Harris brothers' monument shop. Quickly, Leon proved too confining for Gene's wanderlust. At the end of August he purchased eight dollars' worth of luggage and headed west. By September of 1918, he had settled in San Francisco, where he worked as a waiter for a restaurant called Schneider Brothers located at 1891 Haight Street, opposite Golden Gate Park. Living in a single room in a large apartment house at 415 Jones Street, situated in the city's Tenderloin District, Gene was finally on his own in an exciting city. Three years earlier, in the summer of 1915, this cosmopolitan metropolis had hosted over nineteen million visitors during the Panama-Pacific International Exposition. Recovered from the devastating 1906 earthquake, San Francisco was promoting itself as "The World's Favorite City." Gene Harris doubtless agreed.

By February of 1919, Gene had moved to San Francisco's financial district, living at 447 Bush Street, then the Hansa Hotel, which rented rooms by the week. An upgrade from Jones Street, some of the rooms had private baths. That month, he wed waitress Bessie Agnes Mahoney, an Irish immigrant a few years his senior.

Their marriage was brief. After moving to San Diego, where they continued to wait tables, the couple separated. Bessie returned to San Francisco and lived with her married sister. Gene headed for Los Angeles and, according to his cousin, Elizabeth "Babe" Harris, used the city as a jumping off point to roam the world. By 1922, he was back in Los Angeles, where he registered to vote. Occupation: Waiter. Party: Democrat. That year, Uncle Julian Harris concluded his job as guardian, closing Gene's accounts in Leon and sending $53.70 to his nephew in Los Angeles.

Then, something or someone unknown took Gene to Chicago. In 1923, the Chicago city directory included the following listing: Eug. Harris, waiter, renting, 524 E. 44th Street. For the next forty years, Chicago would be home to the affable waiter, maître d', and entrepreneur—Gene Harris.

In 1923, Harris' employer is unknown. His rented room was in a middle class house on 44th Street. The South Side Elevated railroad, with its 24-hour service for those who worked around the clock, stopped at 42nd Street, convenient to transport the energetic young man north to Chicago's Loop. There his future business partner, Dan Blanco, was in charge of entertainment at the Moulin Rouge Café. How and when they first met remains a mystery.

By early 1928, however, when Gene Harris' name appeared in "Our Town," he was firmly established as the headwaiter at the Club Alabam and the adventurous boy from Leon, Iowa had found his permanent home.

◆ ◆ ◆

The year started smoothly at 747 Rush Street. In February of 1928, the current show received a nice mention in a round-up of entertainment in

Chicago. Eddie South and his Club Alabamians were cutting records, further spreading the nightclub's visibility.

Then, Prohibition Administrator E. C. Yellowley launched an unprecedented attack against a dozen of Chicago's most popular nightspots. His primary goal may have been to expose the widespread tolerance of "hippos," though, it was suspected that the federal government was digging into connections between the café business and Chicago gangsters. Reported targets included Hollywood Barn, Jeffery Tavern, Cymac, Parody Café, Sunset, Blackhawk, Plantation, Alamon, Club Bagdad, Samovar, Rainbo Gardens, Mike Fritzel's Club Ansonia, Rendezvous Café, and Chez Pierre. A raid at Mike Bloom's Midnight Frolics did not result in an injunction. Many others displayed injunction notices on their front doors. By April, The Rendezvous, Jeffery Tavern, and Sunset were padlocked. Several major clubs including Midnight Frolics, Club Ansonia, and Chez Pierre continued to be scrutinized. The majority of the establishments were exonerated—no booze found on the premises. Some reports included Club Alabam on the watch list.[121]

Variety reported the bold raid: "For the first time in the history of local prohibition enforcement no search warrants were used, and every guest that had a highball glass, ice, ginger ale, or charged waters at their tables were given the once over. Names and addresses were taken and verified before the people were permitted to leave."[122]

The patrons caught with hipflasks or bottles of liquor were not arrested nor would they be prosecuted, though they were asked to testify that they purchased setups at the café. The largest assortment of bottles was found at Rainbo Gardens and Rendezvous.

A year earlier, Mike Fritzel (Friar's Inn), Bill Rothstein (Moulin Rouge) and Al Tierney (Tierney's Town Club) had banded together, attempting to organize fellow nightclub owners and operators. Briefly, Fred Mann, proprietor of Rainbo Gardens, and others considered joining forces to form a local trade association with the intention to take Prohibition officials to court to contend that raids required search warrants and that Yellowley's agents specifically targeted the outlying clubs while sparing the downtown hotels. Within days, Mann announced that he was retaining an attorney and planned to fight his own battle. It was every café proprietor for himself.[123]

Summer saw the addition of a cozy open-air, garden annex to Club Alabam, where Gene Harris supervised the tables. *The Chicagoan*, the city's answer to *The New Yorker*, deemed the atmosphere jolly, yet orderly. A novel Moorish room was inviting and "Professor" Tyler led his band of African-American musicians. Described as rustic, not in a derogatory way, there was no padlock on the door at 747 Rush Street. Nice people, and apparently a dry atmosphere, abounded at Dan Blanco's popular club.[124]

Gaiety–Prohibition Style

New Year's Eve 1928/1929 came and went. Snow fell before midnight and soon the Chicago streets were full of wet slush, but few inebriated revelers. There were 14,000 lively celebrators in the Loop alone. This holiday, Administrator E. C. Yellowley placed 200 prohibition agents throughout the town. Once again as café proprietors and managers across the city pledged their cooperation, Yellowley assured the press that hotel and café owners stood ready to cooperate with federal agents and would prohibit drinking at their tables. Patrons, however, had entered into no such agreement.

Yellowley ordered his prohibition agents to confiscate hip flasks, which is exactly what they did at Club La Boheme on South Wabash Avenue. There, half a dozen patrons lost their liquor. At the College Inn, in the Loop's Hotel Sherman, patrons weren't even hiding bottles under the tables. A whopping thirty flasks were seized. Assistant Administrator George Hurlburt, who was in charge on New Year's Eve, stated: "This is the quietest New Year's [Eve] I have ever experienced. I think the people have grown tired of bootleg and gangster wars and are reconciled to the fact that we have a prohibition law."[125]

The Administration certainly turned a blind eye to the city's Near North Side. There, Dan Blanco's establishment hummed with business. Clubs in the district, including Chez Pierre, Turkish Village, Vanity Fair, and Club Alabam, were packed, turning guests away.[126]

In that section of Chicago, pervasive drinking was not reported. Why? No prohibition agents showed up on the North Side and the police found the district orderly.

1929 began well for Club Alabam. The kitchen offered both Chinese and Southern dishes, supervised by chefs Jim Foo Park and Monroe Cowart.

Eddie Jackson's "colored band" was now featured. Headwaiter Gene Harris was the man to know if you wanted a stage-side table. This was a late night resort where the fun lasted until dawn or after.

Moving from the Loop to Chicago's North Side had several advantages for Dan Blanco and Gene Harris. Young singles and couples were much more likely to cruise clubs on Rush Street than dress up for the Loop. The general atmosphere was Bohemian, allowing for a relaxed nightlife rather than high-tone restaurants with chorus lines and orchestras. Here Blanco's entertainment could be drawn from vaudevillians and cabaret artists, with whom he was intimately familiar. Additionally, Rush Street was out of Al Capone's territory. George "Bugs" Moran, who had replaced the murdered Dion O'Banion, was now boss of the "North Side Gang." Dan Blanco had dealt with this mob during his tenure at Northern Lights and, at least in 1924, was on friendly terms with them.

Not that this part of Chicago was peaceful. Far from it. A full-fledged gangster war had been raging for months when Capone's men, likely in an attempt to kill Moran, executed seven men in a North Clark Street garage on February 14, 1929. Forever to be known as the St. Valentine's Day Massacre, Capone was not convicted and Bugs Moran dug in, holding his territory through the end of Prohibition.

Following the Massacre, 1929 did not go so smoothly for Dan Blanco and the Club Alabam. In May, an extremely small notice was carried by the Associated Press, printed in newspapers across the country. The blurb stated that Judge Joseph L. McCarthy of the Chicago Avenue Court discharged Dan Blanco on a liquor charge but held the woman arrested with him—an entertainer identified as Miss Mary L. Harris. Police told the court that they discovered the twenty-two-year-old Mary Lee Harris pouring alcoholic drinks for Club Alabam guests on the night of April 29. While Harris is a common name, especially in the South, it is an odd coincidence. Was there a connection between this entertainer and Gene Harris?

Next, it was illegal gaming devices that brought Club Alabam to the attention of State's Attorney John A. Swanson. At 2:30 a.m. on the morning of June 16, 1929, police raided the club, battering in the door of a third floor room with axes. Three men and a girl were reportedly playing roulette. Neither the dancers nor the diners in the café were disturbed when Dan Blanco was taken away for questioning. A total of seven arrests were made, including Blanco's croupiers who gave their names as William Herrington and Charles (Carl) M. Smith. William Fuller, son of Leroy Fuller, vice president of the Chicago Car Seal company, and his companion, Vivian Baker, were, apparently, doing the betting. The roulette wheels were seized but later returned because police officer Capt. John Ryan broke into the room without a warrant.

A later report stated that Gene Harris, a waiter, and Otto Jones, a "colored porter," were also taken to the station. Were Harris and Jones arrested because they were in the upstairs room? This may not have been the first time that Gene Harris was apprehended for questioning. It most certainly would not be the last. Late night or early morning conversations at the neighborhood precinct went with the Rush Street territory.

Evelyn Nesbit: Ups And Downs

In September of 1929, Dan Blanco announced that Evelyn Nesbit and Her Atlantic City Beauties would appear at the Club Alabam—"Chicago's Intimate Nite Club." Apparently, despite the turmoil of her most recent engagement under Blanco's direction at the Moulin Rouge, they worked well together and Nesbit brought in customers. This invitation to perform at the Club Alabam would ultimately last four months and cement a relationship between the aging entertainer and the Rush Street cabaret which included Gene Harris, soon to be Blanco's partner and the club's eventual sole proprietor.

It had been almost four years since Evelyn Nesbit's Chicago suicide attempt and her life had been typically rocky during that period. Among her legal actions, Nesbit came to the defense of her minor son, Russell, when newspapers printed that he had thrown unsupervised private parties in Chicago's Congress Hotel, suing the hotel corporation for $50,000 damages in slander and liable against Russell.[127]

Rumors flew that Nesbit planned to remarry Harry K. Thaw. During their reconciliation, Thaw, in a generous mood, purportedly bought her a bungalow in Tudor Terrace, eight miles from Atlantic City. The deed was filed in her name. The cost: $22,000–25,000. Nesbit told reporters, "It's a simple white frock and a kitchen for me. I'll be glad to get out of the cabaret." That dream didn't last long, either because she was not cut out to be a homebody or because she needed to work to afford the house and other expenses.[128]

Despite ups and downs, Atlantic City became a comparatively secure base for Nesbit. She made money. She lost money. In early February of 1927, she lent her name to the Evelyn Nesbit Supper Club near Miami, Florida at Hialeah. The club, which occupied the former Montmartre, was almost immediately raided for gambling, though no arrests were made. When the summer season opened in Atlantic City, Nesbit returned north and worked at the Follies Bergere, with the Eddie Davis Orchestra, featuring Davis on a jazz tenor saxophone.

Next, she decided to go out on her own and, on July 28, started the Evelyn Nesbit Club, taking over the space that was formerly Club Renault on Pacific Avenue, in Atlantic City. She offered a small show, a few acts supported a headliner. In September, she worked with Olga Rilga, Peggy Heavens, Manny King "the Washington boy soprano," and Mayo & Marie. A sensational review included eight beautiful chorus girls, wearing costumes designed by Nesbit. The music of "Joe Frasetto and His Boys" added to the club's initial success.

Financial backing was provided through Nesbit's ex-partner in the failed El Prinkipo. Again, underworld connections brought down the enterprise. One of her behind-the-scenes partners was New York City mob-connected Jerry Daniels, who frightened Nesbit, especially when he was drinking. She believed members of his gang robbed her house not only of cash and jewels but also stole her furs—mink, ermine, and leopard coats—reportedly worth $10,000. Importantly, a safe was taken, which contained legal papers concerning her son Russell. These were never recovered and the smashed safe was later found in a swamp near Absecon Boulevard. It wasn't long before Jerry Daniels and Nesbit's partner had a serious disagreement, giving her an excuse to abandon the club.

By November, the 1927 season was over in Atlantic City and Nesbit returned to Manhattan to open Chez Evelyn (a.k.a. Evelyn Nesbit Club) at 228 West 52nd Street, just a few doors from her failed tearoom. Newly decorated in rose, black, and gold, opening night for Chez Evelyn was set for Tuesday, November 15. She would act as hostess, as well as choreograph a revue featuring a dozen chorus girls. Her agreement was a 50/50 profit split with club manager Jules Martin. Almost immediately there was conflict. Martin received a summons for operating a cabaret without a license, though he insisted he held a permit for the Cameo Club and that "Chez Evelyn" was an alternate name.

Nesbit's former husband, Harry Thaw (who was released from Kirkbride Asylum in April, 1924), was sent an invitation for a stage-side seat on opening night. She wryly told the press, "He probably will be there. You know Harry likes first nights." It was on the fateful opening night of *Mam'zelle Champagne*, playing in the rooftop theater of Madison Square Garden, in 1906, when Thaw shot and killed his rival, and his wife's former lover, architect Stanford White.[129]

Mark Hellinger, syndicated journalist working at the *New York Daily News*, attended opening night at Chez Evelyn and gave Nesbit a glowing review in his Sunday column, "About Town," which specialized in human interest stories, as well as covering news and gossip about Broadway theater. Hellinger insisted that Nesbit looked fifteen years younger than her actual age. Slender and graceful, her eyes were clear, with no indication that she had been to hell and back—more than once. He noted that she had suffered through a grueling murder trial; lived with the abusive Harry Thaw; kicked a morphine habit; made and lost fortunes; and, for twenty years, had seen her name on the front page time and time again. Yet through it all, she persevered, supporting herself and her son Russell. Hellinger deeply admired her dedication as a mother. Now eighteen years old, Russell had grown into a fine young man. Perhaps, for this above all else, Hellinger respected Evelyn Nesbit, wishing her ongoing success as she continued to ride the waves of her cabaret career.[130]

Although, like so many other of Nesbit's ventures, Chez Evelyn lasted only a few weeks, it was open long enough for Harry Thaw to pay a visit, behave erratically, and create headlines. One version maintained Thaw got in a fight with his bodyguard and began pounding the table, sending glassware flying. One of the entertainers was cut by a shattering goblet. Nesbit denied that Thaw's upset was over the size of his check, saying that he just threw one of his mild tantrums. She did admit, though, that at the end of the evening, she presented her former husband with a bill somewhere between $200 and $300, covering food, cigarettes, etc. The "etc." must have been pretty valuable. Nesbit remained unflustered, saying that handling the demonstration was all in a night's work. Thaw countered, claiming a photographer's flash bulb set off his nerves. He stayed until the club closed and, ultimately, paid his check.

The quixotic Nesbit did not remain long in Manhattan. On December 3, she announced that she was quitting Chez Evelyn, claiming that Jules Martin had broken their contract, had not shared the profits equally, and had kept no accounts. She also told reporters that Martin's club was $20,000 in debt when she entered into the agreement. Her work, she said, had paid off Martin's obligations. Unconcerned about where her next job was coming from, Nesbit added that she had offers from eight other nightclubs. *Variety* reported the story with a different twist: "Miss Nesbit walked. Biz n. g., anyway."[131]

Never one to skip a beat, Evelyn Nesbit returned to vaudeville with an act entitled "Personality Personified." In January of 1928, her tour included Boston's Bowdoin Square Theater, which featured continuous movies, Pathe Newsreels, and five vaudeville acts. William Boyd and Bessie Love in *Dress Parade*, along with Alice Terry and Ivan Petrovich in *Garden of Allah*, shimmered on the silver screen. Perched on the piano in the style of Helen Morgan and looked remarkably youthful, dressed in a plunging, beaded Paris gown, Evelyn Nesbit entertained an appreciative audience.

She was likely relieved to be on the road and out of New Jersey during early 1928. There, in March, gangster Jerry Daniels, former backer of the Evelyn Nesbit Club in Atlantic City, was slain at the Corn Exchange (located at North Carolina and Arctic avenues), a "booze dive" he owned. When first reported, the assailant(s) and motive were unknown. In one version, Daniels, who had several nicknames including "King of the Jungle" and "Jerry the Greek," was supposedly with a blonde who "picked a quarrel with him and killed him with a volley of shots."[132] Other reports claimed that four gunmen killed the gangster while he was sitting upstairs with Al McDonald, who had also been Evelyn Nesbit's cabaret partner. McDonald's presence at the Corn Exchange and Nesbit's previous association with Jerry Daniels gave the press a double excuse to bring her name into the story despite the fact that she had nothing to do with Daniels' murder. Ten days later, Samuel "Cappy" Hoffeman, surrendered, confessing he was the murderer.[133]

The following year, another former Nesbit partner, Andre Chatelan, was sent to Sing Sing on two counts of forgery. Tough bunch, the Atlantic City cabaret crowd.

During the month of May, the 1928 season gained momentum. The *Chicago Daily Tribune* printed a friendly warning to all Chicago club owners that Atlantic City presented serious competition when it came to adult entertainment. Despite the national prohibition of alcohol, the island was wet and wild, dotted with nightspots that blatantly ignored the Volstead Act. Here, there were two oceans, just one of which was filled with salt water. Journalist Tom Pettey wrote that a visitor could simply step onto the Boardwalk, turn left or right, getting his feet wet on one side and his throat wet on the other. Beer was conveniently available, imported from Newark and Jersey City. Liquor was brought ashore from ships, diluted, and prepared for sale.

Hip flasks were ubiquitous in hotels and restaurants. Setups of cracked ice and ginger ale could be seen on 90% of the tables in respectable establishments such as the Ambassador, Ritz, and Traymore. The Silver Slipper, which featured a fifteen piece orchestra, was the season's hot spot. All over town drinking and dancing persisted until dawn. Atlantic City was building a reputation as THE convention city and America's playground.

Astonishingly, for the most part, nightclubs and bars were unmolested by the local police. If an occasional padlock went on the door, the proprietors probably catered to tough characters. Speakeasies were unknown because liquor was widely available. In May, the Palais Royal, Follies, and several other clubs on the Boardwalk were about to open their doors. The immediate future of Chez Evelyn was unknown. Boardwalk gossip indicated it might remain closed.[134]

◆ ◆ ◆

In late 1928/early 1929, Evelyn Nesbit's merry-go-round life of opening and closing nightclubs repeated itself again in Manhattan. This time, partner and proprietor Joseph Ward featured Nesbit at his Uptown Club (a.k.a. Swanee Club) in Harlem. Located at 253 West 125th Street (today The Apollo Theater), the club was ready for the 1928 holiday season. Ward engaged Nesbit's chorus girls and Joe Frasetto's band from her recently closed Atlantic City review—a ready-made show.

As a publicity stunt, Harry Thaw was invited for opening night on December 13, 1928. Nesbit acted as hostess and performer, singing popular songs of the day. Joining Thaw at his table, they comfortably indulged in repartee. He stayed until early morning, apparently, leaving the club without incident. Life rarely ran smoothly for Evelyn Nesbit. That month, her only brother, Howard, committed suicide in his home in the Bronx.

◆ ◆ ◆

Following what may have been a fairly quiet New Year's Eve at the Uptown Club, Evelyn Nesbit and Joe Ward were arrested when federal agents raided the cabaret. The charge: violating Prohibition laws. Reports stated that the club was cleared of 400 patrons, while Nesbit and others were taken to the 124th Street police station. They were released on bond and ordered to appear in court the next day before a Federal commissioner. Nesbit gave her age as forty-one, a resident of Northfield, New Jersey. Nesbit's version of the raid included a comical reception in Harlem's police station. A flock of taxicabs dropped off the arrested show people. A sleepy matron pointed to the two Belgian Griffons Nesbit had refused to leave behind in her dressing room, saying: "What's them things you've got? Monkeys?"[135]

A familiar end to the story was the threat of the padlock and a year-long injunction for Joe Ward's club; however, Nesbit was still playing there in March of 1929.

◆ ◆ ◆

Evelyn Nesbit headed back to the comparative security of Atlantic City. There, she and Joe Ward re-opened the Evelyn Nesbit Club on Decoration Day 1929. Referred to as a luxurious nightlife casino, the club sat directly opposite Atlantic City's new Convention Hall. Ward, described as a popular showman, was banking on Nesbit's seemingly eternal popularity, yet theirs turned out to be yet another short-lived business relationship. By September, Nesbit was the hostess at Atlantic City's Follies Bergère. In her memoir, Nesbit claimed that Joe Ward was unprepared for the power of Atlantic City's political czar Enoch L. Johnson, who favored a rival club in the neighborhood. Conventioners were warned against entering the Evelyn Nesbit Club after the 1 o'clock curfew and Ward's business suffered, finally failing.

During her association with Joe Ward, Nesbit had a rare, publicized romance. The love affair was not with Ward, but with Russian-born singer Ivan Alexievitch Romanoff. The couple met while she headed the review at the Uptown Club. Handsome, sporting slicked back hair and a pencil moustache, Romanoff was enthralled when he heard Nesbit sing, "I Must Have That Man."

Following a whirlwind romance of three weeks, on February 6, 1929, newspapers reported that Nesbit was engaged to Romanoff, a twenty-seven-year-old basso then appearing in "The Red Robe" under the name of Ivan Alexis. He claimed to be a Russian Prince, nephew of the late Grand Duke Nicholas, who had died recently at Antibes, France. The singer's father was reportedly a private attaché of the late Czar. Living at the fashionable Whitby (325 West 45th Street), Romanoff had been in the U.S. eight years, training for grand opera. Nesbit, who was staying at the Hotel Manger, commented that she was not sure which she loved best ... the Prince or his voice.

Nesbit prepared a formal statement for the press, calling her fiancé charming, an aristocratic gentleman. "I am still the wife of Jack Clifford ... but I expect to get my divorce in New Jersey very soon. I thought I would never marry again, but this is a real love affair, and when I get my divorce I shall become Princess Evelyn."[136]

Princess Evelyn was not to be. Her divorce from Jack Clifford was not forthcoming. How long the engagement to Romanoff lasted is anyone's guess. As autumn came around, it was back to Chicago for Evelyn Nesbit.

Chicago's Whoopee Belt

With the 1929 Atlantic City season behind her, Evelyn Nesbit agreed to what would become a multi-month engagement at Chicago's Club Alabam, earning a modest $450 per week. Arriving in early October, she witnessed Black Tuesday, October 29, 1929, along with Dan Blanco and Gene Harris. It would take time for the stock market crash to percolate through the general economy. For Club Alabam, a much more immediate threat came in the form of Capt. Charles Essig, who had recently been assigned to the East Chicago Avenue Police Station to clean up the so-called "whoopee belt"—the cafés on the Near North Side.

On November 13, Capt. Essig invited the proprietors of nightclubs and cafes in his district to meet with him. Dan Blanco; Henry Shapiro and David Ablon of the Club Algiers; Pat Nallin from the Turkish Village; Danny Barone of the Club Ambassadeur; and five others showed up for the meeting.[137] Essig made it clear that he planned to eliminate liquor from the Near North Side clubs as well as clean up the nest of gangsters who preyed on the Gold Coast. The back page gallery in the *Tribune* included a photo of a stout and aging Dan Blanco.

Essig meant business and was quoted extensively in the press, saying that he understood the club owners were selling liquor and expected it to stop entirely. If necessary, he threatened to visit establishments in person to see that the law was enforced. He emphatically stated that he wanted all doors opened. *No locked doors.* If any were, Essig would kick them in.

These Near North Side establishments, known as "key clubs," were open to patrons who could "unlock" the door. Whether or not these clubs were opened with a literal key, a membership card, or a password is unknown. However these keys worked, Capt. Essig wanted anyone of legal age to be able to walk into one of these nightspots, unannounced, no secret code required. He concluded: "I don't want you fellows to think I'm a czar.... I'm tough on all law violators, but a hell of a nice fellow to deal with when legitimate businessmen call on me for help."[138]

Presumably, following this meeting, the doors to the Club Alabam were left unlocked and Evelyn Nesbit continued to entertain there through November, sharing the bill with Kitty Cohn, Dorothy Durnell, Billy Meyers, and Bernie Adler, Dan Blanco's longtime associate. Eddie Jackson's band provided dance music.[139]

Then came December and the holiday season. How successful was Captain Essig's no-nonsense campaign? On December 30, 1929, the *Tribune* ran the cheerful headline: "Expect a Wet Dawn of 1930 Despite Drys." The article predicted there would be many opportunities to toast the New Year on the Near North Side, anticipating that ginger ale and setups would be served in hotels and the city's nightspots. While hotels might show discretion in pouring alcohol, open drinking was expected in cabarets such as the Frolics, Granada, Green Mill, and Club Alabam.

The turning of a decade suggested even more celebration than usual on New Year's Eve. The proprietors of hotels and clubs in the Loop District were expecting 20,000 guests and had collected $180,000 in table reservations. Notably, Chicago's famous Palmer House, fearing property damage and, perhaps, a padlock if patrons were observed drinking, decided to close its main dining rooms for New Year's Eve 1929/1930.

While record breaking numbers were expected in the Loop, across Chicago there were significantly fewer places to celebrate than had existed on New Year's Eve 1928/1929. Assistant United States Attorney La Verne Norris noted 511 of Chicago's drinking establishments had been closed by permanent injunction during 1929. Property valued at $5,000,000 now sat unused, padlocked for a calendar year. Norris posed an obvious question concerning the anticipated revelry, "How can there be a bigger celebration when there are more than 500 less places to go?"

The Prohibition Administration was confident it would be a peaceful, law-abiding night. E. C. Yellowley, who decided to leave town for the holiday, predicted a deserted Loop. Yellowley's absence left Assistant Probation Administrator George K. Hurlburt in charge of enforcement. When interviewed by the *Tribune*, Hurlburt denied the rumor that special agents were coming to Chicago to handle drinkers and told the press that he expected another routine New Year's Eve.

Ultimately, the variety of statements describing the night verged on the schizophrenic. The *Tribune*'s front page headline on January 1 screamed: LOOP ROARS FOR NEW YEAR. The article noted that crowds of merrymakers made deafening noise, with shouts and tin horns. On the South Side, shots rang out. And all over town, factory and locomotive whistles heralded the arrival of a new decade. Liquor flowed freely, apparently unnoticed by 100 federal agents, who had been tasked with preventing violations of the Volstead Act.

Conversely, a blasé George Hurlburt issued a statement that was beginning to sound remarkably familiar. He calmly told reporters that this New Year's Eve was the driest in his recollection, believing that most of Chicago spent the evening at the movies. He attributed the remarkable orderliness to the cooperation of hotel managers and nightclub proprietors. Apparently, drinking was done at private parties. There were no arrests.

The major hotels, at least, cooperated with the Administration. At the Hotel Sherman, no setups were served and waiters discouraged drinking from bottles. There, fifteen prohibition agents were on duty. At Edgewater Beach, waiters refused numerous requests for setups, despite the absence of agents at that North Side hotel. Terrace Garden (Morrison Hotel) and the Gold Room (Congress Hotel) refused to serve cracked ice and ginger ale. According to the *Tribune*, both hotels served "mixing beverages" and many high balls were poured under the table.

At Green Mill, located at 4810 Broadway, the vivacious Texas Guinan, formerly of Manhattan's elite speakeasy 300 Club, served as hostess. Demonstrating her signature bravado, she opened the New Year's Eve party by asking prohibition agents to identify themselves and receive a big hand from the stage. Not a man came forward. No doubt hip flasks immediately appeared without hesitation and Guinan's show played until dawn to a capacity crowd of about 400 guests.

What about the Near North Side? Did flagrant scofflaw drinking take place in the whoopee belt as predicted? If so, Dan Blanco did not profit from it. The *Tribune* highlighted his unusual New Year's Eve experience: "Dan Blanco, manager of the Club Alabam, 747 Rush street, nominally one of the gayest in night life of the near north side, his place, which is packed on the average Saturday night, attracted only 20 couples."[140]

Why? Other so-called "key clubs" on the Near North Side did a lively business. Did Dan Blanco leave the door unlocked as demanded by the police, and customers, hesitant to drink with an open door, went elsewhere? Was Evelyn Nesbit still on the bill at the Club Alabam? If so, the small crowd was treated to an unexpectedly intimate evening.

Ruth (Wales) Harris and Eugene Alexander Harris. Rocky Ford, Colorado. c. 1903. (Photo by Wales Photography. Courtesy Ella Richardson Collection)

Eugene Alexander Harris. Rocky Ford, Colorado. c. 1903.
(Photo by Wales Photography. Courtesy Ella Richardson Collection)

In 1897, Ruth Belle Wales married Clayton Eugene "Clay" Harris in Leon, Iowa. Following his death in April, 1900, Ruth and their son, Eugene Alexander "Gene" Harris, moved to Rocky Ford, Colorado, where she was married a second time to Kindred "Wesley" Rose. At that time, Ruth's brother, Charles A. Wales, lived in Colorado and worked as a photographer. For over twenty years, Ruth lived in San Bernardino, California, teaching tapestry, china painting, and other arts and crafts at the Ruth Home studio near El Monte. She died in 1944. Her only son, Gene Harris, was not mentioned in her obituary.

Gene Harris, 1929.
(PUBLISHED WITH PERMISSION OF THE QUIGLEY PUBLISHING COMPANY, A DIVISION OF QP MEDIA, INC., *THE CHICAGOAN*: VOL. 7, NO. 2, 13 APRIL 1929, P. 4.)

This caricature of Gene Harris by Chicago artist Burton Browne appeared in a series of sketches of Chicago's top headwaiters featured in the city's society magazine, The Chicagoan. Later in life, Browne entered advertising and, in 1953, founded the Gaslight Club at 816 Rush Street.

Evelyn Nesbit, 1925.
(Courtesy *Chicago Daily News* negatives collections, Chicago History Museum, DN-007887)

Evelyn Nesbit arrived in Chicago, holding one of her beloved Belgian Griffons camouflaged by her fur cuff. Dan Blanco took a chance on the cabaret star when he invited her to appear at Bill Rothstein's Moulin Rouge Café. She was an unqualified success and it was the beginning of a long association between Blanco and Nesbit.

Evelyn Nesbit's Atlantic City.
(COURTESY THE TICHNOR BROTHERS COLLECTION, BOSTON PUBLIC LIBRARY)

New Wayside Inn, Advertisement. (AUTHOR COLLECTION)

In February of 1930, Evelyn Nesbit and Gene Harris launched the New Way Side Inn, located on West Beach Boulevard in Biloxi, Mississippi. Touted as "The South's Newest and Smartest Night Club," their involvement was short-lived. Nesbit moved on to Panama City, while Harris returned to Chicago and Club Alabam.

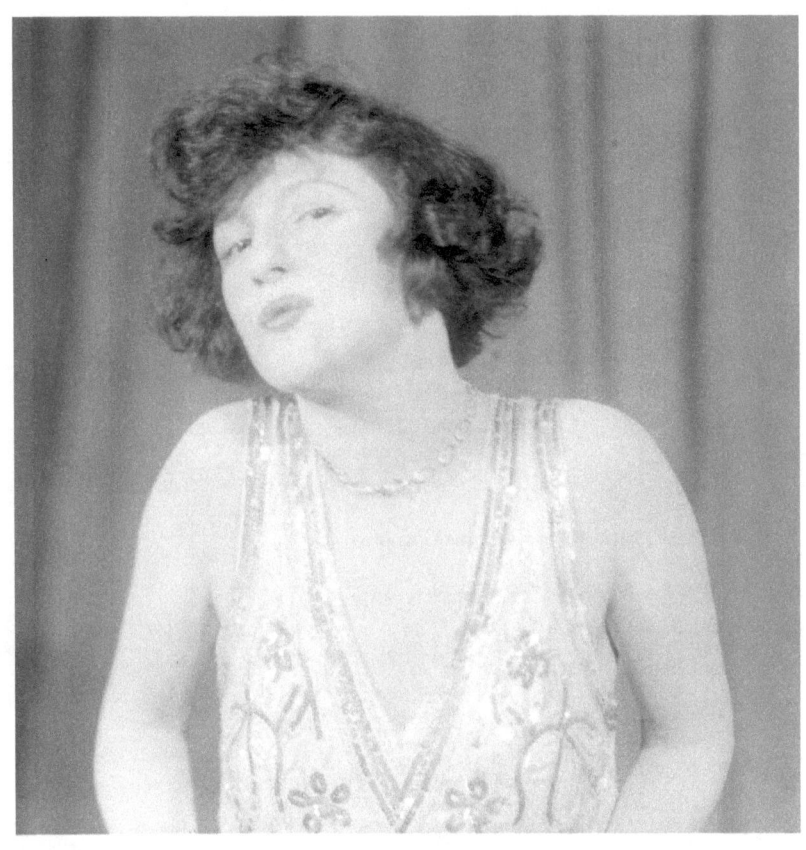

Evelyn Nesbit, Boston Massachusetts, 1928.
(Courtesy of the Boston Public Library, Leslie Jones Collection)

In January of 1928, Evelyn Nesbit played Boston's Bowdoin Square Theater, where her act was captured by Leslie Jones, staff photographer for the <u>Boston Herald-Traveler</u> from 1917–1956. In the early 1970s, nearly 40,000 of his photographic negatives were given to the Boston Public Library by the Jones family.

Kelly's Ritz, Panama City. (AUTHOR COLLECTION)

Kelly's Ritz in Panama City was owned by the infamous Mamie Lee Kelly, who was the inspiration for Cole Porter's "Panama Hattie." Kelly's establishments on the isthmus included a brothel, as well as a cabaret.

George "Bugs" Moran. (Author Collection)

George "Bugs" Moran and his gang controlled Chicago's North Side and Dan Blanco was obliged to buy his liquor from them. In 1930, when Moran's accountant Jack Zuta was killed, Club Alabam was listed in Zuta's accounts receivable, owing the operation $270.

Chicago's World's Fair, "A Century of Progress." (Author Collection)

During 1933-1934, Chicago's World's Fair, "A Century of Progress," was an unqualified Depression-era success. Attendance benefited from the legalization of 3.2 beer and, eventually, the repeal of Prohibition. Pabst Brewing Company sponsored the "Pabst Blue Ribbon Casino," selling foaming glasses of their award-winning product. The Fair's spectacular setting along Lake Michigan was dramatic, especially at night. Midget Village, a particularly popular spot, featured Moulin Rouge Café favorites, "Mike & Ike," among its inhabitants. In 1939, the midget twins would appear as Munchkins in "The Wizard of Oz." Also, working in the Fair's "Streets of Paris," Germaine and Paulette LaPierre sang French songs. The sisters would later work at Club Alabam.

Chicago's World's Fair, "A Century of Progress." (Author Collection)

Chicago's World's Fair, "A Century of Progress," Midget Village.
(Author Collection)

Eddie South, Café Society (Uptown), New York City, c. December 1946. (COURTESY WILLIAM P. GOTTLIEB COLLECTION, LIBRARY OF CONGRESS.)

In 1927, Eddie South and his Club Alabamians came direct from New York City to open Dan Blanco's Club Alabam in Chicago. South was a classical violin prodigy turned jazz musician. Noted writer and photographer William P. Gottlieb covered American jazz during its "Golden Age," documenting its evolution in preeminent publications such as the <u>Washington Post</u> and <u>Down Beat</u> magazine and photographing jazz legends including Louis Armstrong, Duke Ellington, Charlie Parker, Billie Holiday, Dizzy Gillespie, Earl Hines, Thelonious Monk, Stan Kenton, Benny Goodman, Coleman Hawkins, and Ella Fitzgerald.

Club Alabam, 747 Rush Street, c. 1960.
(COURTESY CHICAGO HISTORY MUSEUM, ICHi-051452)

In 1927, Dan Blanco opened the Club Alabam at 747 North Rush Street. Gene Harris became the sole proprietor following Blanco's death in 1937. Club Alabam closed following Harris' death in 1964, when it was deemed Chicago's longest operating, single-proprietor nightclub.

Paulette LaPierre. Photo by Maurice Seymour.
(Courtesy Mary O'Dowd Collection)

Paulette LaPierre. Photo by Maurice Seymour.
(Courtesy Mary O'Dowd Collection)

French songstress Paulette LaPierre was a long-time favorite at the Club Alabam. These photos, utilized for publicity at the club and for advertising in Chicago entertainment publications, were made by Maurice Seymour, Chicago's preeminent celebrity photographer. Seymour opened his photography studio in 1929, specializing in portraiture. His clientele regularly included actors, comedians, singers, and showgirls, though he was best known for his ballet pictures. Over decades, he photographed many of the top entertainers of the day, including Tommy Dorsey, Victor Borge, Anthony Quinn, Edith Piaf, Harry Belafonte, and Carl Reiner. His portraits of Paulette LaPierre perfectly capture her seductive combination of coquettishness and elegance, an ideal blend for the intimate stage at Club Alabam and Gene Harris' microphone.

SELWYN THEATRE

180 North Dearborn Street   Central 8240

It is urged for the comfort and safety of all, that theatre patrons refrain from lighting matches in this theatre.

Beginning Monday Evening, May 8, 1939

Matinees Wednesday and Saturday

RICHARD ALDRICH and RICHARD MYERS

Present

JOHN BARRYMORE

in

"MY DEAR CHILDREN"

A NEW FARCE COMEDY BY

CATHERINE TURNEY and JERRY HORWIN

with

DORIS DUDLEY ★ TALA BIRELL ★ PHILIP REED

Directed by OTTO L. PREMINGER

Setting by DONALD OENSLAGER

"My Dear Children," Selwyn Theatre, Chicago, Illinois. 1939.
(AUTHOR COLLECTION)

For six months during 1939, John Barrymore played Chicago's Selwyn Theater in the comedy "My Dear Children." Following one rollicking evening on stage, the tired thespian found his way to Gene Harris' Club Alabam, where Evelyn Nesbit was appearing on stage. The histrionic Barrymore publically declare his love for her, recalling their unrequited, youthful romance, no doubt receiving shocked applause from the Club Alabam regulars.

John Barrymore, "My Dear Children," *Playbill*, 1939. (Author Collection)

Lillian Bernard and Flo Henri, c. 1928. (AUTHOR COLLECTION)

In 1936, "Lil and Flo" celebrated their thirteenth year in show business at the Club Alabam.

CHAPTER EIGHT

Dixie Bound: Evelyn Nesbit & Gene Harris

Evelyn Nesbit finished her engagement at the Club Alabam and, traveling to Pittsburgh, spent the first weeks of the New Year with her mother, their first reunion in many years. There she gave an extensive interview to reporter Ruth Ayres of the *Pittsburgh Press*, expounding on what was now the focus of her life—Theosophy. After years of reading and serious study, Nesbit felt prepared to lecture on the subjects of philosophy, evolution, theosophy, and religion. Importantly, her son Russell was now self-supporting and Nesbit felt free to pursue the "work closest to her heart" as a possible occupation. As was often the case, Nesbit spoke forcefully, full of conviction. She insisted that she was tired of nightlife and undoubtedly was. Almost immediately, however, she agreed to a new venture with the thirty-year-old Gene Harris in, of all places, Biloxi, Mississippi.[141]

Dixie Bound

Beginning in February, Nesbit was contracted to open the New Wayside Inn, located on West Beach Boulevard in Biloxi. Touted as "The South's Newest and Smartest Night Club," lavish renovations had gone into the café. The club had been rebuilt, redecorated, and landscaped. Designed to seat over 400 patrons, the large oak floor accommodated 100 dancing couples. Merritt Brunies and his orchestra, formerly of Biloxi's Silver Slipper, would provide the music. Filling out the program with Evelyn Nesbit were a lovely, young brunette named Miss Rita Delano, the "Spanish Contralto" of the Keith Vaudeville Circuit, and Miss Jessie James, "New York's Personality Girl." The "Sunshine Chorus" included beautiful and talented specialty dancers from Chicago and New York. There would also be the typical song and dance acts, as well as comedy routines. The club would be under the management of Gene Harris, formerly of the Club Alabam in Chicago, who would offer his patrons three all-star shows every night. While the announcement read like a long-term situation, it quickly became clear that Nesbit's stay would be limited and Gene Harris would soon return to Chicago and his job as headwaiter at the Club Alabam.[142]

Biloxi's *Daily Herald* enthusiastically promoted the new club and Evelyn Nesbit's arrival on the Gulf Coast, letting readers know that the star of stage and screen would arrive at Gulfport's Illinois Central Railway Station. "The Most Talked About Woman in America" was coming directly from a four-month engagement at the well-known Club Alabam in Chicago to open the Wayside Inn.[143]

Preparing for opening night, scheduled for Tuesday, February 18, at 7:00 p.m., the *Daily Herald* ran large advertisements featuring Evelyn Nesbit's picture. The cover charge was set at $1.00. Patrons could expect a wide array of talent, with three shows per night. The bottom of the ad read, in smaller, but very readable typeface, GENE HARRIS, Manager.

On February 19, the newspaper dedicated a half page to congratulatory advertisements for the New Wayside Inn, in part paid for by the builders and renovators of the property, including Manuel & Wetzel, brothers-in-law and longtime general contractors in Biloxi. Gene Harris got what may have been his first mention in *Variety*. He even got top billing! "Gene Harris has taken over the Wayside Inn, Biloxi, Miss., and opens there shortly with a full cabaret policy. Evelyn Nesbit will be the name attraction with Rita Delano, who has been at the Club Forest, New Orleans, also present. A third female entertainer bills herself as "Little Jessie James—New York's Personality Girl."

Biloxi's *Daily Herald* reported enthusiastically on the opening night, praising the internationally famous Miss Evelyn Nesbit as mistress of ceremonies. The small café had been transformed into an elegant nightclub with modernistic, luxurious decor and a particularly effective lighting scheme. The cost of the renovation was estimated to exceed $15,000. By 10 p.m., the house was packed. At midnight, the first floor show went on, accompanied by the Merritt Brunies Orchestra. Nesbit herself sang several songs. Noted among the large number of visitors were many prominent residence of Biloxi and Gulfport, including several county and local officials.

In addition to an attractive chorus line, speciality dancer Joan Manalthe, contralto Rita Delano, and tenor Toney Valencia were received with warm applause. Miss Jessie James lived up to her name and was full of personality. Gene Harris was singled out as the manager. Many of the employees were locals. The enjoyable event continued until 6:00 a.m.

Open day and night, the New Wayside Inn featured Tea Dancing at 2:00 and 5:00 p.m. The Gulf Coast menu was "fixed," a common practice in cabarets at the time. It featured: hors d'oeuvres, celery and olives, Creole gumbo, baked red snapper, half spring chicken a la Louisianne, lettuce salad (with French dressing), and Roquefort cheese with guava jelly. Dessert was vanilla ice cream or cream cheese, served with a demitasse of coffee. There was, of course, no mention of liquor.

The report of the second night was equally positive. The crowd included over one hundred prominent visitors who were staying at nearby Gulf Coast hotels, as well as numerous members of the local society. The show proved thrilling, transcending opening night.

The new venture appeared to be a great success, which makes the next piece of news a bit perplexing. On February 24, Evelyn Nesbit abruptly departed Biloxi and Gene Harris probably left at about the same time. While the local newspaper claimed that Miss Nesbit went back to Chicago, her subsequent engagements indicate she may actually have gone directly around the Gulf of Mexico to New Orleans, where she was interviewed in early March. Harris, who was replaced by Roy Hill as manager, was back in Chicago before April. Previously, Hill had managed nightclubs and "hotel roofs" in New York City and Chicago. He assured his prospective patrons that he would continue offering three all-star shows every night. Importantly, Hill removed the cover charge except on Saturdays. Had business fallen off quickly? If Evelyn Nesbit and Gene Harris had planned to come only for the gala opening, why was this not mentioned in the press? In any case, it seems very unlikely that Gene Harris was prepared to relocate to Biloxi, Mississippi.

Despite attracting large crowds at the New Wayside Inn, Nesbit was quick to move on. Within days of her departure, negative news about the establishment began to seep into the local newspapers. As Mardi Gras approached, problems at the inn deepened. Some of the contracted talent participated in Carnival festivities under the advisement of manager Roy Hill. Then, on March 14, rather shocking headlines reported that the New Wayside Inn was being sued for unpaid bills owed the contracting firm Manual & Wetsell for labor and materials. Claims totaled $1,561.15, a significant sum in Depression-era dollars.

Had Evelyn Nesbit and Gene Harris escaped a quickly deteriorating financial situation? Who were the investors behind the Biloxi venture? Did they include Dan Blanco, who contemplated a winter resort to compliment his Chicago club? Was Roy Hill actually the owner and creator of the New Wayside Inn or simply a replacement manager? Within days, an advertisement in the *Daily Herald* announced that the club was under new management. No names were mentioned, though the cover charge had been completely lifted. Whatever the financial problems, New Wayside Inn was open to celebrate New Year's Eve 1930/1931. Meanwhile, Gene Harris was safely in Chicago, back where he belonged at the Club Alabam. Evelyn Nesbit, on the other hand, was off on a new adventure.

Down To Panama

While precise details remain fuzzy, Evelyn Nesbit went to New Orleans and probably performed at the French Quarter's historic Old Absinthe House. Her stay there was brief.

There is no question that the world-weary entertainer was exhausted. Cabaret work was demanding. Moving constantly was difficult. She wasn't getting any younger. An insatiable reader and self-educator since her youth, Nesbit was deeply interested in Madame Blavatsky's Theosophy and Darwin's theory of evolution, among other topics. In New Orleans, at the Old Absinthe House nightclub, she gave United Press reporter Barry J. Olloway an interview, expanding on what she had told Ruth Ayres in Pittsburgh a few months earlier.

Miss Nesbit's ambitions had appeared in print many times over the years. Sometimes they were actualized, as with her Manhattan specialty shop, and sometimes they were just pipe dreams, whether or not they were fueled by morphine. In March of 1930, Evelyn Nesbit desired to share her personal philosophy with the public. She told journalist Barry J. Olloway that a new religion of wisdom, based in the ancient culture of the Indo-Aryans, would inspire a world experiencing a deepening economic depression. Nesbit saw herself as the ideal person to bring these profound, yet simple, teachings to the American people. "I think it is more perfect than any other conception of God," she said. "It is not a sexed anthropomorphic God."[144]

Did Evelyn Nesbit imagine herself the Aimee Semple McPherson of Eastern Philosophy?

◆ ◆ ◆

Aging may have been the root cause of Nesbit's distress and, as a result, she might have experienced a bit of an existential crisis in the spring of 1930. One article claimed that Nesbit turned forty during this engagement. In fact, that birthday was well behind her. She would be forty-six at the end of the year.

From New Orleans, Nesbit traveled to Panama City. On arrival, she told reporters that she planned never to return to the USA. There, she worked for a month at Kelly's Ritz, owned by the fabulous madam and cabaret owner Mamie Lee Kelly, the inspiration for Cole Porter's "Panama Hattie." Kelly paid Nesbit between $400 and $500 for the month, depending on the recounting. Her show included the Three Jays, a trio of young blonde dancers. *Variety* reported that the blasé Panama natives were unimpressed with Nesbit and her act. It took more than a woman with a past to pique their interest. Famous and notorious persons came and went continually in the jaded capitol.

Consequently, Nesbit's audience was primarily made up of gaping tourists, who visited town about eight days each month. Women were more curious to see Evelyn Nesbit in the flesh than men, perhaps to gloat at her now fading beauty. When international patrons did fill the little tables at Kelly's Ritz, Nesbit mingled, sipped mint-flavored water, and occasionally took the floor to sing the melancholy tune, "Laugh, Clown, Laugh," reminding her audience not to let the world know their sorrows.

Settled in her Panamanian bungalow with her maid and three little dogs, Nesbit reflected on midlife goals, telling one reporter, "I always wanted to come to the tropics…. [And] if one wants and wants unceasingly, one obtains what one wishes for." Part of her attraction to the tropics, she explained, was botany, adding that Panama was a "veritable garden of Eden." Nesbit likely surprised the interviewer when she confessed her desire to make a study of the country's flora and fauna. The article, a special cable to the *San Francisco*

Chronicle, was dated April 1, 1930. Was there a hint of "April Fools' Day" in the interview?[145]

Despite her comparative isolation in vice-ridden Panama City, Nesbit enjoyed the intellectual exchange she craved, including a lengthy conversation with Panama's Governor, Harry Burgess.

Unsurprisingly, Evelyn Nesbit would not escape Panama without a small scandal. On April 13, she was arrested with eleven other Americans, five of them cabaret girls. They were charged with playing roulette in the poker rooms over the Metropole Hotel. Prisoners taunted Miss Nesbit, while the women waited on the jail patio. Later, they were released on $100 bail.

Following a month in Panama City, Nesbit moved to Colón, Panama, where she entertained at Bilgray's cabaret. The management may have been aware of her modest success in Panama City. They offered her $200 a month, room, and 20% commission on receipts. Her month-long contract demanded three appearances each night.

Existing film footage of Nesbit singing at Bilgray's reveals a slightly thick-middled, but well-preserved forty-something chanteuse, swinging a feather boa. The small Panamanian orchestra is elevated behind her. The musicians are backed against a wall. Tables ring the dance floor that accommodates both performers and patrons. The audience appears polite, if slightly bored. Nesbit's number is recorded in long shot, medium shot, and close-up. The footage was intended to be edited, likely for the newsreels.

Nesbit sings, somewhat pathetically, about herself. Even though she remained married to Jack Clifford, they had been separated for many years. She may have first performed "I'm Miss Nesbit Once More," following her divorce from Harry Thaw. Married or not, Nesbit announces that she could do as she pleases, go where she pleases … because she's no man's mama now. There was no question about that. Evelyn Nesbit was not constrained by social convention. By May, she was telling reporters that after she concluded her tour of Panama, she hoped to retire.

It is easy to view Evelyn Nesbit's time in Panama as some kind of descent into a tropical Hades, the bottom of her career. Columnist Mark Hellinger saw it somewhat differently. A longtime admirer of Nesbit, in May of 1930, he described her as an amazing, tireless creature, who had led an exceptionally weird life, played out on the front pages of newspapers. He was sorry to report that Nesbit was dancing in a cabaret in Panama, drawing $200 a week. "As any sailor will tell you," Hellinger wrote, "Panama City is one of the filthiest and wildest towns in the world. I've seen plenty of towns that cater to vice, but Panama takes the cake."[146]

As Hellinger predicted, she was a survivor. Panama was not the end for Evelyn Nesbit. Before the year was out, she was back in Chicago, working at Dan Blanco's Club Alabam.

CHAPTER NINE

"This Is A Nightclub"

When the Federal population census was taken in Chicago in April of 1930, Gene Harris, Dan Blanco and his wife, dancer Marcella Bennett, were all enumerated at 749 Rush Street. The substantial building had two entrances. The street entrance to the apartments was one door up from 747 Rush Street. Census enumerator Mrs. Mary F. Gross noted in the margin: "This is a nightclub." She was certainly correct in that evaluation. Show business atmosphere spilled over into the apartments, filled with employees and friends of the Club Alabam.

Mrs. Gross gave the marital status of Blanco, Bennett, and Harris as divorced. Questions abound. On April 1, 1930, Mrs. Gross wrote: "Dan Blanco, fifty-three, proprietor café, divorced, born Mexico" and "Marcella Bennett, twenty-one, dancer, divorced, born Illinois." Miss Bennett doubtless worked at the Club Alabam. Interestingly, on April 27, the couple was also enumerated as Mr. and Mrs. Daniel B. Leblang (Blanco's legal name), living in an apartment at the Delaware Towers, which they rented for $180.00 per month. There, the couple was recorded as married. Until recently, Marcella Bennett had been Mrs. Neal Phillips. In late 1928, she was a student at De Paul University when she charged her young husband with cruelty.[147]

There is nothing surprising about the Leblangs' double residence. Conveniently, they kept rooms at Club Alabam, as well as an apartment away from the comparative chaos of the nightclub. What about their conflicting marital status? In January of 1931, they traveled to Cuba as husband and wife. A delayed honeymoon? In July of that year, their daughter, Virginia, was born.[148]

Most of Gene Harris' census entry is incorrect and reads as follows: "Harris, Jean; lodger; male; white; twenty-eight; divorced; born California; parents both born Michigan." In truth, Gene's father was born in Virginia and his mother in Iowa, as was he. Significantly, he still might have been a married man.

On February 25, 1919, Gene Harris had married Bessie A. Mahoney in San Francisco. He may or may not have deserted her. They might have separated amicably when they both left San Diego sometime after 1920. But were they divorced? In 1930, Bessie A. Harris was living in San Francisco on Franklin Street with her married sister, Eileen, and her brother-in-law, George Brown. Neither Bessie nor her sister claimed an occupation, not even housekeeper. Her marital status on the Federal population census was given as married. Likely a practicing Catholic, the Irish-born Bessie no doubt would have resisted divorce. With no children, she might have applied to the Church for an annulment. She likely had not seen her husband for most of a decade, however, she did not presume him dead. In that case, her status would have been widow. Bessie was still presenting herself as a married woman, despite a long absent husband. Was she still Gene Harris' wife?[149]

In April of 1930, Aloisia "Babs" Jirik, who would become Gene Harris' second wife, was single and living with her sisters at Chicago's Swiss Apartment House on Winthrop Avenue. Her occupation was given as clerk, cloak room, restaurant. The restaurant was not named. Was she working at Club Alabam?

The former apartment building at 747–749 Rush Street was filled with show people and likely, to some degree, transients, as employees came and went. In the spring of 1930, they included:

Mildred Pickard, twenty-four, dancer, single, born Michigan
Marie Hughes, twenty-four, dancer, single, born Illinois
Jessie Andrew, twenty-four, dancer, single, born Illinois
Elaine Panten, twenty-four, dancer, single, born Iowa
Dorine O'Neill, twenty-five, dancer, divorced, born Ireland
Bernie Adler, forty-nine, musician, divorced, born Illinois
"Ras Puten," forty-five, widowed, prohibition agent, born Illinois

A popular age for dancers, twenty-four. Clearly, Dorine O'Neill was brave to admit to twenty-five and divorced.

Ragtime singer and songwriter Bernie Adler had known Dan Blanco for many years. In 1910, they performed together with Charles Waller and Bert White at Chicago's Alhambra Theater. Like others living at the Club Alabam, Alder had a lively past. In 1911, his wife, Lottie, sued him for divorce, demanding alimony. At the time, Bernie Adler was entertaining in South Side cafés, living apart from his mature wife, and involved with youthful chorus girl Mabel Hadley, who was featured in the "Follies of 1911." Photos in Chicago newspapers depicted Lottie Adler as a lovely, modest woman, with Gibson-style hair piled high on her head and a high-collared blouse covering every inch of her bodice. Conversely, Harry "Bernie" Adler was pictured squeezing a childlike Mabel Hadley. According to Lottie, Bernie was a good husband until he met Miss Hadley, noting: "He bought me expensive rings, took me on tours across the continent, and gave me a luxurious home."[150]

Lottie Adler named Mabel Hadley as co-respondent and the Adlers' divorce became front page news in Chicago. Evidence presented in court included three love songs Adler wrote about his affair. One mentioned the date he met Mabel. Another, "When I am Away," was dedicated to her. Adler, who had provided a furnished flat for his mistress, was far from discrete. Lottie Adler got her divorce. Mabel Hadley's ultimate fate, unknown.

Housemate "Rasputin" was anything but a prohibition agent born in Illinois. Rasputin (sometimes called Harry Rasputin) was born Victor Weinshenker in 1889. Roughly ten years older than Gene Harris, by 1930, Rasputin's experience was long and wide. A *publicity* agent, his clients included Louis Armstrong, whom he accompanied on several European tours, and the popular singer Billy Daniel. Rasputin was described as a bon vivant, go-between, nightclubber, theater-goer, and stage-door Johnny. He loved show business, especially Yiddish theater. In 1933, Rasputin would stand up in court for Evelyn Nesbit, testifying that he was a long-term acquaintance of both her and her soon-to-be ex-husband, Jack Clifford. When Rasputin died in 1957, Herb Lyon remembered him in his long-running column "Tower Ticker," writing that just before Rasputin died, the journalist received an eerie postcard sent from somewhere on the Pennsylvania Turnpike. "Ras" wrote, "See you next week!" A Damon Runyon-type character, Rasputin would drop by Lyon's desk, unannounced, seeking publicity for his clients. His colorful, casual manner would clearly be missed.[151]

Living in rooms at Club Alabam's address—747 Rush Street—were a Filipino houseman named J. L. Decena (age twenty-eight) and his Illinois-born wife, Irene (age twenty-four), who worked with him as the club's housekeeper.

Chicago's Bohemia: The Near North Side

During the early part of the 20th century, the Near North Side, specifically the neighborhood called Tower Town, gradually became home to Bohemian types, including musicians, writers, and artists. During the 1920's, rising rents pushed the community away from Michigan Avenue and the historic Water Tower. Rush Street was ready and waiting to receive them.

Next door to the Club Alabam, the Southern Tea Shop occupied 745 Rush Street. The proprietor, Miss Annie Sara Bock, made her home at 743–745 Rush. A middle-aged divorcee born in Pennsylvania, Bock shared her rooms with the manager of the tea shop, Ada McDannold [sic]; a young artist named Helen Jenkins; as well as Mary and Margaret Henderson, both twenty-four years old, both nightclub entertainers. It should be no surprise that they admitted to that "magic" age of twenty-four. Were they a sister act, working at Club Alabam?

This Rush Street tearoom was the first of several owned by Miss Bock. Chicago dining expert John Drury enjoyed the food at the Southern Tea Shop. Luncheon was priced at 50 cents, dinner at 75 cents. The atmosphere included "intelligent colored waitresses" and a limited menu of regional dishes which attracted a clientele of newspapermen, artists, and musicians who lived in the studio apartments on Rush Street.[152]

One of the artists who was living above the Southern Tea Shop was Erik Magnussen, a Danish craftsman who exhibited hand-wrought silver in his apartment. In 1901, Magnussen debuted his work at the age of seventeen in his uncle's gallery in Denmark, then studied for two years in Berlin. Once in the United States, his jewelry became popular despite the Great Depression. By 1933, he had left Chicago and opened a studio in Los Angeles where movie stars popularized his work.

In The Grip Of Gangsters

In the summer of 1930, Gene Harris was back from Biloxi and on the job as headwaiter, greeting loyal patrons at Club Alabam. Dan Blanco booked top musical talent, including songwriter and orchestra leader Al Handler, whose music floated into the outside garden. Handler's original tunes included

"Nightmare" (1926) and "Phantom Blues" (1927). A popular hot jazz dance band, Al Handler recorded "Pretty Lips" (1926) and "Magnolia" (1927). In the fall, Blanco refreshed his program and Handler's band was followed by Willie Newberger's orchestra, who would remain into 1931.

In the background, Chicago was staging a deadly gangland war. During August of 1930, Chicago's newspapers were filled with headlines announcing the murder of Jack Zuta, a key criminal on the city's North Side. Once the dominion of Dion O'Banion and his second-in-command, Louis Alterie, the liquor trade in the northern territory was now controlled by Bugs Moran, some of whose gang members were slaughtered by Al Capone's men in the St. Valentine's Day Massacre on February 14, 1929.[153]

Jack Zuta was an accountant, a meticulous record keeper and political fixer, first for Capone in the 1920's and then for Bugs Moran's North Side Gang. Zuta had a growing number of enemies. Anyone who kept books for the mob had a lot of incriminating information at his fingertips. Additionally, Zuta operated brothels, considered by many gangsters an undignified sector of the crime world. He may have been connected to the murder of *Tribune* reporter Alfred "Jake" Lingle in June of 1930. Lingle had foolishly tried to extort money from Moran's gambling operations. After Zuta was questioned by the police concerning details of Lingle's violent and very public murder, there was reasonable apprehension on the part of North Side mobsters that Zuta might have shared incriminating information with the authorities in order to save himself. Following an attempt on his life on July 1, Zuta went into hiding on Upper Nemahbin Lake, west of Milwaukee, where he was murdered on August 1, 1930.

Zuta's loose accounting papers, found among his personal effects at the lake resort, revealed that even in hiding he had been selling liquor in Chicago. The *Tribune* reported that the first name on Zuta's accounts receivable (retail) list dated July 23, 1930 was "Albam. $270," a comparatively modest debt to the mob. Other entries mentioned were "Art L. $465.65," presumed to be Art Lowe, proprietor of the Wigwam café; Morrie W. $1,100.00," likely Morrie Wallman, an operator of North Side cafes and one-time partner of Ted Newberry of the Green Mill; and "Jimmie G." was believed to be Jimmie Galligan, another café manager.

While it was no surprise that men associated with nightclubs might be buying liquor from Moran's gang, the *Tribune* article also included a statement by a North Side café owner, whose name was withheld from the newspapers. For months, Capone's men had been pushing north and the informant indicated that power might be shifting. The anonymous proprietor reported being approached by threatening gangsters, who carried guns visibly beneath their belts, warning café owners to buy their product ... or face the consequences.

Officials learned that this unsavory visit occurred shortly after the attempt to kill Zuta on the night of July 1, and that the gun-toting booze salesmen returned several times to see the café owner after he had refused to deal with them on the first call. Chief of Detectives Norton was proceeding on the theory that Capone was behind the campaign to rid the North Side of the gang that for years had forced its liquor on cafes, nightclubs, and soft drink parlors in that territory.

Was the informant Dan Blanco? Surely, the thugs payed a similar call at the Club Alabam.

◆ ◆ ◆

In October of 1930, Evelyn Nesbit returned to Chicago, arriving from New York City on the Broadway Limited. Her companion was Lovey, a tan Belgian Griffon, the perfect size for traveling. By November, she was back acting as hostess at the Club Alabam, where Russian-born playwright and comic actor Alexander Carr threw a party for her and Dan Blanco on November 30, 1930. Carr and Nesbit were likely old friends. At the time, he was touring with his comedy, *Mendle, Inc.,* then playing at the Aldelphi Theater at 11 North Clark Street. Audiences were promised "A Laugh In Every Line." The play had been a solid hit on Broadway, running from November 25, 1929 into June of 1930.

While in Chicago for an extended stay, Evelyn Nesbit decided to file for divorce against Jack Clifford, charging him with desertion ten years prior. Newspapers across the country ran the story. She continued to make exciting headlines, especially if romance, marriage, or divorce were involved. The press was not entirely sympathetic. The *Miami News* quipped, "Evelyn Nesbit charges her husband deserted her 10 years ago and we've been wondering when she dropped in at home to find out."[154] Despite the flurry of excitement, Nesbit would have to wait a while longer for her divorce.

◆ ◆ ◆

Following the death of Chicago "gang lord" Jack Zuta, two incidents at Club Alabam indicate that Dan Blanco and Bugs Moran's North Side gang might not have been on the best of terms.

On December 17, 1930, gangsters Anthony "Red" Kissane and Jack "West Side" Barry were arrested after they openly displayed revolvers inside the Club Alabam. Charged with disorderly conduct, no guns were found on the men when the police arrived. Their hearing was set for December 19 and they were released on an easily obtained $400 bond.

Did Blanco call the police when the men showed their guns? Likely, he did not want a repeat of the Northern Lights incident when thugs fired guns, leaving a policeman wounded and a dead gangster on the sidewalk outside. It is unknown if Evelyn Nesbit was working at the Club Alabam when Barry and Kissane were arrested.

A bulky middle-aged man, Anthony Kissane was a decorated World War I veteran with an impressive criminal record. The press called him a notorious hoodlum. Purportedly once a bodyguard for murdered *Tribune* reporter Alfred "Jake" Lingle, Kissane was suspected of a wide-range of crimes from carrying concealed weapons, to robbery, to bombing and brawling, to murder. In August of 1930, he was among the mobsters questioned about the slaying of Jack Zuta.

Thin faced with a long, sharp nose, Jack "West Side" Barry was an ex-con and racketeer who had muscled his way into dominating the Newspaper Drivers' Union. As secretary-treasurer, he controlled union funds. Earlier in 1930, within a time span of five days, he withdrew $2,500 from the union's bank account. Between May 1 and August 30, Barry virtually drained the treasury, writing checks totaling $17,690, leaving a paltry $8.54 in the union coffers. In court, Judge John H. Lyle read an anonymous letter written by members of the Newspaper Drivers' Union, Local 706, asserting that Barry had forced his way into the union, using armed henchmen. It was also noted that after Barry was "elected" to the office of secretary-treasurer, he purchased a new Cadillac.[155]

Following the murders of Lingle and Zuta in the summer of 1930, State's Attorney John A. Swanson had been working overtime to arrest North Side gangsters. In June, Swanson was pleased when two so-called "big shots" of gangland Chicago were found guilty in jury trials. One of them was Anthony

Kissane, who was charged with carrying concealed weapons, sentenced to one year in the county jail, and fined $300. It was the first time Kissane had been found guilty of any crime. In September, he remained at large.

That month, twenty-six known Chicago criminals, including Al Capone, were charged with vagrancy—one of the few charges that successfully put gangsters in jail. Barry and Kissane were among them. On September 10, they were arrested while loitering at the corner of Polk and Dearborn streets (the location of the Chicago & Eastern Illinois Railway's Dearborn Station) and were taken to the East Chicago Avenue Police Station. The next morning, they appeared in the Town Hall Court before Judge John H. Lyle, who found them guilty of vagrancy, sentencing them each to six months' hard labor, plus a $100 fine. Bail was set at $30,000 for each man. Kissane gave his occupation as salesman, living at 4225 N. Springfield Avenue. Barry gave his address as 180 W. Washington Street (the location of the Newspaper Drivers' Union), admitting he was a "business agent" for the union.

On September 13, Judge Lyle refused a cash bond, demanding real estate as security. He observed, "Gangsters go about armed with ready cash. That is their weapon. I have stopped cash bonds in all these cases and demand real estate funds, and real estate must be scheduled."[156]

A widely-published article reported that Judge Lyle "snorted angrily" in court, saying: "Any gunman has plenty of jack. Every time you hear of one being killed you hear police found a grand or so in his pockets." Did the judge really use such slang or had a reporter peppered his comments with gangster lingo to spice up the story?[157]

The two men were granted a jury trial and sent back to their jail cells to await ample security to cover their bail. They did not remain long.

On November 24, the gunmen again appeared in court and were granted a continuance to December 4 on their vagrancy charges. The following day, Judge Lyle held Barry (now charged with burglary as well as vagrancy), setting his bond at $150,000. Lyle railed against other judges, Judge Joseph E. David in particular, for their lax bond policies. Likewise, Lyle did not feel that the police department was doing its job. During the hearing, Judge Lyle addressed Chief of Detectives John Norton, exclaiming that men like Jack Barry should not be free to roam the streets. The judge found it puzzling that a police force of 5,000 able men was unable to run these "midnight assassins" out of Chicago. Lyle went on to call Al Capone, "a crime wave all by himself." Somehow, despite Judge Lyle's earnest efforts, Barry was soon at large.[158]

On December 16, the day before Kissane and Barry dropped in at the Club Alabam, they were scheduled to appear before Judge Justin McCarthy—not the tough Judge Lyle. Two days after their arrest, on December 19, the men appeared before Judge Leon Edelman, requesting a jury trial. This time, bond was set at an easily attainable $5,000 each. There was no indication that they continued to harass Dan Blanco.

During 1931, Kissane and Barry kept finding their way into courtrooms. In July, Barry was suspected of cold-blooded murder. Ely H. Orr, who had spent twenty-seven years in the circulation department of the *Chicago Herald and Examiner*, had recently become secretary-treasurer of the Newspaper Drivers' Union. While driving his car, Orr had stopped at a traffic light when two or three men with shotguns fired at him point-blank. The killers reportedly drove away laughing. The slaying was national news. The following day, Barry was released on an airtight alibi. By August of 1931, Kissane was finally incarcerated, serving a one-year jail sentence for carrying a gun.

The tale of Barry and Kissane is a shockingly familiar one in Chicago during the Prohibition era. On a daily basis, dozens of men like them got away with a multitude of crimes from racketeering to murder in the first degree. Men like Dan Blanco and Gene Harris had to stay in their good graces, if they were not to end up dead like Ely H. Orr.

◆ ◆ ◆

The holidays came and went. In early January, Dan and Marcella Blanco vacationed in "America's Rivera"—Havana, Cuba. The Dixie Limited and the Dixie Flyer both ran from Chicago's Dearborn Station to Miami, Florida, with passengers continuing by ship to Havana. Leisurely two-week tours offered by the Chicago & Eastern Illinois Railway were priced at $185. The couple was scheduled to return to Miami, Florida on the *S. S. Algonquin* on January 17. Gene Harris was no doubt in charge during Blanco's absence, catering to Evelyn Nesbit, who stayed on at the club into the New Year.

Then, in the early hours of Monday, January 13, five bandits broke into the safe at the Club Alabam, taking $645. The burglars posed as Prohibition agents. The crowd from the previous evening had dispersed. The housekeeper was alone in the club when the men arrived and, unsurprisingly, did not know the combination to the safe.

Did the thieves know Dan Blanco was out of town? Was there a connection between the burglars and the arrests of Kissane and Barry? There was no further mention in the regional newspapers of the robbery or how it was resolved. Evelyn Nesbit stayed on in Chicago and, by February, she had moved to the Club Ambassadeur, housed in an old mansion at 226 East Ontario Street, where Jimmie Noone and his orchestra provided the dance music. Restaurant critic John Drury described the café as intimate and cozy, yet hot. A perfect combination for Nesbit to ply her charms.

Gigi Rene and Dan Blanco's old friend Slater Brockman—quick change artist, monologist, impersonator, and singer of character songs— took over at Club Alabam. Willie Newberger's orchestra provided continuity for the dancing patrons.

Girls Of The Club Alabam

There was never a dull moment on Rush Street. In February of 1931, a singer at the Club Alabam named Etta Murray made the front page of the local newspapers. Murray's boyfriend, William Sullivan (alias William Doyle and William Windsor), was arrested on August 15, 1930 on a gun-toting charge, had spent the last three months in the county jail, and still owed the Cook County Court a $300 fine. Described as a Chicago gangster and one time bodyguard for Tommy Abbott, one of the city's notorious vice racketeers, Sullivan now claimed he was a pauper. Sullivan's attorney, John R. Snively, put Etta Murray on the witness stand to testify to Sullivan's insolvency.

Described as a comely, Titian-haired crooner, Etta Murray didn't seem to know much about her boyfriend. She couldn't attest to his job or profession while he was living in Chicago. She didn't know where he worked. She believed that he didn't have any money and admitted to sending him two or three dollars every week. She didn't know if he owned an automobile or significant property. Apparently, Miss Murray simply never asked Mr. Sullivan details about his life. After all, what Etta Murray didn't know couldn't hurt her. Sullivan's petition to have the fine waved was denied and he went back to the county jail until it was paid or proved conclusively he was unable to pay the $300.

Such was the atmosphere at the Club Alabam, where a revolving door of pretty, youthful, and hopeful showgirls such as Etta Murray mingled freely with underworld characters, doing their best to keep their distance while enjoying the exploits and easy money of these thrill-seeking men. Over the years, stories of their dreams of success—sometimes won, sometimes lost—were occasionally interesting or sensational enough to become public knowledge.

An attractive blonde named Eleanor Witte, from Rockford, Illinois, got her start at the Club Alabam. She had trained with Paul James at the Fraser-James School of Music and Dancing. Hard work and apparent talent paid off and she got a job touring with George White's popular "Scandals." Later, she made it to Broadway and was billed as Eleanor De Witte, a "Girl in the Ensemble," in a musical comedy, *White Horse Inn*.

Miss Margaret Williams, originally of Des Moines, Iowa, was another successful Club Alabam "graduate." A lovely, wide-eyed brunette, she entertained at the Alabam, praised in the *Des Moines Register* as "one of Chicago's smartest nightclubs," and various other venues in Chicago, where she appeared as a solo buck and tap dancer. She also danced with a sister act. An educated young lady, she had graduated from St Joseph's Academy in Des Moines and attended Iowa State College in Ames. In 1931, she proudly returned to the Des Moines stage with the Kurnicker ballet in an act for Paramount-Publix theater chain, as the captain of a troupe of ten dancing girls.

Later in the decade, another Club Alabam veteran met with a less fortunate end. Twenty-two year old dancer Sandra Neal and her friend Lynne Hammond (also twenty-two) left their jobs at the Club Alabam in search of Broadway's bright lights. Once in New York City, Sandra Neal found despair rather than a job. Broke after five months of constant rejection, without even the hope of joining a chorus line, she committed suicide by drinking poison.

Dusk To Dawn On Rush Street

Four years after its inception, Club Alabam had staying power. It had survived the stock market crash and the ensuing economic depression, as well as burglary, carving out an apparently permanent niche on Rush Street. John Drury highlighted the club as a late-night hot spot in his *Dining in Chicago*:

> CLUB ALABAM, 747 Rush Street: More dusk to dawn diversion on the near north side. Evelyn Nesbit Thaw was a big drawing card when she was here recently. Dan Blanco is host, Slater Brockman does the mastering, and Willie Newberger's orchestra furnishes the music—which, by the by, is nothing if not "hot." Floor shows and vaudeville entertainers and Chinese and Southern dishes—what a combination. Cover charge, $1.00. Delaware 0808.[159]

During the summer months, Dave Unell and his band entertained, and, in October of 1931, Dan Blanco took out an ad in the *Chicago Daily Tribune* for the "New Club Alabam." What was new? Dinner was now priced at $2.00 and there was no cover charge to dinner guests, a likely result of the down-turning national economy. On the bill was Anton Lada and His Louisiana Five ("Formerly with the Ziegfeld Follies"); Gypsy Le Nore, danseuse; Lou King, Chicago's favorite entertainer; and Mary Thorn, soprano. Germaine LaPierre (of radio fame) filled out the bill. Born in Quebec and a bona fide French-speaking "songstress," her sister, Paulette, had worked for Dan Blanco at Bill Rothstein's Moulin Rouge in the mid-1920s. The style of cuisine was not mentioned, though, the current talent suggested a French flair. Anton Lada was a drummer and his band, which originated in New Orleans, played Dixieland Jazz.

New Year's Eve rolled around again and, despite the fact that money was tight, it was predicted that hotels and cafés would be jammed for midnight parties. Based on advanced reservations, hotel managers anticipated one of the largest celebrations in years. Crowds for hotels and restaurants were estimated to exceed 20,000 persons—ready to dine, dance, and consume illegal alcohol on New Year's Eve 1931/1932. Prices were lowered to accommodate the tenor of the times, reduced by about 25 percent from the previous year, a discount that successfully lured guests. Packages for a midnight supper, dancing, floor show, a variety of entertainment, and souvenirs averaged $7.50 per person. Beyond the major hotels and private dining rooms, cabarets such as Frolics Café, Colosimo's, Vanity Fair, Rubaiyat, and Club Alabam prepared for the revelers, expecting capacity crowds.

It was no surprise the next morning, when local newspapers reported that the Volstead Act once again had been ignored on December 31, 1931. Liquor was abundant. Every café, cabaret, and restaurant in and around the Loop was crowded. Hotels were packed. Theaters were full. Even intermittent drizzle didn't dampen the festivities. At least in Chicago, on New Year's Eve 1931, there was no Great Depression and no Prohibition. An unidentified witness observed, "The night was pretty wet, and I don't mean rain."[160]

Once again, Chicago's authorities turned a blind eye to the city's revelry. On the Near North Side, the Ambassadeur, Mack, Café de Alex, Rubaiyat, as well as Club Alabam, all welcomed "happy" guests.

◆ ◆ ◆

During 1932, the Great Depression deepened, many businesses failed, yet the Club Alabam stayed afloat, with Frank Frulett and his orchestra taking over the music from Anton Lada and his Louisiana Boys. Rush Street continued to be home to increasingly struggling Bohemians, including the notable silver worker Erik Magnussen, while Chicago prepared for the World's Fair of 1933-1934. Bootlegger Louis Alterie, who had been vaguely connected with the Northern Lights shooting of gangster Johnny Phillips in 1924, was arrested in Denver, charged with the kidnapping of gambler Edward Dobkin.

The year culminated with another successful year-end celebration. Newspapers announced that Chicago nightspots experienced the best New Year's Eve business since the crash in 1929.

Before the month of January 1933 was out, however, Dan Blanco ran into some trouble with federal agents. Blanco was served with a federal dry law warrant following the arraignment of two Club Alabam employees who were arrested during an unexpected raid.

The *Rockford Register-Republic* turned the incident into an eye-catching front page story with the headline, "Modern Paul Revere Sounds Warning Of Federal Raids." Clubs in the Loop were successfully warned that prohibition agents were heading their way. Club Alabam, the Kit-Kat club, the Turkish Village, and an unnamed, exclusive second-floor meeting place on East Chicago Avenue, were successfully raided. This midnight ride found thirty couples happily dancing at Club Alabam. No liquor was discovered. The manager (unnamed) and an assistant were arrested, allegedly having sold liquor to an investigator.[161]

Was headwaiter Gene Harris the arrested assistant?

Ends of stories rarely, if ever, find their way into even the back pages of the newspapers. Fines might be paid. Palms greased. Favors collected. Anything was possible on Rush Street. However the issue was resolved, Club Alabam carried on. By mid-1933, following a treacherous year during which Evelyn Nesbit's health and livelihood were both severely compromised, she would return to Chicago, Dan Blanco, and the Club Alabam.

A Welcome Haven For Evelyn Nesbit

On April 4, 1933, beer was once again legal across the nation and, in the summer of 1933, there were thirty-two major nightclubs, cafes, and beer gardens in Chicago, employing orchestras and specialty talent. *Variety* classified their programs as "cabaret bills." Among them was the eternal draw, Evelyn Nesbit, who had returned to Club Alabam and would remain for months.

In early 1932, Nesbit had become seriously ill while working at the Coconut Club in St. Louis, fighting pneumonia and a serious kidney ailment, possibly Bright's Disease. By the time she headed east in November, Nesbit had lost over forty pounds. While hospitalized in New York City, languishing at a dangerously emaciated ninety-eight pounds, she announced her plans to retire to her New Jersey country home and write a tell-all autobiography which would "blow the Thaw case wide open." Described as frail and penniless, Nesbit doubtless was strapped for money, particularly due to the absence of work during 1932. She announced publically that she never wanted to see the inside of a nightclub again. How many times in her life had Evelyn Nesbit uttered those words?

The idea of responding to Harry Thaw's confessional, *The Traitor* (1926), promised much needed funds from book sales. Thaw's publication had been a financial failure, selling 4,000 copies out of an edition of 10,000, which Thaw himself published. A spicy telling of Nesbit's life story would potentially reach a much larger audience, particularly women readers.

By January of 1933, Nesbit had returned to Atlantic City, where she was reportedly once again ill with pleuropneumonia. A small notice in the *Pittsburgh Press* suggested a larger story behind Nesbit's confinement. Her illness prevented her from aiding authorities in exposing a Pittsburgh-based narcotic ring.[162]

◆ ◆ ◆

In May of 1933, Nesbit lived in the comparative security of Atlantic City; revisited her divorce from Harry Thaw; and again endeavored to establish him as the father of her son. Nesbit's ex-husband had never acknowledged Russell, though the young man used Thaw's name. Nesbit hired Frederick E. Goldsmith of Goldsmith and Felix (New York City) and admitted that the Thaws had been sending her gift money. The sums were small and arrived at irregular intervals. When the family threatened to cut off the funds, Nesbit shared a letter from the Thaws' attorneys, Stone and McCandless of Pittsburgh, with eager journalists. The letter, dated December 14, 1932 and signed by Stephen Stone, stated that the Thaw family was aware that Nesbit was writing a book. Stone offered a strong warning concerning future support, "The monies which we have been sending to you each month, and which we have sent you for many, many years past, are nothing but gifts. It is fair to presume that the giver would hesitate somewhat in continuing to make remittances until he knew the extent to which he and his people are being criticized in your book."[163]

In her typical carefree style, Nesbit found the references to remittances and gifts, to be "a ghastly joke." Living in a small apartment with a girlfriend, she was virtually destitute. Her compromised health threatened her livelihood. While previously she had confidently earned her own living as a performer and a cabaret hostess, she was getting older and needed to seek other forms of income.[164]

Ultimately, Nesbit conceded that the fight against the rich and powerful Thaw family was futile. Having regained her health, she was poised to reemerge, triumphant over adversity. Despite her self-proclaimed wretched state, her youthful personality shone brightly through the careworn years. Her abundant hair was free of gray and her face unlined. She was neither too old nor too tired to travel to Chicago and perform at Dan Blanco's Club Alabam.

◆ ◆ ◆

On June 5, 1933, Evelyn Nesbit opened her new engagement at the Club Alabam. On July 15, she was again national news. In Chicago, Superior Judge

Joseph Sabath granted her a divorce from her husband and former dancing partner, Jack Clifford. Nesbit wore a summery, grey polka dot dress, a white cotton coat, and white sandals. Her testimony was brief. They were married on May 24, 1916, in Elegant City, Maryland. According to Nesbit, Clifford had deserted her within three years of their marriage. She testified that she had treated him kindly and gave him no reason to leave her. Present in court to corroborate her story was her friend and employer Dan Blanco (in the record under his legal name, Daniel Leblang). Also by Nesbit's side was publicity agent Victor Weinschener (a.k.a. Rasputin), who stated he had known both her and Clifford for twenty years. Clifford did not appear. Nesbit did not know his whereabouts. At the time of their marriage, the bride-to-be was quoted as saying, "This time I married to please myself and not my friends. And that means this marriage is for love."[165] Love fades, however. Sometimes rather quickly.

◆ ◆ ◆

Immediately following the court decision, Blanco and Nesbit went to New York City. Ed Sullivan, in his column "Manhattan," dropped an intriguing rumor, "THE EVELYN NESBIT—Dan (Club Alabam) Blanca [sic] attachment was reported here two Mondays ago."[166] Were they just friends, business associates, or a temporary couple?

Whatever the nature of their relationship, Dan Blanco was loyal to his friends and, among them, he counted Evelyn Nesbit. He kept her on the payroll into October. Ultimately, he could not solve her financial dilemma. In December of 1933, she did not or could not pay a $500 storage bill in Atlantic City that was two and a half years overdue. The property included numerous unclaimed furs which were auctioned by a local department store. The collection brought a disappointing $15.00. A pathetic mention in the *New York Times* concluded, "Miss Nesbit was last reported to be in Chicago."[167]

CHAPTER TEN

Happy Days Are Here Again

The summer of 1933 brought the World's Fair to Chicago and with it hundreds of thousands of thirsty tourists in search of a variety of entertainments. The midway and other attractions supplemented the city's cabarets, introducing temporary competition to the clubs on Rush Street. Texas Guinan, Manhattan's infamous Queen of Prohibition, was in high demand and Midget Village featured Club Alabam favorites Mike & Ike. Dubbed the Century of Progress, the Fair provided endless fodder for the Chicago newspapers.

The selection of nightclubs within the fairgrounds ranged from "The Days of '49," a Spanish-style honky-tonk capturing pioneer days in Old California, to an elaborate Pirate Ship, containing multiple bars and dance floors and featuring Texas Guinan's troupe. Guinan was the boisterous Mistress of Ceremonies, her famous cry— "Hello, sucker!"—rang out from the poop deck. Guinan's showmanship and gusto was hard to match, especially when accompanied by an Oriental ballet, a knife throwing act, a trio of roller skaters, and occasional visits from the inhabitants of Midget Village.[168]

How could Club Alabam possibly compete with Texas Guinan's long-honed persona? Blanco and Harris' best hope was that customers would head to Rush Street, nightly, after the World's Fair closed.

In October of 1933, Mildred Harris Chaplin, the former Mrs. Charles Chaplin, followed Evelyn Nesbit at the Club Alabam. The petite entertainer was Chaplin's first wife and a familiar face to Chicago's vaudeville audiences. In the fall of 1933, she toured with her own "Hollywood Revue"—a troupe of twenty—and her California Syncopators. Delivering a few songs and impersonations of famous motion picture stars, Mildred Harris Chaplin's multi-week engagement ended in November and she was followed by a big-eyed, blonde entertainer, Irene Duvall. Her arched eyebrows, button nose, and bow mouth made a charming picture. She, too, had appeared in movies with both

Maurice Chevalier and Charlie Chaplin. The two women even looked alike. Duvall would witness the repeal of Prohibition with Dan Blanco and Gene Harris at the Club Alabam and ring in the New Year.[169]

Legal Liquor At Last

December 5, 1933. Prohibition was officially over. New Year's Eve 1933, would be very wet and, finally, wet would be legal. It was the first time in over a decade that hotels and clubs in Chicago could look forward to honest receipts from liquor. The Palmer House, just eight years old, had never rung in the New Year with champagne and the hotel's officials announced there would be $25,000 worth of liquor in their ballrooms and bars. Record crowds were anticipated. Enticements were offered to encourage advance reservations. Edgewater Beach Hotel, boasting over 2,000 reservations, would give away a bottle of Burgundy to each couple who purchased their New Year's Eve supper.

On January 1, 1934, Chicago's *Daily Tribune* heralded: "IN LEGAL WINE CHICAGO GAYLY WELCOMES 1934. Merriest Revel in Twenty Years." Chicagoans were reborn with "gusto and élan," recalling old times in a hot town. "Downtown the scene resembled a modified armistice night, with crowds in some places packing sidewalks like sardines. Horns, chroniclers, whistles, bells, and other din making contraptions were in everyone's hands—and were used."[170]

The widespread celebration covered Chicago from the Loop to the Near North Side to the suburbs to the glamour of Randolph Street to the seedier Southside. A misty rain, which started about 8:30 p.m., dampened no one's spirits.

Jack Coleman, Club Alabam Doorman

In the summer of 1934, Club Alabam received extraordinary publicity in Chicago's *Sunday Tribune* when the newspaper ran a full-page feature, complete with photo essay, recounting the life story of the club's doorman, African American Jack Coleman, whose broad smile beamed out from the page. His uniform consisted of a white yachting cap (sporting the words Club Alabam), a double-breasted dark blazer (trimmed with light piping), striped white trousers, and black-and-white spectators. A dapper introduction to an evening at Club Alabam.

Born in Mississippi, Jack Coleman dreamed of being a lawyer, however, circumstances left him broke in Chicago, where he took on a long series of jobs. Some were punishing and physical. Some were softer, like his time spent serving the public in a Pullman car. After working as an usher, he was hired as the doorman at Club Alabam. Jack was pleased to have a job without mental or physical strain and stressed the dignity of the position. He told *Tribune* reporter, Guy Murchie, Jr., "When the folks go in they tip the waiter, the shawl dancer, the singers, the cigarette girl, the hat check girl—and when they come out there's little left."[171]

Fortunately, Jack Coleman did not have to rely on tips. The club paid him $1,500 a year for his services.

Coleman was the first and the last person to greet patrons at the Club Alabam, who received a gracious welcome, whatever their walk of life. He was assertive with taxi drivers, telling them to "pull up, Bud—you can stop over there by the alley," as well as unsteady playboys, finding their way to the sidewalk at 4:00 a.m.[172]

Coleman's working hours may have been long but they were relaxed, as evidenced by one photograph which showed him leaning back, reading an issue of the *Tribune*. He got eight hours sleep daily, from eight in the morning until four in the afternoon. His wife brought him breakfast in bed. He took the State Street trolley to work and was on the job from 7:00 p.m. to 7:00 a.m.

Depression Era Demimonde

Despite the fact that Prohibition had come to an end, nightclubs in Chicago's Near North Side were not free from connections to Chicago's criminal element or other unsavory aspects of the city's nightlife. Gangsters continued to provide sensational headlines. On July 22, 1934, John Dillinger was killed in front of Chicago's Biograph Theatre, bringing an end to his bank-robbing career. There was also the revolving complement of playboys, idle rich, and "visiting firemen," enjoying a spree away from home. All were components of the cabaret territory.

The autumn of 1934 once again brought unwelcome headlines for Evelyn Nesbit, who had recently told "all" the previous spring in her autobiography, *Prodigal Days*. In November of 1934, a vast narcotics gang based in West Philadelphia was exposed, including dealer Mrs. Rosa DeMarco, a thirty-five-year-old mother of three. Mrs. DeMarco's little red address book contained clients from Maine to California, including: "Evelyn Thaw, Club Alabam, Chicago."

It was unclear precisely when Nesbit received drugs from Mrs. DeMarco while working for Dan Blanco and Gene Harris. Packages could have been sent to the club anytime over the past five years, where she had been a regular attraction since 1929.

Did Nesbit's connection to this gang go back as far as 1925/1926 when she attempted suicide in Chicago? At that time, the press reported that "Doc R." wrote her: "Damn narcotic gang were pushing me for $150, but could not connect up with friends here or in Pittsburgh. Only have a limited time to send on cash." Later identified as Dr. W. Calvin Roller of Brownsville, Pennsylvania, his explanation that his note was about the payment of a fine may have been as implausible as it sounded. At the time, Nesbit's maid was concerned that she might be using morphine again.

◆ ◆ ◆

One extreme case of misbehaving on Rush Street made national headlines in February of 1935, when the thirty-four-year-old, recently divorced George Eastman Dryden (grandnephew of Kodak camera king, George Eastman) was charged with "parboiling" twenty-one-year-old Vera "Billy" Read and assaulting her twenty-four-year-old sister, Hazel "Sunny" Read, both working as hostesses at Club Alabam. The young women were natives of Tulsa, Oklahoma, though apparently already seasoned in the sometimes dangerous milieu of Chicago after dark.

On the night of January 14, Dryden visited the Club Alabam where he was warmly welcomed, embraced by Vera's sister, Hazel. After several rounds of drinking, Dryden invited Hazel to a party in his apartment. As they were leaving, Hazel noticed that Vera was draped across the club bar, possibly drunk. Deciding to take Vera with them, they hired a cab to drive the one block to Dryden's apartment at 814 Rush Street. There, "East" Dryden, heir to a rubber fortune, was responsible for what journalists dubbed a "gay party," and got himself into some hot water, allegedly dunking Vera Read, fully clothed, in his bathtub. The United Press news service picked up the story, making it national, front page news.

Called "the best-groomed mustache in Cook County," Dryden claimed that Vera Read was not pushed into his bathtub and denied hitting her in the face, causing her pert nose to bleed. However she landed in the tub, the water would have been tepid. At 5:00 a.m., Dryden attested, hot water was a rarity in his apartment.

Dryden maintained that it was Hazel's idea to give Vera a bath, suggesting it was the way to sober her sister. Allegedly, Vera had other ideas and decided to commit suicide, first by jumping out a window, and then threatening to cut herself with a razor blade. Hazel drew the water in the tub and, while they considered how best to undress Vera, she slipped and fell in. Dryden and Hazel pulled her out. End of escapade.

Vera denied Dryden's version of the story, claiming she was not drunk and did not attempt suicide. She also revealed a trade secret, telling reporters that patrons could purchase endless rounds of drinks for a hostess and she would never get drunk. A hostess' glass was always filled with colored water. She and her sister were not paid a salary, rather they received a commission on drinks purchased by their escorts.

Vera's details differed drastically from Dryden's as to what happened in the bathroom, claiming that after East hit her in the nose with his fist, she went into the bathroom for a towel because her nose was bleeding. The tub was filled with hot water and Dryden dumped her in. Fully dressed, scalded and screaming, each time Vera attempted to get out, Dryden pushed her back in. Finally, she was helped out.

East Dryden, likely a regular at the Club Alabam, insisted that he was not drunk at the time of the incident, telling the judge he only consumed seven drinks all night. Dryden's friends corroborated his story. When Dryden was found not guilty, Hazel dropped her assault charges. The Read sisters got their names in the newspaper and the *Tribune* ran photos of the pretty brunettes. Club Alabam got the kind of sordid publicity that rarely hurts a nightclub.

♦ ♦ ♦

By 1935, Chicago had adjusted to post-Prohibition drinking habits, albeit softened by the economic pressures of the Great Depression. Booze was back, bringing a much-needed shot in the arm to the failing receipts of nightclubs, hotels, and restaurants. While the Jazz Age and unbridled prosperity wound down and the Depression deepened, both Dan Blanco and Gene Harris experienced significant changes in their personal lives.

Dan Blanco separated from dancer Marcella Bennett, who remarried and reared their daughter, Virginia.[173] Thelma Garson, another dancer in her early twenties, became Dan Blanco's next romance. She would be his last. Approaching sixty, Blanco's demanding lifestyle was catching up with him and he eased out of managing the club. In August of 1936, he and Thelma traveled by the *S.S. President Pierce* from New York to Los Angeles, cruising through the Panama Canal. In 1936–1937, they may have wintered in Florida. Three months before Blanco's death, the couple married in Fort Lauderdale on March 5, 1937. He died in Chicago, on June 1, following a long illness. Funeral services were held in a chapel at 2701 North Clark Street and Blanco was buried in Chicago's Acacia Park Cemetery and Mausoleum. Details in obituaries conflict. There was no question that Dan Blanco had left his mark on Chicago. The *Tribune* noted he had entertained the city for thirty-five years. *Variety* called him one of the first cabaret entertainers—which indeed he was.

Since Blanco's days at White City, cabaret had grown to become a favorite form of Chicago nightlife. He fostered many talented entertainers, not the least of whom was the reemerging Evelyn Nesbit and an ambitious headwaiter named Gene Harris.

DANIEL LE BLANG, OWNER OF NIGHT CLUBS, IS DEAD

Daniel Blanco Le Blang, owner of the Club Alabam, 747 Rush street, died of a heart attack yesterday in the North Shore sanitarium in Winnetka after a long illness. He was 60 years old. Mr. Le Blang, known as Dan Blanco, had been an entertainer and nightclub operator here for thirty-five years.

For several years he operated the Northern Lights café at Broadway and Devon avenue and for the last eleven years the Club Alabam. His home was at 749 Rush street. Surviving him are his wife, Thelma Garson Le Blang, whom he married in 1935 [sic], and a daughter by a previous marriage, Virginia, 5 years old. Funeral services will be held at 2 p.m. in the chapel at 2701 North Clark street.[174]

Chicago Tribune

DAN BLANCO

Dan Blanco, 69 [sic], one of the first cabaret entertainers, and later a café operator and owner, died at his home in Chicago, June 1, from a heart ailment.

At the time of his death he was half owner of Club Alabam, but had been inactive in the operation for over a year.[175]

Variety

CHAPTER ELEVEN

Gene Harris' Club Alabam

Fortunately, Dan Blanco had been an excellent mentor to Gene Harris, who became a full partner in the club before Blanco's death. Harris was more than ready to be the sole proprietor of Chicago's Club Alabam. Harris' accumulated experience working with Blanco, especially with the establishment of the New Wayside Inn in Biloxi, Mississippi, undoubtedly taught him a great deal about club ownership. Problems with contractors, suppliers of all kinds, backers, and talent, were constants in the nightclub world. Not to mention the inevitable dealings with the criminal element, as well as paying off the police.

By the mid-1930s, Harris found stability in his relationship with Aloisia "Babs" Jirik. An attractive brunette, she had large, sparkling eyes and a wide smile. A native of North Dakota, of Czechoslovakian extraction, she and her talented, pretty sisters had come to the big city, seeking jobs, if not also fame and fortune. Born in 1904, when Babs first met Gene Harris, she lived with two of her sisters in a rented room at the attractive Swiss Apartment House (5230 Winthrop Avenue), not far from Lake Michigan. She worked as a cigarette girl. Her half-sister, Mary J. Hasna, was a cloakroom clerk, while the younger, Irene Jirik, was a more accomplished "theatrical entertainer."

The Harrises lived together in the apartment above Club Alabam, which remained their residence until Gene Harris' death in 1964. The adjacent building, at 749 Rush Street, continued to house a variety of characters, including various club employees. Eventually, these residents would include Irene Jirik and her dance partner, Violet Wilson, employed by Club Alabam, as well as another sister, Rosalie (Jirik) Thompson, who worked in the cloakroom. Under Gene Harris' influence, Club Alabam quickly became a family affair.

By 1936, Harris' name began appearing in advertisements for the club. Dan Blanco's growing infirmity demanded he step down as an active partner and Harris was on his own to develop the club's reputation and choose talent. His personal life reflected his status as a nightclub owner. In the spring of 1936, Gene and Babs enjoyed a trip to sunny Bermuda, sailing on the *Monarch of Bermuda*.

That summer, Harris booked "Lil" Bernard and "Flo" Henrie, sometimes referred to as "The Female Van & Schenck." Like Dan Blanco before him, Harris put in very long days, beginning with luncheon priced at fifty cents. During the summer months, there was dancing from noon until 7:00 a.m. By September, the club had dropped lunch and afternoon dancing, starting the program at 5:30 p.m. Four orchestras were featured and advertisements promised delicious deluxe dinners, priced at $1.00. Charbroiled steaks were a specialty. Importantly, unlike fancier establishments, there was no cover charge and no minimum.[176]

Six months later, Lil and Flo continued as headliners at the club. Featured in the *Tribune* column "Night Club Notes," they celebrated their thirteenth year together in show business at the Club Alabam. Joining them on the bill were the dancing McCune Sisters and Art Williams.

By the summer of 1938, Gene Harris was seasoned as the sole proprietor of Club Alabam. Notices promoting the club's entertainment indicate that Harris did not stray far from the nitch Dan Blanco had established. Changes were made to accommodate both finances and audience taste. The Club Alabam's chorus line, like those at one time ubiquitous across Chicago's resorts, was retired. The days of employing chorus girls for between $25 to $35 per week, with an extra $5 or $10 for costumes was over. They had priced themselves out of the market.

Gene Harris' bill did not feature big names. Draws like popular pianist Eddy Duchin performed at Aragon and Trianon, North Side ballrooms. Club Alabam was where you went after the glamourous shows and where show people gathered after their performances in other clubs. It was the late, **late** night place to be.

"Night Club Hostess Is Found Slain In Chicago"

It wasn't long before Club Alabam owner Gene Harris had a potential public relations disaster on his hands. In early September of 1938, headlines announced: "Cabaret Hostess Found Strangled in Chicago Hotel." Gene

Harris' checker/floor man/bouncer, the husky Frank Raab, had allegedly murdered a former Club Alabam hostess, Mrs. Marie Lamont. At the time of her death, she worked as an assistant in the Drake Hotel flower shop, which catered to high society patrons in the Loop. As recently as the previous week, Raab had been employed at the Club Alabam. Whether he had quit or been fired is unknown.

The attractive, auburn-haired, twenty-seven-year-old Lamont was found dead in Raab's room at the Lorraine Hotel at 411 South Wabash Avenue, an unsavory place that for years had been the home to criminals—from petty thieves, to ex-convicts, to rapists, to depressives contemplating suicide. Half naked, clad in a silken nightgown, red marks on her neck indicated strangulation and an electric light cord was found on the floor by the bed. Some reports claimed that the cord was still around her neck when the body was discovered. She was the mother of an eight-year-old daughter, Joan, who lived with her paternal grandparents in Kendalville, Indiana, and was then enrolled in a convent school at LaGrange. Lamont had also been convent educated.

William F. "Frank" Raab had occupied rooms in the hotel for two years. One reporter called him a "hot spot habitué." During that time, Mrs. Lamont and her husband, Robert, separated and Marie had been living at a "girl's club" at 215 East Erie Street.

She had been dead about fifteen or sixteen hours when her body was discovered. A chamber maid, Charlie Williams, had entered the hotel room for routine cleaning. Miss Williams explained to the *Tribune*: "This woman was lying on the bed with a sheet pulled over her head.... Her hands were crossed, and I thought she was asleep. When I returned again at 3 o'clock and saw she had not moved I knew something was wrong and called the manager." Others reported that the couple had been drinking the night before.[177]

Later the next day, the plot thickened when Frank Raab was found drunk, apparently attempting suicide in Chicago's Garfield Park Lagoon. The police identified him by his soaked Social Security card and realized he was the man sought in connection with Marie Lamont's death. On the way to the detective bureau, Raab incriminated himself when an officer commented, "Do you know Mrs. Lamont? You'll probably see her at the detective bureau." Raab reportedly responded: "What the hell, is she still alive?"[178]

The case was complicated further by a slim brunette named Jean Carlyle, age twenty-six or twenty-seven, who worked as a "dice game girl" at a Fox Lake roadhouse. Jean told police that she loved Frank Raab and planned to marry him, though she suspected he was involved with another woman. She possessed a letter written by Raab, which she interpreted as a possible suicide note. In it he wrote: "Everything is a constant muddle. If I should leave this world voluntarily I wish you the best of luck." Apt advice for a dice game girl.[179]

Jean Carlyle, like so many other young women who populated Chicago's nightlife, had left Little Rock, Arkansas, heading for adventure in the big city. She worked in clubs and, previously, lived with Frank Raab in the very hotel room where Marie Lamont died. Jean had reportedly moved to Fox Lake several months earlier "to get some country air."[180]

Unsurprisingly, Frank Raab had a sordid past. In the early 1920s, he served two years in Joliet Penitentiary for burglary. Paroled in 1923, during Prohibition, he worked in nightclubs and as a beer runner for the ruthless Irish-American gangsters Roger and Tommy Touhy, who entered the bootlegging business in 1925. A thorn in the side of Al Capone's "The Outfit," the Touhy brothers had penetrated the North Side following the St. Valentine's Day Massacre in 1929. By 1934, Tommy was declared "Public Enemy Number One." By 1938, he was dead and Roger was incarcerated. Frank Raab's connection to the brothers is a chilling reminder that Club Alabam, during Prohibition and after, dealt daily with the city's roughest characters. Had Dan Blanco and Gene Harris been friendly with Raab since his beer-running days? Did they owe him a favor when they hired him as a bouncer?

Shortly after Raab was apprehended and sobered up, he confessed to the murder, telling police that his desperate sweetheart begged him to kill her. The coroner's report suggested there may have been a suicide pact between Frank and Marie. An analysis of her vital organs revealed enough hypnotic poison to have caused the death. The same poison was reportedly found in Raab's system. Despite the coroner's findings, Assistant State's Attorney John S. Boyle said there was no evidence of a suicide pact. Raab waved a trial by jury and Judge W. J. Lindsay sentenced him to twenty-one years in jail for the slaying of Marie Lamont.

What did this kind of notoriety mean for Club Alabam? The story was national news picked up from Charleston, South Carolina, to Lexington, Kentucky, to Portland, Oregon. The *Asheville Citizen–Times* ran the headline: "Night Club Hostess Is Found Slain In Chicago." Marie's less flamboyant job in a floral shop was overlooked; her employment at Club Alabam made for a more salacious headline.[181]

In 1943, King Features Syndicate published a compelling retelling of the murder of Marie Lamont, written by Terry McShane and entitled, "The Strange Case of the Red Carnation." In this sensational version, Detective Richard Barry of the Homicide Squad visits the Club Alabam, the "management" cooperates with the law, informing Barry that Raab was no longer employed at the club, having left the week prior to the crime. Was Gene Harris interviewed about Frank Raab, his name withheld from the true crime narrative?

New Lid Law

As the 1930s drew to a close, in March of 1939, "The Amazing Evelyn Nesbit"—"The Most Talked About Woman in the World"—returned for yet another engagement with Gene Harris at Club Alabam. Joining Nesbit on the program was the blonde Harriet Norris, who appeared in an "Interlude of Innuendo," and emcee Jack Irving, designated "Speaker of the House." Old friend, Bernie Adler, was also on the bill. Singer Paulette LaPierre added continental flair to the evening's entertainment and became a longtime fixture. Norris, with her dazzling smile, also became a favorite at the club. Billed as the "Exponent of Sophisticated Songs," she eventually graduated to "Mistress of Ceremonies."

Like Dan Blanco before him, Gene Harris openly displayed a humorous touch in his advertisements. Three bands, Chet Robinson, Dave Unell, and Eddie Roth, played nightly, filling in between four shows, the last set starting at 4 a.m. Dinner remained reasonably priced at $1.50, charcoal broiled steaks and chickens were featured on the menu. Prospective patrons reading Chicago newspapers were reminded that Club Alabam was the place to be for dinner or after the theater.

◆ ◆ ◆

That spring, a new wave of reform in Chicago became a serious problem for establishments like Club Alabam. If new city liquor ordinances stayed in effect, it could mean the end of Harris' club and many more like it. An article by Guy Murchie, Jr. ran in the *Tribune* under a mournful headline announcing: "1 O'CLOCK TOWN! TRADE SKIDS IN GLUM TAVERNS."[182]

At the beginning of May, Chicago police had their eye on 9,200 establishments which were ordered to be closed by 1 a.m. on weekdays and by 2 a.m. on Sunday mornings, the first ordinance of its kind since 1933. Initially, the police found this new "lid law" ignored by many tavern keepers. Some of the bigger nightclubs, like Chez Paree, stayed open after 1 o'clock, skirting the law by not serving liquor.

Proprietors across the city resisted, as they watched thousands of patrons head to suburban roadhouses where the new curfew did not apply. On May 14, thirty Chicago tavern owners were arrested either for opening early or closing late. By mid-month, it was estimated that strict enforcement had put 1,500 bartenders out of work and many dice girls would be fired. By May 22, thirty-two additional proprietors were arrested, most of them for selling liquor after 2 a.m. on Sunday morning. Gene Harris was not reported among them.

Smaller club and saloon owners, waiters, bartenders, musicians, and even taxi drivers stood to lose significant income under the new closing ordinance. For his article, Murchie visited Rush Street to interview those affected. He talked to dice girl Ruth Jurgensen, who explained that the frequent rollers typically showed up after midnight. "My income has dropped a fourth since we began closing at one."[183]

He also spoke to the ever-popular Jack Coleman, "the stout and amiable colored doorman," at Club Alabam, who stated, "They are making a hick town of Chicago." Coleman elaborated that all the nightclubs had both entertainment and food dispensary licenses, meaning they were never required to close their doors. The new law applied to selling intoxicating liquors after 1 o'clock. If they were caught, their licenses would be revoked. Coleman went on to observe that, "Folks now are afraid to go to nightclubs after midnight. They're afraid of getting a ride in a patrol wagon. I watch the traffic in Rush Street, and I've noticed that since this law's been enforced, you could shoot a cannon down Rush Street without hitting an automobile."[184]

Next, Murchie stepped inside the club to talk to a gloomy Gene Harris. "I'm laying off 75 percent of my help on Sunday," he said. "Convention men just aren't going out much. They come to town to have a good time. Now they are going to roadhouses out in the country. Niles Center [Skokie] gets a lot of business." Harris also noted that so-called beer flats were springing up everywhere. All these proprietors had to do was fix up a room and start selling beer. One of Harris' showgirls told him she was in a beer flat that was doing a big business until 7 o'clock in the morning.[185]

Interestingly, a cabbie provided Murchie with an inside scoop, telling the journalist that he had lost a lot of business due to the new curfew. The driver was looking ahead to July when licenses would come up for renewal. He predicted that there would be two grades of licenses: one for clubs willing to close before 1:00 a.m. and a more expensive one for those wanting to operate late into the night. When Murchie asked the cabbie where he got his information: "O, we fellers get around, you know."[186]

The cabbie knew what he was talking about. By mid-June, Chicago's City Council had adjusted their opinion on late night entertainment in Chicago, proposing increased licensing fees for clubs that wanted a 4:00 a.m. closing. Proprietors along Rush Street were asked by the *Tribune* for comment. Colony Club (744 Rush), Rose Bowl (865 Rush), Kit-Kat (871 Rush), Pit (875 Rush), 885 Club (885 Rush), Isbell's (940 Rush), and Gay 90's Music Hall (1022 Rush) all stood ready to pay the additional fee. Their business didn't heat up until midnight. Gene Harris commented for Club Alabam, "The proposal is very good."[187] On July 10, new so-called "owl privileges" were available at $700 per year. The adjusted curfews were 4:00 a.m. on weekdays, 5:00 a.m. on Sunday mornings.

Evelyn Nesbit's Swan Song And A Reunion With John Barrymore

During the lid law crisis, Evelyn Nesbit was playing the Club Alabam. Her timing was, as usual, slightly disastrous. She had arrived in Chicago for an extended engagement in one of her favorite nightclubs only to find Rush Street and the city's tavern owners in a tizzy.

In 1939, Nesbit toured with a burlesque act. She kicked off the year at Cleveland's Roxy burlesque theater in a show entitled "Memories." The notice in the *Plain Dealer* was lukewarm. She told the press she hoped to be regarded as a singer. The review claimed Nesbit's singing fell short for radio but was okay for the Roxy. Billed as Evelyn Nesbit Thaw, she sang "Them There Eyes," published in 1930 and popularized by Bing Crosby and The Rhythm Boys. In 1939, Billie Holiday made it her own. The reviewer also found Nesbit's quips dated, noting that Roxy regulars might be surprised when she didn't "drop a stitch." She shared the bill with a stripper named Rose La Rose.

While in Cleveland, Nesbit gave an interview which reflected her always abundant humor. If she had learned anything in her decades as a media darling, she knew how to throw out a provocative line or two, generating a headline that would entice editors across the country to run her story. "I wish I were a strip teaser," she admitted to the Ohio reporter. "I wouldn't have to bother with so many clothes." At fifty-four, those days were likely behind her. She explained that there was nothing risque about her act, though she had completely changed her patter. "Noël Coward stuff doesn't go here."[188]

Nesbit criticized people who defended burlesque as Art, though she found some of the strippers beautiful to watch. She admitted needing a job to support herself and help her mother, financially; she didn't particularly care what that job was. "I'd work in a sheep pen in Central Park if I had to," she said frankly.[189]

At the end of January, Nesbit moved on to an engagement in Cincinnati. It was her first appearance in the city in many years. This show was entitled "Venus and Vanity," presenting "a bevy of burlesque stars," including a stripper named Vilma Joszy and eighteen chorus girls. Full of stamina, Nesbit was on stage for four shows daily, with a special midnight performance on Saturday. One evening, Nesbit slipped on a step, falling and breaking two bones in her wrist. Two hours later, she appeared on stage, sporting a blue silk sling donated by Miss Joszy, proving that she was ever the trooper.

In February, Nesbit played Detroit, appearing at the Avenue burlesque theater. Her arm in a cast, she was particularly proud of the fact that she had not missed a single show, even going on stage under the effects of ether. The *Detroit Free Press* ran a feature article detailing Evelyn Nesbit's attitudes about aging in which she commented that a woman is as old as her skin. The reporter kindly added that Nesbit's skin was as youthful as on the night her former husband, Harry K. Thaw, shot and killed Stanford White. Was it? Or did the journalist see an opportunity to mention the old scandal?

Lighthearted as ever, Nesbit refused to apologize for touring in burlesque. "Don't be surprised if you see me sometime in a Chinese juggling act," she said. "It's the only thing I haven't done on stage."[190]

By early April, Nesbit reached Chicago and the Club Alabam, where she was a solo act once more and remained until late May, despite the nearly month-long early closing curfew. Gene Harris may have struggled to meet her salary. By mid-June, Nesbit was booked in Milwaukee, playing the Miami Club—"Milwaukee's Finest Theatre Restaurant." Even if she had wanted to stay longer with Harris in Chicago, his extreme loss of revenue under the new ordinance may have forced her to leave.

In the spring of 1939, while Evelyn Nesbit was playing the Club Alabam, John Barrymore opened in his play, *My Dear Children*. One night after the show, he found his way from Chicago's Selwyn Theater to Rush Street and Gene Harris' Club Alabam. There, he was dazzled by Evelyn Nesbit. According to legend, Barrymore announced to the room that she was his first love. Their brief romance, in 1902, had ended before it could sour. "Jack" was twenty-one and Evelyn was seventeen. Nesbit's mother did not approve and ended the budding affair. In May of 1939, a tearful reunion at Club Alabam followed Barrymore's public declaration of love. If we could only turn back the clock to hear the unrecorded reminiscences of these aging thespians, both nearing the end of long and challenging careers....

On May 30, Barrymore suffered a heart attack. After three weeks rest, he returned to the stage. Like Evelyn Nesbit, he took his commitment seriously and continued to mount the popular play in Chicago into the first week of January, 1940.[191]

As the 1930s ended, Evelyn Nesbit's name increasingly appeared in columns entitled "Remember When" and "Twenty-five Years Ago Today." Burlesque was the end of the theatrical road. She spent the summer of 1939 with her mother, renting a New Jersey farm about four miles outside historic Flemington, living adjacent actress Sylvia Sydney. In August, Nesbit came to the aid of an old friend, Princess Wana, to launch her new supper club in Dunellen, New Jersey, performing there for four weeks.

Reporter Mary P. Elliott interviewed Nesbit, describing her dark red hair and her now husky voice. Laughing as she talked, Nesbit explained she had no desire to become a torch or blues singer, she wanted to make people laugh. Not every singer could deliver a comedy song and Nesbit felt this was her calling.[192]

In early 1940, she was hospitalized with reported gallbladder issues; she rallied briefly in 1942 and was strong enough to celebrate thirty years in show business at Brooklyn's Aloha Club; and, finally, appeared in Manhattan at Ernie's Three Ring Circus (an ultra-modern restaurant and bar, featuring circus murals on the walls). Perhaps hitting the thirty-year mark satisfied Nesbit. Age and poor health sapped even her youthful energy and she quietly slipped into retirement.[193]

Illegal Gambling At "Chicago's Oldest Dinner and Supper Club"

By the autumn of 1939, Gene Harris was claiming that Club Alabam was Chicago's Oldest Dinner and Supper Club. It may well have been. Who could resist the "sensational" food and easy-going talent (four shows nightly), as well as a generous, affable host? Harris promised there was never a cover or a minimum charge. Patrons could count on action from 6 p.m. until closing. His large newspaper advertisements oozed with excitement for his establishment printing eye-catching lines like: **"Maybe We're Crazy ... but you won't be when you try our sensational Flaming Crater Dinner."**

The Flaming Crater Dinner included a choice of several entrees; chicken, duck, chops and prize-winning steaks. A complete dinner was available at the unbelievably low price of $1.50. AND for parties of four, the meal included the quart of famous Renault Champagne or Sparkling Burgundy—compliments of your host, Gene Harris. A party of two received a pint of wine. Harris challenged his prospective patrons: "If you don't agree that our FLAMING CRATER DINNER ... Plus a quart of Renault Champagne or Sparkling Burgundy is the finest dinner you've ever eaten ... **We'll GIVE you the dinner ... AND $5 IN COLD CASH."**

Bernard and Henrie continued to top the bill, which included Rio and Rita, that scintillating international dance team, and Effie Button, "The Duchess of Rush Street." Harris bragged that he was "packing them in" and, as far as he was concerned, every night was New Year's Eve at Club Alabam.

There was one significant attraction at the Club Alabam that Gene Harris did not mention in his newspaper advertisements—illegal gambling.

In the early hours of March 6, 1941, Club Alabam was raided for the first time in twelve years, having enjoyed a long immunity from any police interference with its casino "sideline." The raid included Colony Club, located across the street at 744 Rush. Manager Henry "Sonny" Goldstone maintained he was the Colony's sole owner, denying that powerful gangster and ex-convict Nicholas Circella, better known as Nick Dean, actually owned the club.[194]

Gambling paraphernalia was seized at both establishments. Nine men were arrested. At Club Alabam, police found one roulette game and one blackjack game running on the second floor and another blackjack game operating in a side room off the cabaret on the first floor. Fifteen patrons were "chased out." Leo Harky, the club's manager, was arrested, along with three other men described as his assistants: George A. Stein, Lou Rossman, and John Schmid, who had previously served two years in prison for auto theft. Where was Gene Harris?

A slick, plainclothes detective named James Ryan posed as an out-of-town shoe salesman, winning the confidence of a Club Alabam hostess who was sitting at the bar. When he "flashed a sizable roll," she suggested he might like to play the roulette wheel in the upstairs gambling room, confessing that it was for regular customers but he might be an exception. Then, she made a critical error, confiding, "I can tell you're not a cop. I got ways of telling." Chances are good that one hostess lost her job that week.[195]

In April, Leo Harky and the three other Club Alabam employees appeared in Judge George B. Weiss' South Street Racket Court, where they faced multiple state and city charges. The judge imposed fines totaling over $900. Manager Harky was charged with permitting gambling in a tavern, an offense that carried with it a revocation of the tavern license. Where **was** Gene Harris?

Reminiscent of the days when Dan Blanco held the cabaret license for Northern Lights' owner Andy Craig, did managers typically hold tavern licenses, placing a buffer between the owners and the law? Does this partly explain why Colony Club's manager, Sonny Goldstone, could claim to be the club's sole proprietor?

In late summer, Pulitzer Prize-winning Westbrook Pegler, a popular and controversial columnist during the 1930s and 1940s, wrote about the depths of corruption at Chicago's Colony Club, and offered one explanation as to why club owners might not own tavern licenses—Nick Dean, the real backer of the nightspot, had a criminal record, disqualifying him as a licensee. Pegler knew firsthand the kind of "joint" the club was. On one visit, he was approached by the headwaiter on behalf of prostitutes, who loitered in the shadows. He had personally seen gaming rooms. Shockingly open illegal activity. "The Colony Club is a dump," wrote Pegler, "under criminal ownership and assurance of this fact may impart a special thrill to the radio audience the next time the announcer's mooing notes advise the unseen multitude that they are listening to music by one of Jimmy Petrillo's union orchestras from the beautiful and exclusive Colony Club on Chicago's famous Gold Coast."[196]

In mid-May, a front page story in the *Tribune* revealed that padlocks went on the doors of both Club Alabam and the Colony Club. Mayor Edward Joseph Kelly had instructed the city collector not to reissue tavern or restaurant licenses to either establishment and went on the warpath against racketeering. In one week, 300 arrests were made in the Loop and outlying sections of the city. On May 19, local press printed a long list of so-called gambling resorts which had been raided and taverns whose licenses had been revoked. The raids at Club Alabam and the Colony had kicked off a wave of reform in Chicago. State's Attorney Thomas J. Courtney commented, "These fountains of easy money have been dried up."[197]

By July, manager Francis Roush was in place at the Club Alabam, ready to reopen, in possession of a six-month tavern license. Curiously, local press reported that the club had been sold, yet Gene Harris would own it until his death. In mid-July, typically amusing and enthusiastic advertisements for Club Alabam claimed *new* management and *new* owners, who had invested in improvements—a cozy cocktail lounge and a "few new gadgets." Had Harris found different financial partners, as well as a replacement for the embarrassed Leo Harky?

◆ ◆ ◆

Reporter Will Davidson helped stimulate business, writing: "Club Alabam has bounced back in the café scene with new lights, new decorations, a new bar, and new bosses. The same kitchen staff is turning out the famous Flaming Crater dinners, but a new cast is dishing out entertainment."[198]

The club continued to focus on fine food, which now included Maine lobster, fresh Florida Pompano, "the aristocratic fish," and succulent Louisiana frog legs. The price of dinner remained a remarkable $1.50. Dinner started at 5 p.m. and there was no change in the club's moderately priced drinks. Even a packed show had room for Dan Blanco's old friend Bernie Adler.

Interestingly, as the months went on, Gene Harris' name was conspicuously missing from Club Alabam's innovative advertisements, but his anecdotal style was unmistakable.

DO YOU RATE WITH WOMEN?

Brother, one sure way to score heavily with the ladies is to take 'em where the real smart folks go. And the wife or girlfriend is pretty smart about good food, too. You'll get a big kick out of watching the ladies gush, coo, and gurgle with delight when you bring them to the CLUB ALABAM. They know it's really "the place to go" because they have heard their enthusiastic girlfriends rave about the CLUB ALABAM's food. Score a smash hit with your lady tonight, treat her to the CLUB ALABAM's famous

FLAMING CRATER DINNER

PRESTIDIGITATORS!!

Yes Sir, that's what a customer called the CLUB ALABAM chefs the other night. We didn't know just how to react to this until our Athens University headwaiter, Peter, explained that our enthusiastic guest was taking the "hard way" to call our chefs magicians at the art of preparing delicious food.

No matter what you call 'em folks, you'll agree with our thousands of delighted diners that the CLUB ALABAM chefs prepare food that is really "out of another world." Come in tonight and thrill to some CLUB ALABAM magic as served on our sensational

FLAMING CRATER DINNER

"PARADOXICALLY"

Said one of our guests, "The CLUB ALABAM serves the finest in America at a ridiculously low price. How can you do it?" Well Brother, it sure is a paradox and sometimes we wonder too, how the old Alabam does it. But while we're wondering, thousands of connoisseurs of fine food are taking advantage of a truly unusual situation and are flocking each night to thrill to the CLUB ALABAM's nationally-famous sensational

FLAMING CRATER DINNER

♦ ♦ ♦

Clearly, Club Alabam valued a strong menu over an impressive floor show. In the summer of 1941, Harris announced two significant additions to his staff, straight from unoccupied France: Sylvestre Delanoeye, a famous European chef, and François Charpentier, a continental maître d'hotel. According to advertisements, the men were famed throughout Europe at the Crillon (Paris) and the Adlon (Berlin) and known to Americans via their connections to prestigious New York establishments, including the Waldorf-Astoria and the Knickerbocker Hotel.

Late-night crowds at Club Alabam were boisterous. Many came after the theater or after seeing a top-line entertainer at a posh club. In the wee hours of the morning, show people found their way to the Alabam, to relax and drink and chat with Gene Harris, who wisely kept the club air-conditioned all year round—"maintaining 68°." When the band was hot and the dancing exuberant, a cool atmosphere was a definite selling point!

Paulette LaPierre: Sunny France In Old Alabam

A hallmark of the Club Alabam was continuity, not only of its unique "speakeasy" atmosphere but also of its talent. Gene Harris' warm personality inspired loyalty in his employees and he was, in turn, loyal to them. Performers such as musician Bernie Adler, "Bernard and Henrie," Harriet Norris, and pianist Two-Ton Baker remained at the club year after year. Another exemplary, long-term employee was singer and dancer Paulette LaPierre. Billed across her career as a "Frenchy songstress," a "French Comedienne," a "Parisian dynamo," and "A Bit of Sunny France," LaPierre's French songs were especially popular in the post-World War I milieu, when many returning doughboys fondly remembered a Mademoiselle ... or two.

Born in Montréal in 1895, Paulette LaPierre was just four years Gene Harris' senior. From the early 1920s, she worked steadily in vaudeville, first touring with her talented sisters: Germaine, who later worked with Paulette in Chicago at Mike Fritzel's Frolics, where they entertained tableside, singing French songs between acts; Anita, who specialized in "Parisian songs" and worked with Paulette in Miami, Florida; and the youngest, Geraldine. Life was far from glamorous on the vaudeville circuit. Managers could be unscrupulous.

Pay checks irregular. To supplement their income, the LaPierres sold sheet music featuring their pictures.

After the sister act dissolved, Anita toured Europe, including a "command performance" in England, and married Frank Ross, the voice of Daddy Warbucks in the enormously popular radio show *Little Orphan Annie*. Likewise, Paulette continued to work in vaudeville with her husband, Dave O'Dowd, who specialized in a soft-shoe routine.

In the 1920s, Paulette LaPierre bobbed her hair and rouged her lips, invoking the coquettish look of silent film favorites Renée Adorée and Clara Bow. In Chicago, she sang at Bill Rothstein's Moulin Rouge Café, contributing to the French ambiance. There she worked with then stage manager Dan Blanco and appeared along with Evelyn Nesbit when she made her successful Chicago comeback in 1925.

As the years went by, life on the road became less and less attractive. With two sons to rear, LaPierre permanently switched from touring in vaudeville to engagements in nightclubs and cabarets, putting down roots in Chicago. Like Club Alabam, Paulette LaPierre had staying power and became one of the city's perennially popular, hard-working entertainers. A life-long practicing Catholic, LaPierre entered show business because she was talented, not because she sought an exciting life. When a patron offered to toast her with champagne, she drank ginger ale, though the customer likely paid champagne prices.

She worked at a variety of venues, including the Kit Kat Club; Club Royale ("Chicago's Foremost Supper Club, Where Celebrities of Stage and Screen Meet") where she appeared on the program with Texas Guinan; and the Colony Club, where she was honored on the menu, which featured a romaine lettuce salad called the "Paulette LaPierre."

During 1933–1934, along with Club Alabam favorites Mike & Ike, Paulette and Germaine LaPierre could be found at the Chicago World's Fair, singing French songs in "The Streets of Paris" exhibition. Nearby, the sensation-causing Sally Rand performed her ostrich-feathered fan dance to the soothing strains of Debussy's "Clair de Lune."

A seasoned professional who worked for many bosses in towns across America, Paulette LaPierre liked the relaxed and familial atmosphere of Club Alabam best of all. In addition to a steady pay check, performers (as well as their families) could count on Gene Harris' kitchen for good meals, a much appreciated perk.

By 1939, Paulette LaPierre was a fixture on the bill and had found a home as a member of the Club Alabam family. She was there, supporting Evelyn Nesbit, when John Barrymore publicly declared his love, as well as the unlucky night, in 1941, when Club Alabam and the Colony Club were raided for operating illegal gambling. Allegedly, Club Alabam was targeted because Gene Harris was behind in paying his "protection money" to the police. Furious, LaPierre was taken to the local station with other employees. Within thirty minutes, however, they were released and she held no grudge against her employer, continuing to work for Gene Harris through World War II, ringing in many a new year. She was still performing at Club Alabam in the autumn of 1946, having lasted in the spotlight beyond her fiftieth birthday.

◆ ◆ ◆

Years later, in 1962, Chicago *Sun-Times* columnist Irv "Kup" Kupcinet explained Club Alabam's uniqueness and recipe for longevity, quoting Gene Harris at length:

> "We always have catered to a fun-loving group. In the early days, it was millionaires who wanted to get out 'on the town.' The millionaires are gone today, but we still have many of our old-time customers. They like to get rowdy, sing out loud, walk across the stage during the floor show, and call out to one another. You can't do that with high-priced talent. Some of them won't even let you serve during the performance. So our policy is to hire the kind of entertainers who don't mind these little interferences. What kind of acts permit this? That's why I say, and say it proudly, we have the world's worst floor show. My customers come first, the entertainers second."[199]

Gene Harris was exaggerating, of course. He hired dependable, professional talent, well-loved across Chicago for their personable delivery, as well as their desire to please his sometimes rowdy crowd. Harris also neglected to say that he served some of the best food in town. Kup added that the private room, upstairs at the Club Alabam, greatly enhancing its popularity. Over the years, many prominent people had relaxed there, away from prying eyes. In the 1930s, and perhaps beyond, that relaxation may have included a little gambling.

Evelyn Nesbit Thaw, 1907.
(Courtesy George Grantham Bain Collection, Library of Congress.)

Millionaire Harry K. Thaw called his wife "the dearest girl in the world." Plagued by drug addiction and obsessive jealousy, on June 24, 1906, Thaw murdered Nesbit's former lover, Stanford White, atop Madison Square Garden in front of dozens of theatergoers who were attending the opening night of a frothy musical called <u>Mam'zelle Champagne</u>.

In 1907, Evelyn Nesbit Thaw testified in her husband's defense in what became known as "the crime of the century." On the witness stand, Nesbit detailed White's seduction of her in his sumptuous apartment, which included a red velvet swing suspended from a high ceiling. He delighted as she kicked at a Japanese paper parasol, shredding it to pieces. The erotic nature of this "game" was not lost on the jury, journalists, nor the public and Nesbit became known as the girl in the red velvet swing. In 1955, 20th Century Fox released a film version of Nesbit's life by that title and, over the decades, countless articles, several books, and the Broadway musical <u>Ragtime</u> have perpetuated the nickname.

Johnny Sircy, 1959. (AUTHOR COLLECTION)

Gene Harris and his business partner, Charles E. Houston, co-owned the Fashion Club Pony Farm located in Libertyville, Illinois. In 1959, little Johnny Sircy enjoyed a ride on one of their Shetland ponies.

Gene Harris and Shetland pony, c. 1955. (AUTHOR COLLECTION)

In Iowa, at the Fashion Club Pony Farm in Garden Grove Township, Iowa, near Gene Harris' hometown of Leon, the nightclub proprietor was known as "Cowpuncher." His partner, Dr. Wayne Munn, once president of the American Shetland Pony Club and chairman of the Herd Registration Committee of the American Guernsey Association, lent valuable expertise to the breeding of the Shetland pony stock.

Dick "Two Ton" Baker, 1944. Photo W-G-N Press Department. (Author Collection)

Chicago celebrity Two Ton Baker found lasting success both in radio and with live performances. In 1944, his fifteen-minute program aired on Chicago's widely broadcast W-G-N. A devoted employee of Club Alabam, Baker taught himself piano, never taking a lesson. During the 1950s and 1960s, he kept Gene Harris' patrons happy singing an enormous repertoire of nostalgic tunes.

Club Alabam, 1964. (AUTHOR COLLECTION)

When this photo was taken in July of 1964, just months before Gene Harris' death, the main dining room at Club Alabam was known as the "Epicure Club." The original red and white checked table clothes, which in the 1920s reflected the speakeasy's Dixieland atmosphere, had long been replaced with the double white table cloths associated with fine dining.

Evelyn Nesbit, "Tired Butterfly," 1903.
(Photos by Rudolf Eickemeyer, Jr., Author Collection)

From artist model to accomplished artist, another aspect of Evelyn Nesbit's creative life was finally actualized in Los Angeles, California where she created and taught sculpture.

Evelyn Nesbit. c. 1910.
(Courtesy George Grantham Bain Collection, Library of Congress.)

In 1913, a similar image illustrated Evelyn Nesbit's syndicated memoir, "The Story of My Life" by Evelyn Thaw. Drawn to sculpting, Nesbit knew an artistic career was an impractical way to support herself and her son, writing: "My enthusiasm for my sculpture never waned. Day after day, week after week, I worked and read and reflected with the single aim of being found worthy in the field that had been so unexpectedly opened up to me. I had never been 'stage struck,' nor was I now work struck. I was grasping at a great opportunity to save myself, to justify my continued existence."

CHAPTER TWELVE

Fashion Club Stables & The End Of An Era

Following the reorganization forced by the gambling charges, Gene Harris turned his attention to his lucrative side business: horses and ponies. While his name disappeared from the advertisements for Club Alabam, it now appeared in similarly styled ads for "Gene Harris' FASHION CLUB STABLES."

In 1937, Gene Harris' deep Virginia roots were showing when he purchased the Fashion Club Stables, located on North Cleveland Avenue, one block west of Clark Street. The stables remembered a horse named "My Fashion." At that time, fourteen miles of bridle paths wound through Lincoln Park and along Lake Michigan's shoreline. Chicago's elite kept horses in town, while members of the middle class took riding lessons and rented horses on weekends.

Snappy advertisements (sounding very much like the fun-loving Gene Harris) encouraged prospective equestriennes to "Do as thousands of smart, chic women are doing.... Ride Horseback!" Fashion Club Stables promised a "core of expert instructors" capable of making anyone a confident rider in no time. It was a chance to meet interesting, sporty people and make friends, while finding "excitement, adventure, fun, and rejuvenated beauty." There was a large indoor ring, which promised to be the safest and most beautiful in the city—open a very accommodating twenty-four hours a day. Harris, himself, built the 55 x 150 foot arena, one of the largest of its kind in Chicago.

Horses were also sold through the stables. Harris devised an unusual "single price" system. There were new arrivals daily, with dozens of horses to choose from. Potential customers could view any horse, at any hour, on any day. Interested parties could request a circular with complete details from: Gene Harris' Fashion Club Stables, 2223 N. Cleveland Ave.

A single price horse does not imply a finely bred animal and, in 1944, Harris found himself implicated in a law suit brought by Lawrence P. Bardin (described as a fancier of show horses) against W. C. Mountjoy, operator of a training stables at Devon Avenue and Dee Road in Park Ridge, Illinois. Bardin accused Mountjoy of operating a "confidence game," calling him a "Yankee horse trader." Bardin paid $5,500 for two horses and complained that he was stuck with "two plugs, full of worms." Mountjoy had purchased the animals from Gene Harris, presumably trained them, and sold them to Bardin at a hefty markup.[200]

Fire Destroys Fashion Club Stables

In 1945, tragedy struck the stables when an electrical fire blazed out of control, suffocating a total of eighty horses. Some were blooded horses boarding at the stable, many of them ribbon winners, valued up to $10,000 each. Gene Harris lost fifty horses, estimating his financial loss at $100,000 [over 1.3 million in 2019 dollars]. Newspaper reports indicated even higher losses, perhaps as much as $200,000 total. In addition to running the stables, Harris showed gaited horses. Two of his prized animals, Golden Sensation and Intruder, a five-gated horse, were lost in the fire. It was rumored that Harris had once refused to sell Intruder when offered $10,000. Recently, the stables had been completely remodeled. The fire was discovered by a groom named Robert June, age twenty, when he was feeding the animals. Five horses were led to safety. June, who was handicapped from infantile paralysis, was unable to sound an alarm.[201]

Other headaches came with owning the stables. In 1946, Harris was sued for $2,500 worth of damages for the alleged mutilation of a horse boarded at Fashion Club. The mare's owner charged that its tongue had been cut out, claiming that animal could no longer eat without assistance. Harris' response was, "the horse either bit off the end of its own tongue or some other horse did it, so far as we can figure it out."[202]

The Pony King

After the devastating fire at Fashion Club Stables, Gene Harris shifted to a less toney, though remarkably lucrative, business breeding Shetland Ponies. Herb Lyon, in his column "Tower Ticker," noted: "Gene Harris, known all over the country as the owner of Rush st.'s Club Alabam, makes more money raising and selling Shetland ponies. [The night spot's a hobby.]"[203] It wasn't long before Gene Harris was known around town as the Pony King.

Following the war, Harris observed Americans moving to rapidly growing suburbs. Many returning GI's had grown up on farms, raised a variety of animals, and might want something beyond the family dog for their children to enjoy. Suburban parents quickly found ponies made excellent pets. They cost less to feed than a dog, were gentle, easy to train, played nicely with children, and even mowed the lawn. Importantly, Shetlands required only about half an acre of ground, making it feasible to keep one at a suburban home. There was something appealing about looking through a plate glass window to see a pony kicking up his heels.

Ponies were lovable and Harris argued they were a good investment, maintaining that breeding was an ideal sideline for a speculative businessman. More lucrative than cattle, hogs or other livestock, ponies consumed less than $50 worth of feed a year. They scrounged for themselves and required little oversight.

The world's smallest horse, a Shetland pony could weigh up to 400 pounds. Spotted ponies were popular with children, while their parents preferred Palomino, sorrel, or dapple chested. By 1955, the breeding, raising, selling and showing of Shetland ponies was a $31 million industry in America. Harris expected demand to double.

Illinois became the world's capital of Shetland Pony breeding and, by 1958, Gene Harris described himself as the "world's largest pony dealer" and Fashion Club ponies continued to sell like proverbial hot cakes throughout the United States. Harris' breed stock descended from the renowned Shetland Stallion, King Larigo, a world champion once owned by Diamond Jim Brady, who won 896 blue ribbons, had 144 "sons and daughters," and died in 1929.[204]

Harris and his partners owned two farms, one in Libertyville, Illinois, and one near his birthplace in Leon, Iowa, where he was known as "Cowpuncher," a peculiar moniker since Harris didn't breed cattle. Dr. Wayne Munn, at one time president of the American Shetland Pony Club and chairman of the Herd Registration Committee of the American Guernsey Association, was Harris' partner in the Leon farm. Dr. Munn, known as the father and, later, the grandfather of the Shetland pony breed in America, was a dignified and expert partner, who worked tirelessly to increase the breed's popularity.[205]

The Leon farm, managed by Walter Strover, was home to 100 registered Shetland brood mares. The ever innovative Gene Harris sold his ponies via mail-order catalogs, including Sears, Montgomery Ward, and Spiegel. An early advertisement read: "You may choose my name. I am a male pony (gelding) 40 inches tall. I am black in color and 5 years old. I'm very gentle and affectionate—very much of a pet. I am suitable for a child 4 to 12 years of age. I am in good health. $250 is my price—$50 to be sent with the order and $200 C.O.D. when I arrive."

In 1954, ponies were available in five colors from Fashion Club Pony Farm, priced at $299.50. They ranged from 41 to 46 inches high at the saddle, delivered ready to ride. Colts were sold for $149.95, poised to mature with their youthful owners. Ponies were shipped within twenty-four hours of the order being received. Satisfaction was guaranteed. In the mid-1950s, Harris sold about 2,000 ponies per year from the 440-acre farm in Leon. By the early 1960s, he and Charles E. Houston co-owned the Libertyville, Illinois farm and were selling 3,000–4,000 Shetland ponies each year. Several brought a price of $10,000 apiece.

Approximately ten years into the business, Gene Harris was selling all of his ponies before they were weaned. In 1955, he predicted, "This year's crop is sold before it's even foaled." That's how popular Shetland ponies were. Fashion Club Pony Farm even offered a "lay-away" plan, enabling customers to pay 25% down and reserve a pony a year in advance. That year, Harris added Mexican Burros to his offerings, selling them direct from Mexico for $99.00. Described as lovable, soft-eyed little fellows, Harris claimed they were as easy to care for as a dog. If the buyer lived within fifty miles of Chicago, there was no extra charge for shipping.

In 1959, Harris had another round of bad luck at the Iowa farm when Brush Creek flooded and valuable ponies were washed away. This setback may or may not have influenced Harris to sell the farm in 1960.[206]

World War II, "Colonel" Harris, And The Cabaret Tax

Businesses boomed everywhere during the war years and, likely, Club Alabam was no exception. Cities and towns across America operated twenty-four hours a day, with everything from banks to movie theaters to nightclubs providing servicemen and war workers with necessities and entertainment at all hours. Gene Harris continued to run his amusing and eye-catching advertisements for Club Alabam, promoting fine and affordable dining. In 1944, the club offered a "Super Breakfast Special" for potential patrons who had been "joint-hoppin'." There was a choice of meat—ham, bacon, or sausage—and eggs, toast, and coffee for a reasonable $.75. Beginning in March of 1943, meat had been rationed in wartime America, making eating breakfast out, complete with meat, an appealing option, especially if, as Club Alabam's advertisements suggested ... you might "feel the need of food for blotting paper" after a night on the town!

By 1944, club owners across America were also challenged by whiskey rationing. Distilleries were commandeered for war work—the production of industrial alcohol. Manhattans and whiskey sours gave way to rum and Coca-Cola and The Andrews Sisters had a mega hit, singing the praises of the newly popular drink.

During the 1940s, Gene Harris' name appeared in local newspapers, connected to more than one *cause célèbre*. In January of 1944, Harris was one of eleven men arrested for wearing a uniform and insignia that mimicked the US Army. He was released on $1,000 bail. At the time, Harris held the rank of Colonel in a nationwide, pseudo-military organization known as the Military Order of the Guards, headquartered in Chicago. He defended the organization to the press, asserting that it was patriotic in nature and promoted military fitness among its members. The organization also claimed to train women to assume police duties during war emergencies. The arrested men were reprimanded in the Chicago Court, paid small fines, and agreed to disband for the remainder of the war, though it was reported that the FBI conducted a two-year investigation of the group. Among other charges, the organization allegedly carried on a number of petty rackets, which included the selling of commissions and securing extra gasoline rations for members.

Gene Harris may or may not have been involved in these illegalities. Still, he potentially profited from the organization. By 1942, Harris had advanced to the rank of Major, was active in recruitment, and enlistment blanks were available at his Fashion Club Stables. Anyone who enlisted had to be willing and able to ride once a week, as well as pay $1.00 for the rental of a horse at the stables.

Simultaneously, beginning in 1944, Harris had to contend with an onerous, Federal cabaret tax, created to help reduce the national debt. On April 1, the existing cabaret tax was increased from 5% to 30%, negatively affecting business, throwing entertainers out of work, and actually reducing government revenue due to decreased nightclub business. Senator Sheridan Downey, a Democrat from California, claimed that revenues for clubs and restaurants in his state had fallen off 70% since the establishment of the 30% tax, emphasizing that the levy applied not only to big hotels and resorts but also to any drugstore owner who featured a juke box, encouraging teenagers to dance while sipping a milkshake.

By May, the U.S. Senate favored dropping the cabaret tax to 20%, while exempting all uniformed service men and women from paying the levy. Congress revised the bill, agreeing to 20%, without exempting men and women in uniform. On June 7, 1944, the new bill was sent to the White House for President Roosevelt's signature, to be effective on July 1.

With a bit of swagger, Club Alabam addressed the cabaret tax publically, pointing out that the famous Flaming Crater Dinner remained a bargain at $1.98, federal and state tax included. In addition to a delicious meal, there was orchestra music and dancing from 7:00 p.m., plus four floor shows a night. There was still never a cover, admission, or minimum charge. The pre-war, prize-winning prime sirloin steak was a thing of the past, though the menu featured beef in the form of a chopped tenderloin steak.

In June of 1944, the club got some free advertising in, of all places, Brownsville, Texas. In a letter to the editor of the *Brownsville Herald*, a man named Tom Phillips enclosed a clipping of an advertisement for the Club Alabam, featuring all the mouth-watering details of the Flaming Crater Dinner. The editor reprinted the menu, claiming, if he hadn't seen it in black and white, he would never have believed that, despite the terrific cabaret tax, the club could offer so much food and entertainment for a mere $1.98.

New Year's Eve 1944 at the "Nationally Famous" Club Alabam was an all-inclusive event. Dinner, a spectacular show, and free noise makers, all for $6.10, taxes included. It was a chance to ring in the New Year at Chicago's Oldest Club.

As 1944 turned into 1945, the cabaret tax persisted and the Club Alabam created a brand new policy for the brand new year. A blanket 20% would not be added to the patron's check. If guests arrived between 5:00 and 9:30 p.m., they paid no tax. If they ate or drank after 9:30 p.m., they paid tax only on what they consumed *after* that time. The price for dinner had been dropped to an enticing $1.75. Gene Harris had effectively turned one venue into two. During the dinner hour, Club Alabam was a restaurant, featuring fine dining. The first floor show began at 9:30 p.m. and, presto, Club Alabam became a cabaret.

From the World War I-era cabaret wars that plagued Gene Harris' mentor, Dan Blanco, to the World War II-era cabaret tax, nightclubs continued to cope with and, sometimes, evade government intervention. Following the war, in 1952, the Club Alabam, at least one hotel, and sixteen other clubs and cafés in Chicago were charged with unpaid back sales tax. The Hotel Sherman owed an assessment of $63,806. The Blackhawk, known for its prime rib and famous spinning salad bowl, owed nearly as much, and The Ivanhoe, once one of Al Capone's favorite restaurants, was also included. Club Alabam was in arrears for over $12,200. In July of 1953, Gene Harris' establishment remained on the sheriff's list.

Fine Dining With A Dash Of Nostalgia

During 1945, across Chicago, nightclub owners supported the war effort in an unusual way. The American Guild of Variety Artists requested that its members work only a six day week, instead of the typical seven. The goal was to free up more citizens for part-time work in war plants. Larger nightclubs employed enough acts to divide across seven nights and stay open all week. In Chicago alone, this applied to 6,800 people working in cafés, cocktail lounges, nightclubs, hotels, and taverns. All types of performers were affected from singers to dancers to magicians to jugglers.

During the war, 747 Rush Street welcomed extended family members. Relatives from Leon, Iowa, had a place to stay if they visited Chicago. When

Cousin Elizabeth "Babe" Harris, a professional dancer, came through Chicago with the USO, she was feted by Gene and Babs Harris.

Babs' family members continued to work at Club Alabam. She and Gene helped rear her niece, Merrilee Thomson. In 1940, Merrilee (age fourteen) was living with the Harrises. Her mother, Rosalie (Jirik) Thomson, was divorced and rooming next door at 745 Rush, as was Marrilee's aunt, Irene Jirik. Rosalie was employed in the club's check room. Irene and her roommate, Violet Wilson, were entertainers at the club, possibly a duo-act or members of the "scintillating, intimate all-girl show."

Merrilee took Gene's name and, as Merrilee Harris, acted in dramatic shows on Chicago's widely broadcast radio station W-G-N and, in March of 1947, launched her singing career at the Club Alabam. By autumn, she was the club's emcee, introducing the popular Marie Shaw, dubbed a "young Sophie Tucker." Merrilee soon left for Hollywood to pursue a career in show business. In 1952, she married Graham "Grey" Stafford, son of radio star Handley Stafford. In Babs Harris' obituary, Merrilee Harris Stafford was named as her "beloved daughter."[207]

◆ ◆ ◆

In 1946, a devastating fire at Chicago's La Salle Hotel killed at least fifty-nine people. Mayor Edward Joseph Kelly immediately padlocked establishments in violation of fire ordinances. These included two theaters, the Shubert and the Great Northern located in the Loop, as well as several nightspots, one of which was Club Alabam. The barroom remained open, however, the restaurant closed until changes were made to meet ordinance requirements. The story of the La Salle Hotel fire, including the closing of five nightclubs, was national news. Later reports indicated that the building itself presented a problem for Gene Harris and Club Alabam, something only a revision in the building code could address. By the end of June, that was accomplished and a revised code permitted nightclubs to occupy buildings with wood floors and wood beams, providing that the owners safeguarded against fire.

Postwar, the club continued to be a Rush Street classic, with plenty of regulars enjoying an old-fashioned good time. In 1948, Chicago columnist Dale Harrison commented that while nightclubs typically came and went pretty quickly, a notable exception was Club Alabam. Harrison praised the club's support of their talent, "When they get a new singer, they really go to town for her. For instance, that cute Judy Talbot, quite the name in radio for years, is now in her third month at Club Alabam, and proving more and more popular each night.[208]

In 1950, reporter Jack Lait (devoted friend of Evelyn Nesbit) and Chicago columnist Lee Mortimer published the underground guide *Chicago Confidential*, giving Club Alabam a nice nod. In a short directory of headwaiters, Alabam's Jerry Elsner, who had covered for Gene Harris while he ventured to Biloxi, topped the alphabetical list. Other establishments were among Chicago's most famous: Blackhawk, Chez Paree, College Inn, Drake Hotel, Edgewater Beach Hotel, Palmer House, and "Phil" was the man to know at the Pump Room. The floorshow at 747 Rush was described as "hot."

The immediate postwar years brought numerous changes to the Club Alabam, not the least of which was the advent of television. Ever the inventive marketer, Gene Harris broadcasted an inside preview of the club's entertainment. In March of 1950, "Bound For Alabam" aired on WGN-TV, Mondays at 8:15 p.m., and featured Judy Talbot singing "Memory Lane." The diminutive Talbot, like Helen Morgan (and Evelyn Nesbit) a generation before her, sang perched on the piano, taking audiences back to the Roaring Twenties and Morgan's torch songs. Judy Talbot was a hit, bringing in business and keeping conventioneers happy into the wee hours of the morning.

In the spring of 1953, the successful Broadway revival of the musical *Pal Joey* took to the road and played Chicago' Shubert Theatre. Set in the late 1930s, antihero Joey Evans' was the fictional emcee at a second-rate Chicago nightclub. The musical found an eager audience and Chicago's journalists wrote nostalgically about John O'Hara's character. Journalist William Leonard recalled that during the Depression there were plenty of jobs for nightclub emcees, naming now vanished clubs—Midnight Frolics, 606, Colosimo's, Gay '90s, Sonny Goldstone's Yacht Club, and the Miami. Among the talent, Leonard recalled Harriet Norris, once the Mistress of Ceremonies at Club Alabam.

By 1953, Club Alabam was an almost singular holdout of the old-style cabaret, with four shows a night. William Leonard noted that in Pal Joey's day, Chicago cabarets thrived on the Near North Side. The orchestra leader was still a big draw and big name entertainment was just getting started. Patrons came to "dance, drink, gamble, and table hop, instead of sitting as spectators in judgment on the floor show."[209] In the 1950s, after a night at the theater, particularly after enjoying *Pal Joey* at the Shubert, Chicagoans could still segue to the nostalgic Club Alabam for drinks and more entertainment.

◆ ◆ ◆

Gene Harris had long been interested in offering fine food at the Club Alabam. Once the war and rationing were over, he again featured steaks on his menu. Special Cut Juicy Sirloin Steak, $3.00. Special Filet Mignon, $3.00. Choice Top Sirloin Steak, $2.00. America loved beef and Harris promised, "We never run out of steaks." In 1950, he insisted that every steak he served cost him money. His steaks were purported to be six inches thick, of aged, trimmed, eye-of-sirloin served at the table sizzling on a bed of glowing coals. That was a lot of steak on the plate. Harris must have also stocked a large supply of doggie bags.

In 1958, Gene Harris remodeled the main room at the Club Alabam, creating the Epicure Room, dedicated to fine dining. Initially, Jules Reiser was announced as Maître d' and there would be no entertainment or dancing until after midnight. Reiser had risen through the Chicago restaurant ranks, beginning as a bus boy in Carson Pirie Scott's tearoom. A bona fide gourmet, he had worked at the posh St. Hubert's Grill and at the elegant Colony Restaurant in the Churchill Hotel before agreeing to work for Harris.

In early 1959, Terry Hunter reviewed the Epicure Room for the *Chicago Sun-Times* and opened by stating that nightclubs and good food didn't always go together. In the case of Gene Harris' restaurant, however, the name epicure was no misnomer. Skillful Maître d' Jules Reiser prepared an outstanding tableside salad. Breast of chicken, served in a delicious Madeira sauce, was paired with Virginia ham "Eugenie." Portions were generous. A plate full of Canadian walleye was big enough for two diners. The salad was "a work of art" and dessert, a Vesuvius, was ice cream topped with flaming cherry sauce, seated in dry ice, and steamed like a volcano. Dinner prices ranged from $4.50 to $6.50. The Epicure Room sat fifty patrons. Hunter advised reservations.[210]

A year later, Harris hired a trio of chorus girls for the first time in twenty years, bringing another touch of nostalgia to his program, and Art Carter took over as Maître d'. In 1956, he came to the US from London, where he had satisfied the tastes of Princess Margaret and Queen Elizabeth. His resume included the dining rooms of Café de Paris and Pigalle, the Ambassador Hotel's Buttery, and Imperial House. Recently employed by Chicago's Drake Hotel, Carter attracted discerning diners and positive press.

Carter was praised as a culinary genius, who served dishes at the table with flair, including Châteaubriand "a la press" (Carter's personal sauce), made from blanched beef knuckles, sliced mushrooms, seasoning, and Madeira. His soufflé potatoes were "light as air" and the Châteaubriand was accompanied by asparagus hollandaise. His salad dressing was, apparently, extraordinary. A notable specialty was French fried strawberries, with sabayon (a.k.a. zabagilione) sauce. Celebrity restaurant reviewer Kay Loring could not imagine a more delectable dessert.[211]

In addition to an ever-congenial atmosphere, Gene Harris sold continuity. His menu announced, "As always ... the same Old Club Alabam," and featured an image of his irresistible and time-honored striped awning. His neon sign with the kicking chorus girl, stretched back towards Prohibition days, now romanticized in the minds of his older patrons.

Harris continued to encourage audience participation with his performers. For fifteen years, Dick "Two-Ton" Baker played piano at the club, specializing in tunes of yesteryear. The ebullient pianist sang enthusiastically and Club Alabam's audience sang along. It was not unusual for patrons to leave their tables and cluster around his piano in the middle of the dance floor. During the 1950s and 1960s, Baker recorded old-fashioned favorites such as "Five Foot Two," "I'm Forever Blowing Bubbles," "My Blue Heaven," and "You Must Have Been a Beautiful Baby."

Entertainment columnist Will Leonard was a big fan of Club Alabam. In 1959, in his column "On The Town," he wrote at length about the club's staying power. Leonard observed that Gene Harris' floor show, like his neon sign, was straight out of the 1920s. The bill included a lusty vocalist at an old-fashioned microphone and a sister act, kicking up a storm. Harris was amused that his out-of-date entertainment had lasted long enough to come back in style. Other cabaret producers around town were mounting Herculean efforts to stage vintage shows, emulating The Roaring Twenties, while Gene Harris and Club Alabam had never left the era. The main lounge featured semi-circular leather booths and classic round tables, draped in double tablecloths. Leaves wound through a dropped, open lattice ceiling. Desert landscapes, including one of Monument Valley, covered the walls. An odd backdrop for gourmet dining, yet for Harris' patrons, it worked.

While Gene Harris and the Club Alabam appeared to stand still, entertainment in Chicago had moved on with the times. In late 1963, Herb Lyon's column featured news about celebrities such as Peggy Lee, Nichols and May, and the Hilton Hotels' dashing boss, Conrad Hilton. In November, Lyon wrote: "Hey, here's a distinction never noted by the national mags that do those ridiculous run-downs on our town: Gene Harris and his colorful Club Alabam are launching their 39th year of fine food and action. This makes the Alabam the nation's oldest, continuous nightclub without a doubt."[212]

Within a few weeks, on December 3, 1963, Lyon mentioned Gene Harris again. This time his name appeared at the top of the column. Harris had been hospitalized with a mild heart attack. News was optimistic. Lyon claimed that Harris was perhaps Rush Street's best known figure. Doubtless Harris heard from many well-wishers and, by January, Lyon reported that Harris was "chipper, and back in action as host" at Club Alabam. His second wind did not last long and, in March, popular Maître d' Hoppy Blage greeted guests at the club in Harris' stead.[213]

In May of 1964, Harris made a radical shift in entertainment, bringing jazz back to the club. During Prohibition, he and Dan Blanco had engaged many jazz bands. Now Bob Ballard and his six-piece Dixieland Stompers heated up the night at 747 Rush Street. Gourmet dinners were still featured, ranging from $3.50 to $5.50, announced in simple, dignified advertisements. Doubtless Harris' energy for outlandish advertising had diminished with his ill health. By early June, the ailing Harris closed the club, ostensibly to reorganize the business. Later that month, Herb Lyon let his readers know that they could find Club Alabam talent working elsewhere in Chicago—Flo Henry, loyal to Harris for twenty-three years, had moved on and Art Carter was now at Delmonico's, Essex Inn, Michigan Avenue.

Gene Harris and his nightclub had been inseparable for nearly forty years. It was doubtful that anyone else could successfully take his place. Surprisingly, Harris told reporters that he was dead broke. If he was, the club had lasted as long as he did. In August, Harris suffered a serious stroke. In critical condition, it was unlikely he would ever return to work. In early December, Stanley Reed quietly reopened the club and old friend, columnist Herb Lyon wrote optimistically that Harris was recovering nicely. If he was improving, his upswing was not to last. He died on December 25 and a mass was held for him at Holy Name Catholic Cathedral on December 28.

The Associated Press wire service carried the news of Gene Harris' death. Reported across the country from Washington DC to Omaha, details of his biography varied, though, most noted that Harris first worked at the Club Alabam in 1926, purchasing it in 1937. Among his famous customers were Jimmy Durante, Phyllis Diller, Tony Curtis, Carol Channing, and Danny Kaye.

In "Tower Ticker," Herb Lyon recalled once taking visiting titans, columnists Walter Winchell, Earl Wilson, and Hy Gardener, to see Club Alabam's remarkably preserved, speakeasy-like setting. "As others before them, they were totally charmed by Gene's fascinating stories and the whole atmosphere. All ran to their typewriters and did pieces on Harris and 'The most unique spot in America.' We are going to miss the warm and rare Gene Harris."[214]

◆ ◆ ◆

Years ago, a yellowing newspaper clipping piqued my curiosity. Who was this kinsman, this Gene Harris? A beloved nightclub proprietor of a Rush Street institution called Club Alabam. Why had I never heard his name mentioned in connection with my family? The answer was simple. Among my upstanding, Midwestern relations, the affable Gene Harris definitely qualified as a black sheep.

Especially during the first half of the twentieth century, law-abiding, tax-paying, conservative citizens did not associate with the likes of Dan Blanco, Evelyn Nesbit, and Gene Harris. Their circles were not our circles. In that progressive age of reform, organizations such as the Catholic Legion of Decency and the Anti-Saloon League strove to impose morality on the masses, advocating social controls from censorship to the national prohibition of alcohol. Meant to uplift a population of the less fortunate and correct the behavior of wrongdoers, some movements backfired, especially Prohibition, which turned millions of Americans into scofflaws and left the nation with entrenched, pervasive, organized crime.

Today, with the distance of time, the colorful lives of Blanco, Nesbit, and Harris (and many of their associates) become enchanting. The once risky, if not outright deadly, world of Chicago after dark now evokes alluring cabarets depicted in Hollywood B movies. Crawling the Whoopee Belt or cruising the Rush Street "strip" of days gone by poses no threat. Dangerous criminals, long deceased, are elevated to celebrities. Chicago's most famous son may well be Al Capone, still recognized around the world.

The multi-talented Dan Blanco was representative of many performers in his generation. A nice guy on the one hand. A flagrant lawbreaker on the other. He rubbed shoulders with murderers, paid off police as well as gangsters, was married and divorced over and over. His was a completely unacceptable lifestyle in small-town (and some might add, small-minded) America. From a distance, his contribution to the history of entertainment easily outweighs his flaws. His performances delighted thousands and he introduced European cabaret to a less judgmental, fun-loving class of Midwesterners.

On a much grander scale, America was entranced with the naughty and mercurial life of Evelyn Nesbit. Watching safely from afar, newspaper readers and theater-goers were dazzled by her beauty, impressed by her daring, appalled at her arrests. Her painful struggle against morphine addiction was as compelling as it was scandalous. Her life read like a work of fiction. Exciting fiction! As a member of your family, however, she might quickly qualify as the blackest of sheep. Chastised and forgiven, admired and reviled, Evelyn Nesbit's roller coaster of a life sold both respectable and tabloid newspapers. She was *the* media cash cow of the twentieth century, providing gossipy "news" fodder for decades. Fortunately for her, a light heart and innate intelligence kept her head above water and her life in some kind of perspective.

Gene Harris, and many of his cohorts, lived on the edge of decency, skirting the constraints of a strictly law-abiding society. Looking back over decades, freed from direct association with the man or the need to impose moral judgement, Harris' adventures in Chicago unfold as another romantic tale. His vagabond ways and celebrity friends fascinate. His brushes with criminals thrill. His good points—generosity, loyalty, and easy-going showmanship—outshine his code of situational ethics. Now reclaimed from what became dozens and dozens of yellowing newspaper clippings, Gene Harris and his amiable smile will continue to light up the Rush Street of the imagination like no one before or since.

EPILOGUE

Evelyn Nesbit...
Peace at Last

Over the decades, Evelyn Nesbit's life story swung from that of a media darling to a sympathetic victim of life's slings and arrows to a phoenix rising from the ashes of a lost career. Consistently, and rather remarkably, she often took charge of her life story as it reached the public.

In 1942, when Evelyn Nesbit celebrated thirty years in show business, retirement was finally on the horizon. In early 1944, her mother, Mrs. Florence Holman, died of influenza in New York. Eighty years old, she had long ago married Pittsburgh stock broker Charles J. Holman, who had been dead for twelve years. Her death would not have been national news except for her daughter's notoriety. Journalists employed any excuse to remind newspaper readers that Evelyn Nesbit was the "cause" of Stanford White's murder. Later, Nesbit commented that she officially retired when her mother died in 1944. This did not, however, mean that journalists and sensation seeking reporters left her in peace. They would continue to capitalize on her name until her death.

"Murder at the Marguery"

In 1945, Nesbit's life became national headlines once again in connection with the slaying of the wealthy textile executive, Albert E. Langford, which papers dubbed "Murder at the Marguery." Two unidentified men forced their way into Langford's Park Avenue apartment, and shot and killed him while his wife was in the adjoining room. Nesbit's name was found in the address book of the victim's wife, Mrs. Marion Langford, along with about thirty other friends, many of whom were socially prominent. One reporter seized the opportunity to take a jab at Nesbit's faded stardom, saying that the police located her in a tavern across the street from New York City's Carnegie Hall.

When questioned, Evelyn Nesbit explained her limited connection with the couple: "The Langfords were charming and generous people. My contact with them was purely social."[215] Mrs. Langford was a well-known patron of the arts and had been the benefactress of numerous protégés. Despite Nesbit's retirement from show business, at sixty, she still provided vivacious companionship enjoyed by the Langfords and other socialites.

Mrs. Langford told the press that during the previous year an apparent blackmailer pressed her for money and Nesbit admitted that she had been with Mrs. Langford during one of these encounters. Nesbit had a strong alibi for the night of the murder. She was on Long Island visiting friends and had not been in Manhattan for five or six weeks. She told the press that she had not seen the Langfords in months and was last with the couple when she attended a party in their suite at the Hotel Marguery on New Year's Day, adding that it was a nice, quiet party. Despite implications that Nesbit might be down and out, she was enjoying the company of wealthy art patrons like the Langfords and spending weeks with friends on Long Island.

It was never suggested that Evelyn Nesbit was in any way connected with the murder of Albert Langford, rather, her connection to the Langfords became another opportunity to use her name to sell newspapers. The single witness to the murder was Mrs. Langford's black Pekinese, Wendy, who was helpless to identify the killer. The case remains unsolved.

◆ ◆ ◆

When Harry K. Thaw died in Florida at the age of seventy-six on February 22, 1947, it was the end of a very long road for Evelyn Nesbit. Newspapers printed that she was depressed and deeply sorry about his death, however, there was little more to say. In his will, he left her $10,000 (roughly $100,000 today). Given the value of his estate it was viewed by many as a pittance. Longtime friend, journalist Jack Lait, defended Nesbit's sacrifices for the Thaw family, mentioning specifically that her candid testimony saved Thaw from the electric chair for the murder of Stanford White. Lait also took the opportunity to applaud Nesbit's devotion to her son, Russell Thaw.

Lait recalled once visiting Nesbit in her Greenwich Village apartment, surrounded by artists, show people, writers, and other Bohemian types, some of whom were bona fide intellectuals. Their relationship had been a close one.

Lait twice served as ghostwriter for her memoirs—the so-called "Death Bed" serialized memoir (1926) and, likely, her book-length autobiography *Prodigal Days*. At the time of its release, a review in the *Brooklyn Daily Eagle* stated: "This book is aptly titled and certainly does not spare the author. It is written in a sensational tabloid style which has in all probability been ghosted."[216]

Jack Lait believed that Evelyn Nesbit got a "raw deal" when she received 1% of her former husband's estate, however, that $10,000 held the potential to change the course of the remainder of her life.

Despite perceptions that Nesbit's life was in ruins, when she learned of Thaw's death, photographers captured her walking in Central Park, fur-clad, coiffed, sporting a fashionable hat, and exercising Hedy, her current Belgium Griffon. That year, the six-year-old reddish-brown dog proved to be a little Broadway star, earning between $16.00 and $20.00 a day "acting" in an operatic version of Edgar Rice's *Street Scene*, with music by Kurt Weill, at the Adelphi Theatre. The Griffon, who won the part over one hundred competitors, was presented to the press by her proudly smiling owner.[217]

Grant Beach School Of Arts And Crafts

Following Thaw's death, Nesbit left New York City and moved to Southern California. Her son, Russell W. Thaw, lived in West Los Angeles and she chose to live downtown in what was sometimes referred to as Los Angeles' Greenwich Village, a Bohemian neighborhood located just north of Bunker Hill. She lived and studied at the Grant Beach School of Arts and Crafts, which offered a variety of classes, including jewelry making, weaving, ceramics, and even puppetry.

Beach and his mother had renovated a Victorian house at 413 North Figueroa Street at the intersection with West Temple Street, and rented studios to a wide variety of creative types. The house was surrounded by a cluster of buildings some called cottages. Others referred to them as tenements. The complex was aptly called an art colony, which included writers. During the 1940s, science fiction author Ray Bradbury lived there and was friendly with the Beaches. A decade later, Evelyn Nesbit occupied a small apartment adjacent the school and studied sculpting while the new Hollywood Freeway rumbled nearby.

At the time arts and crafts were enjoying a renaissance in Southern California, particularly mosaics, and Beach's school taught techniques that could become a paying hobby. Talented students might actually sell what they created. Ceramic bowls and vases, cloisonné plates, even flowers fashioned from modeling clay and fired into corsages and earrings, were purchased at craft fairs and in stores. The school earned a national reputation. In 1952, *Popular Mechanics* featured it in a richly illustrated article, "Fused-Enamel Finishes." Grant Beach showed his own work internationally, including in Japan.

In 1952, Nesbit graduated from Grant Beach's school, completing a one year course in ceramics. She had long delayed formal study in an art form she loved. In about 1909, following Harry Thaw's commitment, Nesbit discovered she had a talent for sculpture. Living in a furnished, studio apartment in midtown Manhattan, she began working with modeling clay and plasticine. Photographer Alfred Stieglitz praised her efforts, encouraging her to study.

As the creator of Manhattan's gallery 291, Stieglitz was an art connoisseur and showcased what was then the avant-garde—Matisse, Rodin, Cézanne, Picasso, and other contemporary greats. Nesbit admired Rodin and was philosophical in her approach to sculpting. As was often the case, she was surprisingly articulate and self-aware when discussing topics she was passionate about. She could recite from memory Rodin's challenge to his critics who did not understand his style of realism.

As much as Nesbit enjoyed working with clay, in 1909, she was a woman on her own, needed to support herself, and sculpture was unlikely to provide a livelihood for herself and later for her son, Russell. So, while her enthusiasm for the art form never waned, she turned to vaudeville and silent motion pictures for an income. Looking back forty years later, she marveled that neither Stanford White nor the many artists she posed for ever recognized or fostered her innate talent. In 1954, she proclaimed, "This is what I was intended for.... I could sing a little, dance a little, do a monologue, but for art I had genius. Why, I ask myself, didn't someone discover this genius?"[218]

At another crossroad in her life, Evelyn Nesbit was again on her own, exploring a long dormant aspect of her innate creativity. She stayed on at the Grant Beach School to teach sculpting, limiting her pupils to those who showed distinct talent. She was completely at home with the Bohemian atmosphere, reminiscent of her days in Greenwich Village. Three humorously named cats—Weirdie, Alley Khan (she had known the Aga Khan in Paris), and Stumpy—had replaced her beloved Belgium Griffons. Her belongings were minimal. Her personal satisfaction was higher than it had been in years.

Nesbit was serious about her newest career. In 1954, the *Los Angeles Time*s ran a lengthy article, delineating her past, as well as her present. At sixty-nine, she insisted she had at last found peace and happiness, content to be displaying her sculpture in a ceramic show at the Long Beach Municipal Auditorium. Despite a sign identifying her as Evelyn Nesbit, many visitors walked by her booth, not noticing the famous Gibson Girl. It was the oldest attendees, recalling the trial of 1907, who stopped to have a word with the once glamorous woman who fascinated them in their youth. They saw through the iron gray hair, thickened waist, and schoolmarm eyeglasses, focusing on Nesbit's still bright hazel eyes. She may have been wearing a baggy Chinese smock, woolen slacks, bobby socks, and loafers, but those elderly women still envisioned her dripping in diamonds, ermine slung across her shoulder.

By the mid-1950s, more than sculpture calmed Evelyn Nesbit's once restless soul. She had long been a student of esoteric religion and philosophy. While journalists were loath to let her forget the past, Nesbit maintained that she lived in the present, stating, "I live each day for what it brings. I'm happy. I'm at peace."[219] A self-proclaimed Theosophist, she deeply admired the work of Helena Blavatsky (1831–1891). For decades, Nesbit read widely in Western and Eastern philosophy. In the early 1950s, she was absorbing *The Mysteries of the Qabalah*. Before the decade was finished, she would convert to Catholicism and regularly attend mass.

The Girl In The Red Velvet Swing

When 20th Century Fox purchased the rights to Evelyn Nesbit's life story, paying her a reported $50,000, she was thrust once again into the spotlight. Based on Charles Samuels' unauthorized biography, *The Girl in the Red Velvet Swing*, the film focused on Nesbit's relationship with Stanford White, climaxing with Harry K. Thaw's trial for murder. Joan Collins played the breathtakingly beautiful young Nesbit. Ray Milland was cast as the predatory White, with Farley Granger as the unstable Thaw.[220]

By the summer of 1955, the film was in production and it was time for Evelyn Nesbit to meet the press one last time. Her story appeared in Hedda Hopper's column and she was interviewed by popular Hollywood reporter, Bob Thomas. The film's screenwriter-producer, Charles Brackett, found her charming, an amazing beauty. Photos appeared in newspapers and magazines, picturing her sculpting and visiting the movie set. By late July, the seventy-year-old Nesbit was exhausted. She collapsed, was hospitalized, and, several days later, her physician, Dr. Clyde Landers, released a statement saying that overexertion and excitement led to her attack.

When the film opened in October, Nesbit was again sought for comments. While in Manhattan, she was asked about her memories of the city. She shared mouthwatering descriptions of eating terrapin at Sherry's, drinking German beer at Luchow's with Stanford White, and her longing for a big, broiled Maine lobster. Most of the press coverage was fluffy and repetitive, with an outstanding exception—a six-part series written by journalist Adela Rogers St. Johns, who recounted Nesbit's life story in detail, thoughtfully comparing her glamourous years in turn-of-the-century Manhattan to her simple, Bohemian existence in Los Angeles. St. Johns' snappy prose brought Nesbit's studio and colorful neighborhood to life, complete with a Greenwich Village-style café, which she frequented. It took little imagination to see how far this local pub was from Nesbit's youth spent at world-famous restaurants like Rector's, where the oyster-devouring Diamond Jim Brady was a regular.

St. Johns pulled no punches writing about what she clearly viewed as Nesbit's reduced circumstances, calling her pets "alley cats" and describing her home as a dark, bare little studio. The journalist even revealed that, years ago, she had seen Nesbit punch drunk and baulked at her belief in Karma, The Wheel, and Fate, concluding that her story involved a lot of bad luck. Perhaps St. Johns felt that Nesbit's philosophy whitewashed what had been a life full of tragedy and disappointment. Still, the writer admitted that she had proved to be an indomitable woman, concluding that, if reincarnation was a reality, Evelyn Nesbit had learned many lessons and would likely come back as "somebody terrific."[221]

In June of 1956, Evelyn Nesbit suffered a stroke, leaving her too compromised to care for her cats. A heart-wrenching notice ran in the *Los Angeles*

Times. Nesbit had asked the Pet Assistance Foundation to help her place Cuffie, a gray and white Manx, and Weirdie, a tortoiseshell Manx, in a good home.

In 1962, author Gerald Langford capitalized on Nesbit's biography in his book, *The Murder of Stanford White*. Published by Bobbs-Merrill, it ran 270 pages, priced at $5.00. In a book review for the *Los Angeles Times*, Robert R. Kirsch observed, "Langford keeps his interpretations to a minimum; when given they are cogently made."[222]

Despite renewed interest in the notorious trial, Evelyn Nesbit quietly slipped from the headlines, to become national news one last time when she died on Tuesday, January 17, 1967, in a Santa Monica, California nursing home. A Requiem Mass was held at St. Martin of Tours Catholic Church in Brentwood, attended by her son Russell, grandchildren, and great-grandchildren. She was buried in Holy Cross Cemetery in Culver City, California, the final resting place of many Catholic celebrities, including Bing Crosby, Rita Hayworth, and Loretta Young.

Lengthy, illustrated articles appeared across America, recounting Evelyn Nesbit's celebrity and, as always, focused on her role in the scandalous murder of Stanford White. The rest of Nesbit's travails, which few seemed to care about—her talent for survival; her astounding ability to rebound and reinvent herself; and her sensitive, beautiful, but beleaguered soul which she spent decades developing for the world beyond—fell to the cutting room floor.

NOTES

1. Will Leonard, "Gene Harris Dies: Managed Club Alabam," *Chicago Tribune*, 27 December 1964. Will Leonard's "On The Town" had appeared in the *Chicago Tribune* since 1952.
2. *Chicago Sunday Tribune*, 12 April 1908.
3. *Wichita Daily Eagle*, 1 July 1909.
4. The copyright for "King of the Mafia" was filed by Dan Blanco.
5. Richard Henry Little, "Round about Chicago: Among the Untamed Rathskellerians," *Chicago Daily Tribune*, 18 August 1910.
6. Ernie Erdman also contributed to Al Jolson's hit "Toot Toot, Tootsie, Goodbye" (1922, with Dan Russo, Ted Fio Rito, and Gus Kahn) and "Sail On, Sil'ry Moon" (1912).
7. Bert White, known for the ragtime hit "Canadian Capers" (1915), worked with Dan Blanco and Gene Harris for many years.
8. On July 4, 1914, the *Chicago Daily Tribune* reported: "Warrants for other saloons will be issued today. Evidence against Jordan was secured by Policewoman Frances Willsey, who spent three nights in the saloon buying drinks after hours. The arrest of Jordan caused uneasiness among saloonkeepers in the old red light district. There are a dozen saloons in this district which, it is said, pay no attention to the 1 o'clock closing law." See *Chicago Daily Tribune*, 4 July 1914.
9. *Player*, 4 July 1913. The weekly *Player* was published in New York City and was "The Official Organ of the White Rats Actors' Union of America and the Associated Actresses of America."
10. *Chicago Examiner*, 25 May 1913.
11. *Inter Ocean*, 19 June 1913.
12. Gene Morgan, "SUMMER PARKS as YOU LIKE EM," *Chicago Sunday Tribune*, 27 July 1913.
13. Ibid.

14 *New York Clipper*, 26 July 1913. The *New York Clipper* was the oldest theatrical journal in America. Founded in 1853, it covered news in the legitimate theater, vaudeville, burlesque, circus, carnivals, minstrel shows, fairs, parks, and, eventually, motion pictures.

15 Arthur Collins (1864–1933), "King of the Ragtime Singers," and Byron G. Harlan were white performers who entertained in black dialect and preferred to call their songs "Ragtime Tunes," avoiding the racial slur "coon." The duo made the first recording of another novelty, "jungle" hit "Aba Daba Honeymoon," featuring monkeys and chimps. "Aba Daba" enjoyed a long life. Debbie Reynolds and Carleton Carpenter performed it in *Two Weeks with Love* (1950). Their recording rose to #22 on the 1951 Billboard charts. In 1951, Boop Girl Helen Kane also released a version. Dixieland and Alabam came up frequently in Ragtime music. In 1913, Collins and Harlan had a hit with "When the Midnight Choo-Choo Leaves for Alabam," later performed by Judy Garland and Fred Astaire in *Easter Parade* (1948).

16 *New York Clipper*, 29 November 1913.

17 A few months later, Morris Beifeld died at his Chicago home, 5172 Michigan Avenue. Described as the founder and "guiding genius of Chicago's big South Side amusement park, White City," the Hungarian immigrant was the brother of Joseph Beifield, who owned the Hotel Sherman. See *New York Clipper*, 28 February 1917. "Collins'" may have been Ben Collins' café, located at 23rd and Cottage Grove. Likely a converted saloon, it was reportedly packed with prostitutes and sold drinks after hours.

18 *Brook Reporter* (Brook, IN), 13 October 1916; *Des Moines Register*, 19 June 1916.

19 *Inter Ocean*, 16 April 1914.

20 *Chicago Daily Tribune*, 6 April 1911.

21 *Chicago Daily Tribune*, 3 June 1911.

22 *Chicago Daily Tribune*, 31 October 1912.

23 *Chicago Daily Tribune*, 13 October 1912. In 1915, the Belvidere was owned by Albert Bouche, restauranteur and Dan Blanco's future employer. The McGovern brothers, Williams and John, were North Clark Street fixtures, always maintaining at least one saloon. In 1915, they reopened a backroom cabaret at 659 North Clark Street for "men only." In 1916, the *Chicago Examiner* called McGovern Bros.' cabaret "one of the most vociferous in North Clark Street."

24 *Chicago Daily Tribune*, 17 July 1916.

25 The Belvidere, Grand Café's neighbor at 838 North Clark, was among numerous other cabarets accused of being in complete disregard of the law, violating various ordinances. In July of 1916, Arsonia Café's musical entertainment was shut down by police.

26. North Clark Street was replete with snares. In August, *Variety* printed this quip: "Lately North Clark street hotels have been visited by secret service agents and quite a number of actors have been reported as having trouble proving that they were past the draft age maximum." See *Variety*, 31 August 1917.

27. *Chicago Daily Tribune*, 1 September 1917.

28. *Chicago Examiner*, 1 September 1917.

29. *Chicago Daily Tribune*, 16 September 1917. A list of North Clark Street cabarets identified the establishment at 601 North Clark Street as the Ohio Café. Judge Barasa's decision was a fascinating reversal of the attitude prevalent in 1914 when Roy Jones' place was the scene of a fatal shooting and both Jones and the police were guilty of attempting to cover up the murder.

30. Concurrent with the war on cabarets, the Twenty-first Ward, which encompassed the Lower and Near North Side, exploded with the exposure of deep-rooted graft. At the helm was the "Generalizzimo of Vice" Francis A. Becker, the "invisible" North Side Chief of Police and a member of the Republican State Central Committee. More than 1,000 letters seized from Becker's office revealed the complex web of graft on the North Side and Cook County State's Attorney Maclay Hoyne took on one of the biggest vice cases in the city's history. Bits of some of the letters were printed in the newspapers, making it clear who were among "our boys" and who were not. Hoyne said, "Everything was fish that came to his net. In his list of graft prospects he did not except fruit stands, peanut stands, and bootblack stands. He evidently tried to find out who owned these places or who was responsible financially for their operation." See *Chicago Daily Tribune*, 17 September 1917.

31. *Chicago Daily Tribune*, 28 September 1917.

32. *Chicago Daily Tribune*, 28 October 1917.

33. *Chicago Examiner*, 28 September 1917; 29 September 1917.

34. According to the *Chicago Examiner*, McCloskey was fined $25.00 and court costs for six charges against him. Eight additional charges were dismissed when the minors involved failed to appear in court. The *Chicago Daily Tribune* printed a different story, initially reporting that McCloskey was booked on four charges of contributing to the delinquency of minors, six counts of selling liquor to minors, plus six additional charges for allowing minors in a cabaret, which was a state charge. See *Chicago Examiner*, 9 October 1917; *Chicago Daily Tribune*, 1 October 1917.

35. *Chicago Daily Tribune*, 9 October 1917.

36. *Chicago Examiner*, 17 October 1917.

37. *Chicago Daily Tribune*, 22 October 1917.

38. *Chicago Daily Tribune*, 21 October 1917.

39 *Chicago Examiner*, 26 October 1917.

40 *Chicago Daily Tribune*, 25 October 1917.

41 *Chicago Examiner*, 26 October 1917.

42 *Chicago Daily Tribune*, 27 October 1917.

43 In a 1911 vice investigation, O'Bryne's, one of Dan Blanco's former employers, was named among the disreputable saloons. The mingling of customers, dancers, and professional prostitutes was facilitated in cabarets. The Leader, Hastings, and Athenia Café, all on the 1911 list of offenders, were still in business in 1917.

44 *Chicago Daily Tribune*, 24 October 1917.

45 *Chicago Daily Tribune*, 6 October 1917.

46 Ibid.

47 *Chicago Daily Tribune*, 10 November 1917.

48 *Times* (Munster, IN), 26 September 1918.

49 *Indianapolis Star*, 4 February 1919.

50 In 1920, the "old" Drexel, a well-known South Side cabaret, had been remodeled into a "high class dance hall." The reported investment was $50,000. In 1923, it was "new" again.

51 *Variety*, 27 January 1922.

52 *Chicago Daily Tribune*, 25 February 1922. The Chicago courts were jammed with cases concerning violations of the Volstead Act. By October of 1923, Federal Judge Adam C. Cliffe was waging a war on crooked lawyers—commonly known as "fixers." Judge Cliffe claimed there were more than 1,000 Prohibition-related cases on the docket.

53 Albert Bouche (born Abramo Laurini or Laurin) may have been a cook, but it is highly unlikely that this Italian immigrant was ever a Parisian chef. In 1951, Chicago columnist William Leonard recalled Bouche's earliest ventures: "He claims he originated the theater-restaurant when he built the Moulin Rouge, at Clark st. and Lawrence av., in 1917, as a continental cabaret that was short lived and became the Rainbo Garden. Another Moulin Rouge, at Wabash av. and Van Buren st., had rough sailing in the early prohibition years. When it wasn't being closed by revenooers it was being bombed by competitors, until Bouche gave up." Leonard also noted that Bouche came to Chicago from the Riviera, "right between Italy and France." See *Chicago Daily Tribune*, 7 August 1951.

54 In May of 1930, Harry McKelvey was the manager at the Little Club, located at 945 North State Street, when a bomb went off, shortly after midnight. A comparatively small explosion, neither he nor owner Leon Schweitzer could offer a motive for the attack. See *Chicago Daily Tribune*, 7 May 1930.

55 *Evening News* (Harrisburg, PA), 17 June 1924.

56 *Indianapolis Star*, 17 June 1924. Frank Kinney, a theatrical promoter from New York, was cut in the face. Other newspapers identified the headwaiter as Harry "McElvey."

57 Dorothy's last name was reported as Kester, Kestner, and Kessner.

58 *Chicago Sunday Tribune*, 16 November 1924.

59 *Chicago Daily Tribune*, 23 November 1924.

60 *Daily Illinois State Journal*, 16 November 1924. Years later, Louis Alterie was extradited from his Colorado ranch.

61 *Chicago Sunday Tribune*, 16 November 1924.

62 *Chicago Daily Tribune*, 30 November 1924.

63 It is highly probable that the Northern Lights never reopened. In 1929, the property was sold by Adolph W. Waldman to William Lange for a reported $225,000. The *Tribune* called the two-story building one of Broadway's former "bright light spots." Waldman originally constructed the building for Keeley Brewing in about 1899. There, a man named Joe Miller ran a well-known café during the pre-Prohibition era. In 1929, the site was occupied by the Palm Grove Chinese restaurant, which held a ten-year lease. Waldman still owned the property through the Northern Lights period, indicating that Andy Craig must have owned the Northern Lights business but not the property. See *Chicago Daily Tribune*, 17 September 1929. In 1931, Fleur de Nor, occupied the building. John Drury wrote: "The famous old northern lights café, on the far north side, redecorated it then renamed. The usual music, floor shows, and food." See John Drury, *Dining in Chicago* (New York: The John Day Company, 1931), 248.

64 "Guns Edit Gangland's Who's Who," *Chicago Daily Tribune*, 10 June 1925.

65 *New York Times*, 1 November 1925.

66 *Variety*, 25 February 1925.

67 Ernie Young was not universally liked. In 1927, he and his wife, Pearl, were robbed while in their apartment at the Davis Hotel. The loss, mostly in jewelry, was estimated at $16,000. They were eating dinner when burglars broke in. Both of them were bound, while the criminals searched the apartment. Telephone wires in the room were cut. The Youngs were told to remain in their apartment and not to attempt to go into the hall for help. They followed instructions and some time passed before the incident was discovered. See *Chicago Daily Tribune*, 16 September 1927.

68 By September of 1926, Dan Blanco was working at the Moulin Rouge Café for Bill Rothstein and had likely been hired months prior to that.

69 Evelyn Nesbit's biography has been extensively published over the decades, typically focusing on the trial concerning the murder of architect Stanford

White. While newspapers and other periodicals followed Nesbit's life and career throughout the 20th century, that story has only been cursorily preserved. For more about her early life see: Michael Macdonald Mooney, *Evelyn Nesbit and Stanford White: Love and Death in the Gilded Age* (NY: Morrow, 1976); Paula Uruburu, *American Eve: Evelyn Nesbit, Stanford White, the Birth of the "It" Girl and the Crime of the Century* (NY: Riverhead, 2008); Simon Baatz, *The Girl on the Velvet Swing: Sex, Murder, and Madness at the Dawn of the Twentieth Century* (NY: Mulholland Books, 2018).

70 *Chicago Daily Tribune*, 7 May 1925.

71 *Winston-Salem Journal*, 31 May 1925.

72 *Chicago Daily Tribune*, 24 November 1913. Looking back, Nesbit remembered the show drew $37,000 in a single week. In 1913, newspapers reported a take of $28,000.

73 *Motion Picture Directory*, 1919.

74 In 1921, prima donna Lydia Lipkowska charged Sam Schepps with usury when he refused to return her pawned diamonds, valued at $30,000. Schepps had loaned her $8,000, demanding a $2,500 "bonus" in addition to six percent interest. See *Daily News* (New York, NY), 23 October 1921.

75 In September of 1920, the dressmaking firm Madame Frances & Company sued Evelyn Nesbit for a balance of $2,960 worth of gowns, hats, wraps, and capes purchased in October of 1919. In March of 1921, Madame Frances brought suit again for the original bill, plus interest.

76 *Milwaukee Journal-Sentinel*, 10 April 1921.

77 Richard Harding Davis was an admirer and defender of Stanford White's reputation. Following White's murder, Davis wrote a lengthy and widely read memorial that was published in *Collier's*.

78 R. H. Whitney, "Evelyn Nesbit, Coffee Vender," *Lansing State Journal*, 25 April 1921. One headline announced, "Evelyn Thaw Sells Coffee. Leaves the Stage Forever." Both Miss Nesbit and the press frequently made absolute statements about her career plans; usually, they proved to be anything but permanent.

79 *Baltimore Sun*, 16 March 1921.

80 In June of 1921, one of Evelyn Nesbit's dogs died suddenly. Given the criminal activity that plagued Nesbit in the coming weeks, it is possible that someone poisoned the dog. Her pet was buried in Hartsdale Pet Cemetery (New York's largest) near two dogs which once belonged to popular dancer Irene Castle.

81 *Winnipeg Tribune*, 12 July 1921.

82 The men's names were reported as: Joseph Daly (24), John Wardmer/Wardner (28), James Dunn (25), and William Hayes (23). Daly was likely criminal Joseph "Spot" Leahy.

83 Evelyn Nesbit maintained that their father, Sam Shubert (1878–1905), had been her friend and, had he been alive, this fiasco over rent would not have happened.

84 *New York Times*, 29 October 1921.

85 *Washington Times*, 30 October 1921.

86 *Wisconsin State Journal* (Madison, WI), 1 November 1921.

87 *Arizona Republican*, 14 November 1921. Alice Rohe (1876–1957) wrote for popular magazines, as well as daily newspapers. In 1913, Rabindranath Tagore (1861–1941) won the Nobel Prize in Literature. *Personality*, from which Nesbit quoted, was published in 1917. Arthur Schopenhauer (1788–1860) influenced Nesbit, particularly "On Suicide," included in his *Studies in Pessimism*.

88 *Evening Public Ledger* (Philadelphia, PA), 15 April 1922; *Herald* (New York, NY), 31 July 1922.

89 *Trenton Evening Times*, 16 May 1922; *Gulfport Daily Herald* (Gulfport, MS), 5 June 1922.

90 *New York Times*, 13 December 1922.

91 *Washington Post*, 18 December 1922.

92 During January of 1923, the series ran in the *Lincoln Evening Journal* under the following headlines: "Drug Victims Are Growing;" "Evelyn Tells Dope History;" "Had Craving For Narcotic: Evelyn Nesbit Tells How Drug Got Hold;" and "Is Cured by Hard Fight: Evelyn Nesbit Gives Credit to Good Doctor." Ironically, immediately following Nesbit's confession, Wallace Reid's death due to narcotics was national news. See "Wally Reid Loses Fight: Hollywood Stirred by Death of Popular Actor," *Lincoln Evening Journal*, 19 January 1923.

93 In *Prodigal Days*, Evelyn Nesbit expanded on her descent into "Hades." In this version she claimed that facial neuralgia rather than a toothache started her on morphine. She went to New Jersey for a milk diet cure which lasted about six weeks. There, she educated herself on the effects of the drug and realized that Harry Thaw had been likely both a morphine and cocaine addict, the cocaine driving his sadistic attack on her prior to their marriage. See *Prodigal Days*, 281–86.

94 Nucky Johnson was one of Atlantic City's most colorful characters. See Frank J. Ferry, *Nucky: The Real Story of the Atlantic City Boardwalk Boss* (ComteQ Publishing, 2013); Grace Anselmo D'Amato, *Chance of a Lifetime: Nucky Johnson, Skinny D'Amato and How Atlantic City Became the Naughty Queen of Resorts* (Harvey Cedars, NJ: Down the Shore Publishing, 2003); Nelson Johnson, *Boardwalk Empire: The Birth, High Times, and Corruption of Atlantic City* (Medford, NJ: Plexus Publishing, 2010). The HBO series, *Boardwalk Empire* (2010–2014), relates a fictionalized story of the Atlantic City boss, renaming him Nucky Thompson (portrayed by Steve Buscemi). A highly imaginative

version of Evelyn Nesbit's days in Atlantic City is a subplot, featuring Gretchen Mol as the drug-addicted showgirl, Gillian Darmondy.

95   On February 1, 1924, the *New York Clipper* noted that Evelyn Nesbit was "at liberty." Poor business had forced her to close El Prinkipo Café.

96   In 1923, entertainer Evan-Burrows Fontaine became a household name when she sued Cornelius Whitney for breach of promise, asking $1,000,000 in damages.

97   *Chicago Daily Tribune*, 16 April 1924. In 1922, Julia Harpman had married prize-winning journalist Westbrook Pegler, who at that time was a sports writer for the *Tribune*.

98   *Variety*, 3 February 1926. In 1925, "Wade's Moulin Rouge Syncopators," included musicians Edwin Jackson, Anthony Spaulding, Arnett Nelson, Billy Paige, Walter Wright, Stump Evans, Eddie South, Ray Whitsett, Stanley Wilson, William Dover, and Jimmy Wade. They recorded on the Puritan label as Wade's Moulin Rouge Orchestra. Jazz violinist Eddie South, Wade's musical director, would later lead his own orchestra, "The Alabamians," at Club Alabam.

99   Ed Lowry, *My Life in Vaudeville, The Autobiography of Ed Lowry*, ed. Paul M. Levitt, (Carbondale, IL: Southern Illinois University Press), 99–100. Ed Lowry continued to work for Bill Rothstein until the Moulin Rouge was padlocked in early 1927. Over the years, Paulette LaPierre and Evelyn Nesbit became friends and worked together at various venues across Chicago, including the Kit Kat Club and, later, Club Alabam.

100 *Chicago Daily Tribune*, 12 September 1925.

101 Ibid.

102 In 1931, John Drury described the Frolics: "When other places have folded up for the night, the Frolics is just beginning. Charles Kelly and his orchestra. Dine and dance until dawn, Earl Rickard is master of ceremonies. Four shows nightly and Theatrical Night, featuring visiting stage celebs, on Wednesdays. Sixteen girls in the chorus and all lively and good to look upon. The place was recently remodeled. Always a lot of Chicago notables at the tables. Mike Fritzel and Ralph Gallet are the well-known managers." See Drury, *Dining in Chicago*, 245.

103 *San Francisco Chronicle*, 6 January 1926.

104 In the *Bellingham Herald*, her name was given as Jessie Accoos, of Brooklyn. The *Chicago Daily Tribune* called her "Gussie Accooe, the dancer's colored maid."

105 *San Francisco Chronicle*, 6 January 1926.

106 *Chicago Daily Tribune*, 6 January 1926.

107 *Variety*, 6 January 1926. Evelyn Nesbit's so-called deathbed memoir was not withheld from the public until her death. Published in the autumn of 1926, the ten-part, heavily illustrated series ran in Hearst newspapers across the county. The final installment revealed that journalist Jack Lait (1883–1954) was the man who encouraged her to sell her story. See *Evening Journal* (Hamilton, OH), 9 October 1926.

108 *Rockford Republic*, 6 January 1926.

109 *Evening Star* (Washington, D.C.), 22 January 1926.

110 Ed Lowry mentions that while he was working at the Moulin Rouge Café, Bill Rothstein had a shadowy partner named "Frankel." See Lowry, *My Life in Vaudeville, The Autobiography of Ed Lowry*, 99.

111 *Prodigal Days*, 300–303.

112 *Variety*, 3 February 1926.

113 *Chicago Daily Tribune*, 24 August 1926.

114 In 1920, Karyl Norman and Evelyn Nesbit toured together on a vaudeville bill. Nesbit, with several silent motion pictures under her belt, was the headliner, in a new act—singing and dancing, as well as displaying new dramatic ability. Norman was described as a "genuine novelty"—a delineator of songs and fashions.

115 *Chicago Daily Tribune*, 9 February 1927.

116 *Chicago Daily Tribune*, 18 October 1927. After the padlock went on the Friar's Inn, Mike Fritzel (known as the "Dean of Chicago nightclub proprietors") opened Chez Paree, which operated from December of 1932 until 1960, booking big names such as Louis Armstrong, the Andrews Sisters, Danny Thomas, Lena Horne, Ella Fitzgerald, Nat King Cole, Sammy Davis, Jr., and Tony Bennett. Located at 610 N. Fairbanks Court, in contrast to Rush Street's gritty atmosphere, it was a glamorous nightclub, featuring a chorus line of Chez Paree Adorables; cigarette girls who also carried cameras to snap pictures of the patrons enjoying a night on the town; and irresistible dice girls. The establishment included a Key Club located behind the bandstand which required an actual key if a customer wanted access to the back room.

117 *Inter Ocean*, 29 June 1911; *Chicago Daily Tribune*, 30 July 1911.

118 *Chicago Daily Tribune*, 29 January 1928.

119 *Leon Reporter*, 19 June 1913.

120 Eugene A. Harris Guardianship Papers, 12 July 1913, Leon, IA.

121 During the spring of 1928, lists of affected nightspots were printed in the weekly publication *The Chicagoan* included Club Alabam. Assistant District Attorney Elder estimated that the total property value of the proposed offenders was

$15,000,000. If these bright spots were padlocked and dark for a year, the action would have a significant impact on the local economy. See *Chicago Daily Tribune*, 16 February 1928.

122 *Variety*, 8 February 1928.

123 In *Jazz Age Chicago*, Scott Newman writes, "Following the February 1928 raid, federal authorities ordered Rainbo Gardens closed. Soon thereafter, [Fred] Mann was arrested on gambling charges. Authorities alleged that Mann sponsored illegal pari-mutuel betting at the Rainbo Fronton. In February 1929, with the Rainbo still padlocked, Mann fell into bankruptcy." See jazzagechicago.wordpress.com.

124 Neil Harris, *The Chicagoan: A Lost Magazine of the Jazz Age* (Chicago, IL: University of Chicago Press, 2008).

125 *Chicago Daily Tribune*, 1 January 1929.

126 In 1931, restaurant critic John Drury wrote: "VANITY FAIR. 803 Grace Street. Other nightclubs come and go but the Vanity Fair remains forever. Or so it seems. Occupying the site of the once famous Marigold Gardens. Has a large following on the north side of Chicago, particularly in the uptown district. Four floor shows nightly and no cover charge. The food is good and high-class people come here. Leo Wolf and his orchestra contribute much toward the popularity of this place. Otto E. Singer, likable and hearty, runs the Vanity Fair. Buckingham 3254." Drury described the Turkish Village Café at 606 North Clark Street: "A snappy orchestra; entertainers sing at your table; food if you get hungry; Turkish the decorations; and George Mason to see that you are enjoying yourself." See Drury, *Dining in Chicago*, 244, 248.

127 As evidence in the libel suit against the Congress Hotel, Evelyn Nesbit claimed a photograph was taken of Russell in Atlantic City the day he was supposed to be in Chicago. See *Prodigal Days*, 303–304.

128 Years later, Evelyn Nesbit told a slightly different version of how she acquired her house in Northfield. She recalled that the deed was not in her name and that Thaw demanded $100 in rent each month, even though he initially gave her an allowance of $300 per month. Whatever funds came from Thaw, they were not sufficient for her to retire and she continued to work in nightclubs. See *Prodigal Days*, 304–305.

129 *New Orleans States*, 13 November 1927.

130 In addition to being a widely read columnist, Mark Hellinger wrote short stories and screenplays. By the late 1930s, he was producing motion pictures in Hollywood.

131 *Variety*, 7 December 1927. Evelyn Nesbit wrote that Harry Thaw became upset when a customer kissed her on the cheek. See *Prodigal Days*, 305.

132 *Shamokin News-Dispatch* (Shamokin, PA), 5 March 1928.

133 *Daily News* (New York, NY), 5 March 1928; *Trenton Evening News*, 15 March 1928.

134 Tom Pettey, "Atlantic City Hands Chicago Wide Open Grin. Bars and Cabarets Running Wild," *Chicago Daily Tribune*, 17 May 1928. In September of 1928, Evelyn Nesbit was working at Atlantic City's Silver Slipper when a carelessly dropped cigarette started a fire in the club, causing $2,000 worth of damage. Hangings and dresses were damaged, possibly including some of Nesbit's personal property. See *Brooklyn Daily Eagle*, 3 September 1928.

135 *Prodigal Days*, 308.

136 Hotel Manger was located in Manhattan, adjacent the Roxy Theater, at 7th Avenue, between 50th and 51st. The Whitby, today a co-op in Hell's Kitchen, has an esteemed history. Completed in 1923, the building is noted for its three impressive bays and rippling brick cornice. Located on West 45th Street between 8th and 9th Avenues, in the heart of New York City's theater district, Doris Day and Betty Grable were once residents. "Room 1411" by Benny Goodman was named after his suite number at The Whitby, where he lived in the late 1920s.

137 John Drury wrote that the Club Ambassadeur at 226 East Ontario Street was "a real sun-dodgers Mecca, east of Michigan Avenue and but five minutes from the Loop. The boys and girls call it a 'hot spot.' It occupies one of those old mansions and is very cozy and intimate. Jimmie Noone and his orchestra provide the music for the floor shows—and for you. And there is an after-theater menu in case you get hungry. No cover charge. Delaware 0930." See Drury, *Dining in Chicago*, 244–245.

138 *Chicago Daily Tribune*, 14 November 1929.

139 Years later, Chicago artist and ad man, Burton Browne, remembered these Prohibition Era key clubs when he founded his Gaslight Clubs. Later, Hugh Hefner would follow suit with the Playboy Club and his rabbit-headed metal key.

140 *Chicago Daily Tribune*, 1 January 1930.

141 *Pittsburgh Press*, 12 January 1930. The article was widely reprinted, frequently with misleading headlines implying that Evelyn Nesbit had "found religion" in conventional Christianity. Nothing could have been further from the truth. One Missouri newspaper ran the article under the headline: "Girl Dancer Forsakes The Stage For Religion. Evelyn Nesbit, Famous Star, Finds Solace in Bible Now." See *Springfield Leader* (Springfield, MO), 17 January 1930.

142 While Gene Harris was absent from Club Alabam during early 1930, Jerry Elsner filled in as headwaiter. Orchestra leader Merritt Brunies (1895–1973) was a jazz trombonist and member of a well-known, New Orleans musical family.

He worked in New Orleans, at Friar's Inn (Chicago), and, later in life, played with his brothers in a Dixieland jazz band in Mississippi, dying in Biloxi.

143 *Daily Herald* (Biloxi, Mississippi), 13 February 1930.

144 *Rockford Register-Gazette*, 3 March 1930.

145 *San Francisco Chronicle*, 2 April 1930.

146 *Tennessean* (Nashville, TN), 12 May 1930. As it did for many Americans, 1930 brought financial hardship to Evelyn Nesbit. In November, her bedroom suite was reclaimed by an Atlantic City furniture company which claimed that she made only one payment and still owed them $411.75.

147 In 1926, Marcella Bennett was twenty-one years old when she married Neal Phillips.

148 According to the 1930 census record, Dan Blanco married for the first time in about 1898. In 1910, he was married to a woman named Letta. In 1913, he married Rose Marks. In January of 1931, Marcella (Bennett) Phillips and Dan Blanco traveled to Havana, Cuba as Mr. and Mrs. Leblang. Sometime before 1936, they were separated and, on March 5, 1937, in Fort Lauderdale, Florida, Blanco married divorcee Thelma Garson (b. 1911, Buffalo, New York), who would be his widow three months later.

149 To date, no records have been located indicating that Gene Harris' marriage to Bessie Mahoney was dissolved, nor has a record of her death been discovered.

150 *Chicago Daily Tribune*, 9 September 1911. Bernie Adler co-wrote Sophie Tucker's first hit, "Dat Lovin' Rag" (1908). His "The Dying Rag" was published by Irving Berlin in 1911.

151 *Chicago Daily Tribune*, 10 October 1957; Ed Lowery, *My Life in Vaudeville, The Autobiography of Ed Lowry*.

152 In 1931, Miss Bock owned another tea shop at 47 East Oak Street. John Drury described it: "A quiet and charming tea room in a brownstone front, where prices are very reasonable and the colored waitresses are polite and attentive. Such specialties of the Southland as Southern fried chicken, date torte, and hot Southern biscuits are popular items on the menu. The table d'hotel luncheon is 50 cents and the dinner is 75 cents. This is No. 2 of the tea shop chain established by Miss Annie Sara Bock, a well-known Chicago restauranteur. Delaware 0817." See Drury, *Dining in Chicago*, 186–87.

153 In January of 1932, Lewis Alterie was finally apprehended and indicted on a kidnaping charge. He had enjoyed several years of peaceful living following the incident at the Northern Lights. See "Louis Alterie Is Indicted On Kidnap Charge: Five Others Accused in Second Abduction," *Chicago Daily Tribune*, 7 January 1932.

154 *Miami News* (Miami, FL), 6 February 1931.

155. By applying the vagrancy law, gangsters, and possibly witnesses of Jake Lingle's murder, could be brought into court, placed under oath, and questioned on a variety of matters.
156. *Chicago Sunday Tribune*, 14 September 1930.
157. *World-Herald* (Omaha, NE), 14 September 1930.
158. *Chicago Daily Tribune*, 26 November 1930.
159. Drury, *Dining in Chicago*, 244.
160. *Chicago Daily Tribune*, 1 January 1932.
161. *Rockford Register-Republic*, 27 January 1933.
162. *Pittsburgh Press*, 1 January 1933.
163. *Idaho Statesman*, 3 May 1933.
164. Ibid.
165. *Chicago Daily Tribune*, 25 May 1916.
166. *Detroit Free Press*, 26 July 1933.
167. *New York Times*, 14 December 1933.
168. Later that year, Texas Guinan was front page news when she died in her sleep, of ulcerated colitis, in Vancouver, British Columbia.
169. Irene Duvall came to the Club Alabam complete with notoriety. In early 1933, she accused Edmund J. Casey of robbing her of $10,000 worth of property. Then, following her appearance in Chicago, she and a man named Dr. Burton Eder were injured when hit by a car in Detroit. Both suffered fractured legs. It was the second time that year that Duvall had been struck by a car as a pedestrian. Considering the criminal element connected with nightclubs, somebody may have been threatening Irene Duvall.
170. *Chicago Daily Tribune*, 1 January 1934.
171. *Chicago Sunday Tribune*, 26 August 1934.
172. Ibid.
173. Marcella Bennett married attorney Ira Kirkland.
174. *Chicago Daily Tribune*, 2 June 1937.
175. *Variety*, 9 June 1937. Dan Blanco's World War I draft registration card records his birth date as January 3, 1877. The same issue of *Variety* reported the death of Jean Harlow from uremic poisoning.
176. Gus Van and Joe Schenck were an extremely successful singing and comedy act, working in vaudeville primarily from the mid-1910s through the 1920s.
177. *Chicago Daily Tribune*, 8 September 1938.

178   *Rockford Register-Republic*, 8 September, 1938.

179   Ibid. A slightly different version was printed in the *Illinois State Journal:* "This has been a topsy-turvy old world for me and, should I decide to leave it voluntarily, it probably would be all for the best." See *Illinois State Journal*, 9 September 1938.

180   The dice game called "26" was a Chicago innovation, invented to skirt gambling laws. Games operated in taverns from the Gold Coast to the Loop to suburban roadhouses. A pleasant bonus were the attractive, score-keeping "dice girls." In 1962, the *Tribune* mourned the end of a decades' old Chicago institution: "The game is played on small tables behind which the '26' girl stands, smiling and cooing, with a cup of 10 dice in her hand and a score pad by her elbow. The customer engages her in small talk and rolls out the dice 13 times." Bets ranged from $.25 to $1.00. Winners collected merchandise—typically drink chits which encouraged more drinking and, hopefully for the management, more betting. See *Chicago Tribune*, 7 January 1962.

181   *Asheville Citizen–Times*, 9 September 1938.

182   *Chicago Daily Tribune*, 28 May 1939.

183   Ibid.

184   Ibid.

185   *Chicago Daily Tribune*, 28 May 1939.

186   Ibid.

187   *Chicago Daily Tribune*, 14 June 1939.

188   *Journal-Sentinel* (Milwaukee, WI), 10 January 1939.

189   Ibid.

190   *Detroit Free Press*, 4 February 1939.

191   John Barrymore's stay in Chicago during the run of *My Dear Children* was fraught with personal and public drama. See John Kobler, *Damned in Paradise: The Life of John Barrymore* (New York: Antheneum, 1977), 327–351.

192   Evelyn Nesbit's hair was sometimes referred to as "Titian." In 1934, she described her natural hair color as "copper" and her eyes as hazel.

193   A relatively new venue, Ernie's opened in 1940, not far from Washington Square, in Greenwich Village at 76 West 3rd Street and operated until 1962.

194   In 1943, the Colony Club was also associated with the gruesome and unsolved murder of "dice girl" Estelle Carey.

195   *Chicago Daily Tribune*, 7 March 1941.

196 *Daily Mail* (Hagerstown, MD), 28 August 1941. In 1941, Westbrook Pegler became the first columnist to win a Pulitzer Prize for exposing racketeering in Hollywood labor unions.

197 *Chicago Daily Tribune*, 19 May 1941.

198 *Chicago Sunday Tribune*, 27 July 1941.

199 Irv Kupcinet, *Kup's Chicago* (Garrett County Press, 2012), digital edition.

200 *Chicago Daily Tribune*, 30 September 1944.

201 Fashion Club Stables were rebuilt at the same site and dubbed "New Fashion Club Stables." It is unclear, however, how long Gene Harris remained invested in the business. In 1946, his interests shifted to breeding Shetland ponies. In 1966, Fashion Club Stables were demolished, making way for a sixteen unit apartment building.

202 *Chicago Daily Tribune*, 8 March 1946.

203 *Chicago Daily Tribune*, 21 February 1956.

204 In 1958, Gene Harris may have used proceeds from his pony farms to remodel Club Alabam.

205 In 1987, Walter Munn was inducted into the American Shetland Pony Club Hall of Fame.

206 In the late summer of 1962, a "Closing Out Farm Sale" advertisement ran in the *Des Moines Tribune*, indicating there were only eighteen Shetland ponies left on the Leon, Iowa farm.

207 Gene Harris also helped support his wife Babs' stepfather, "Dad" Honsa, who was living at the club when he died in 1961.

208 *Chicago Daily Tribune*, 28 April 1948.

209 *Chicago Daily Tribune*, 17 May 1953.

210 *Chicago Sun-Times*, 4 January 1959.

211 *Chicago Daily Tribune*, 14 July 1961.

212 *Chicago Daily Tribune*, 10 November 1963. Another sign of the changing times came in January of 1962, when Chicago police finally put an end to the city's popular dice game known as "26." Taverns had featured this form of law-skirting gambling since Prohibition days and, over the decades, Club Alabam likely employed their share of "26 girls." An article in the *Chicago Tribune* indicated that nightspots in Rush Street, as well as other North Side districts, protested the shutting down of "26."

213 Chicago Daily Tribune, 2 March 1964. While Gene Harris was recovering from his heart attack, police put pressure on the Club Alabam. On March 6, three men were arrested at 5 a.m. and charged with operating a tavern after hours.

Victor Glagic (maître d'hotel), William Purdy (bartender), and Napoleon B. Damianides (waiter) were arrested. Purdy was also charged with resisting arrest. The article did not mention maître d' Hoppy Blage. In May, Judge Gordon B. Nash found them not guilty, concluding that the state had failed to prove that Edward Roche, who held the tavern license for Club Alabam, knew that drinks were being sold.

[214] *Chicago Daily Tribune*, 28 December 1964. Following Gene Harris' death, Steve DeKosta reopened Club Alabam, retaining its speakeasy atmosphere. Columnist Will Leonard opined, "And maybe some night soon there will be a key club upstairs, in Gene Harris' famed old second floor barroom." (*Chicago Tribune*, 11 September 1966.) By 1967, the legendary neon sign, with its kicking chorus girl, was missing and, in 1968, employees and about thirty customers escaped a significant fire in the building. The exact closing date of Club Alabam is currently unknown. Gene Harris' widow, Babs, died in 1979 and, in March of 1996, the building was raised.

[215] *Pittsburgh Press*, 8 June 1945.

[216] *Brooklyn Daily Eagle*, 3 June 1934.

[217] In 1945, Evelyn Nesbit's Belgian Griffon was called "Haidee," which she identified as a Hindu name. Hedy was described as brown, while "Haidee" was described as red and mistaken for a Pekinese. They were likely the same dog.

[218] *Los Angeles Times*, 28 June 1955.

[219] Bill Dredge, "Evelyn Nesbit Thaw, Once Famed, Has Booth In Show," *Los Angeles Times*, 30 July 1954.

[220] Hedda Hopper, "Evelyn Nesbit Meets Press, Discusses Past," *Los Angeles Times*, 28 June 1955. Conservative estimates, including one by syndicated Hollywood columnist Bob Thomas, set Evelyn Nesbit's payment at $30,000 for her life story.

[221] Adela Rogers St. Johns, "The Girl in the Red Velvet Swing," Conclusion, *News-Herald* (Franklin, PA), 19 November 1955.

[222] *Los Angeles Times*, 28 September 1962.

Selected Bibliography

"Evelyn Tells Dope History," *Lincoln Evening Journal* (Lincoln, NE), 11 January 1923. [Part One of a multipart, syndicated series.]

Abbott, Karen. *Sin in the Second City: Madams, Ministers, Playboys, and the Battle for America's Soul*. New York, NY: Random House, 2008.

Allen, Robert C. *A Horrible Prettiness: Burlesque and American Culture*. Chapel Hill, NC: The University of North Carolina Press, 2006.

Baatz, Simon. *The Girl on the Velvet Swing: Sex, Murder, and Madness at the Dawn of the Twentieth Century*. New York, NY: Mulholland Books, 2018.

Bair, Deirdre. *Al Capone: His Life, Legacy, and Legend*. New York, NY: Anchor Books, 2017.

Binder, John J. *Al Capone's Beer Wars: A Complete History of Organized Crime in Chicago during Prohibition*. Amherst, MA: Prometheus Books, 2017.

D'Amato, Grace Anselmo. *Chance of a Lifetime: Nucky Johnson, Skinny D'Amato and How Atlantic City Became the Naughty Queen of Resorts*. Down The Shore Publishing, 2003.

Drury, John. *Dining in Chicago*. New York, NY: The John Day Company, 1931.

Ferry, Frank J. *Nucky: The Real Story of the Atlantic City Boardwalk Boss*. Margate, NJ: ComteQ Publishing, 2013.

Ganz, Cheryl R. *The 1933 Chicago World's Fair: A Century of Progress*. Urbana, IL: University of Illinois Press, 2012.

Gifford, Barry. *The Phantom Father*. New York, NY: Harcourt Brace & Company, 1997.

Hainey, Michael. *After Visiting Friends: A Son's Story*. New York, NY: Scribner, 2014.

Harris, Neil. *The Chicagoan: A Lost Magazine of the Jazz Age*. Chicago, IL: University of Chicago Press, 2008.

Hoffman, Dennis E. *Scarface Al and the Crime Crusaders: Chicago's Private War Against Capone*. Carbondale, IL: Southern Illinois University Press, 2010.

Johnson, Nelson. *Boardwalk Empire: The Birth, High Times, and Corruption of Atlantic City*. Medford, NY: Medford Press: Plexus Publishing, Inc., [2013].

Keefe, Rose. *Guns and Roses: The Untold Story of Dean O'Banion, Chicago's Big Shot Before Al Capone*. Nashville, TN: Cumberland House, 2003.

Keefe, Rose. *The Man Who Got Away: The Bugs Moran Story: A Biography*. Nashville, TN: Cumberland House, 2005.

Keller, Craig. "Supper Time," *Chicago Social* (October 1999): 90–94.

Kobler, John. *Damned in Paradise: The Life of John Barrymore*. New York, NY: Antheneum, 1977.

Kupcinet, Irv. *Kup's Chicago*. Garrett County Press, 2012. Digital edition.

Lait, Jack and Lee Mortimer. *Chicago Confidential*. New York, NY: Crown, 1950.

Lerner, Michael A. *Dry Manhattan: Prohibition in New York City*. Cambridge, MA: Harvard University Press, 2008.

Lesy, Michael. *Murder City: The Bloody History of Chicago in the Twenties*. New York, NY: W. W. Norton & Company, 2007.

Levi, Vicki Gold and Lee Eisenberg. *Atlantic City: 125 Years of Ocean Madness*. Berkeley, CA: Ten Speed Press, 1979.

Lindberg, Richard. *Chicago by Gaslight: A History of Chicago's Netherworld: 1880-1920*. Chicago, IL: Chicago Review Press, 2005.

Lowry, Ed. *My Life in Vaudeville, The Autobiography of Ed Lowry*. Edited by Paul M. Levitt. Carbondale, IL: Southern Illinois University Press, 2011.

Mooney, Michael MacDonald. *Evelyn Nesbit and Stanford White: Love and Death in the Gilded Age*. New York, NY: Morrow, 1976.

Nesbit, Evelyn. "Evelyn Nesbit's Own Story," *Indianapolis Star* (Indianapolis, IN), 1 August 1926. [Part One of a ten-part, syndicated memoir.]

Nesbit, Evelyn. *Prodigal Days: The Untold Story*. New York: Julian Messner, Inc., 1934.

Newman, Scott. "Jazz Age Chicago." jazzagechicago.wordpress.com.

O'Brien, Gillian. *Blood Runs Green: The Murder That Transfixed Gilded Age Chicago*. Chicago: University of Chicago Press, 2015.

Okrent, Daniel. *Last Call: The Rise and Fall of Prohibition*. New York: Scribner, 2011.

Schmeal, Jacqueline Andre. "Iowa's Historic Shetland Pony Farm," *Iowa Barn Foundation Magazine* (Spring 2013): 6.

Shaw, Randy. *The Tenderloin: Sex, Crime, and Resistance in the Heart of San Francisco*. San Francisco: Urban Reality Press, 2015.

Slide, Anthony. *The Encyclopedia of Vaudeville*. Jackson, MS: University Press of Mississippi; Reprint edition, 2012.

St. Johns, Adela Rodgers. "The Girl In the Red Velvet Swing," *Times* (Cumberland, MD), 30 October 1955. [Part One of a six-part, syndicated series.]

Thaw, Evelyn Nesbit. "The Story of My Life," *Times-Dispatch* (Richmond, VA), 28 September 1913. [Part One of a sixteen-part, syndicated memoir.]

Uruburu, Paula. *American Eve: Evelyn Nesbit, Stanford White, the Birth of the "It" Girl and the Crime of the Century*. New York, NY: Riverhead Books, 2009.

Weller, Sam. *Listen to the Echoes: The Ray Bradbury Interviews*. Chicago: Stop Smiling Books, 2010.

Periodicals

Chicago Daily Tribune

Chicago Examiner

Cleveland Plain Dealer

Chicagoan

Daily Herald (Biloxi, Mississippi)

Day Book

Des Moines Register

Detroit Free Press

Illinois State Journal

Inter Ocean

Los Angeles Times

Lincoln Evening Journal

New York Clipper

New York Times

Philadelphia Inquirer

Pittsburgh Press

Player

Rockford Daily Register-Gazette

Rockford Register-Republic

Rockford Morning Star

Rockford Republic

San Francisco Chronicle

Trenton Evening Times

Variety

Washington Post

Acknowledgements

Research for *The Blackest Sheep* began in the mid-1990s, when I discovered Gene Harris' obituary in my mother's filing cabinet. A nascent Internet meant I began my inquiry the old-fashioned way, writing to the Chicago Historical Society and asking if their files contained anything about the Club Alabam. Photocopies of newspaper clippings promptly arrived in the U.S. Mail. I read them with interest, putting them aside as I dove into my Harris family's history.

Little did I realize, the next twenty years would be spent investigating Gene Harris' backstory in order to fully understand why my grandmother's half-brother was born in Leon, Iowa and not in Buckingham County, Virginia. Taking a circuitous route, researching and writing about 300 years of my family's place in American history, I finally made my way back to that little town in southern Iowa where Gene Harris' beginnings had been waiting patiently.

Family members, particularly Marjorie M. (Harris) Reynolds, Elizabeth "Babe" (Harris) Ryan, and Doris Harris, came to my aid with recollections, genealogical connections, and photographs. Al Golding shared the papers of Ella Smith Richardson. Elizabeth Redman, who knew many of my Harris kinsman in Leon, Iowa, conducted valuable research at The Decatur County Historical Society. Bob Bixby continued the quest for Harris tracks in Leon and Decatur County. Catherine Turney, co-author of the play "My Dear Children," shared her experiences of working with John Barrymore. And, at the eleventh hour, Mary O'Dowd, granddaughter of "French songstress" Paulette LaPierre, generously provided memories and memorabilia.

This book could never have been written without searchable historic newspapers, particularly those available at the California Digital Newspaper

Collection, Chicago Public Library, the Internet Archive, Illinois Digital Newspaper Collection, Library of Congress, and several subscription services.

Illustrations were provided not only by members of the Harris family, but also from numerous institutions. My gratitude goes to Arron Schmidt, Boston Public Library; Bob Cullum and the family of Leslie R. Jones; Katie Levi, Chicago History Museum; the digital collection at Library of Congress; the staff at the Billy Rose Theatre Division, The New York Public Library; and Bill Quigley, Quigley Publishing Company.

Many thanks go to my production team: editor Zan McGreevey; indexer Kate Mertes; designer Craig Ramsdell; and David Braughler, who once again steered this project to fruition with abundant expertise.

Index

Accoo, Gussie, 97, 98, 206n104
Adler, Harry "Bernie"
   at Club Alabam, 124, 163, 171, 172
   divorce, 136–137
   at Grand Café, 35
   performances with Dan Blanco, 7, 11, 13
   repertoire of, 11–12
   songs co-written by, 210n150
Adler, Lottie, 136–137
adolescents, delinquency of, 22, 23, 27–34, 37, 41
alcohol. *See also* Prohibition
   dancing and, 36, 37, 40
   death resulting from, 110
   evasion of laws regarding, 15, 16, 121
   licenses for serving, 6, 7, 23
   minors served with, 27–29, 31–34, 37, 41
   mob control of, 49, 54, 139–140
   music and, 18, 32, 37, 40
   prices during Prohibition, 105
   taxation on, 37, 38
Alexander, Max H., 8–9
Alterie, Louis, 54–58, 139, 147, 203n60, 210n153

anti-cabaret ordinance, 29–30, 36–40
Atlantic City (New Jersey)
   alcohol availability in, 121
   cabarets in, 75–81, 88–89
   criminal activity in, 75, 77
   gambling in, 118
   liquor raids in, 80, 83, 89
   political boss in, 80, 122
   vaudeville shows in, 84

Baker, Dick "Two Ton," 172, 185, *plate xlviii*
Barry, Jack "West Side," 141–143
Barrymore, John, 167, 174, 212n191, *plates xlii–xliii*
Beach, Grant, 193–194
Beifeld, Morris, 3, 11, 200n17, *plate xii*
Bennett, Marcella. *See* Blanco, Marcella Bennett
Bernard, Lillian, 160, 168, 172, *plate xliv*
Black Tuesday, 123
Blanco, Dan (Daniel Leblang, Daniel Le Blang). *See also* Club Alabam
   arrest on liquor charges, 116

birth and early years, 3, 211*n*175
children of, 135
in copyright infringement suit, 42–43
death and obituary, 156–157, *plate xxxix*
Grand Café opened by, 13, 22, 25, 41
"Has Anybody Seen My Cat" by, 42, *plate xv*
"King of the Mafia" by, 5, *plate xiv*
marriages, 135, 156, 210*n*148
as mentor to Gene Harris, 2, 159
mob connections of, 12, 116, 188, *plate xxxv*
at Moulin Rouge, 43, 48–49, 63, 84, 89–91, 102, 203*n*68
Nesbit's relationship with, 84–86, 98, 101, 150
at Northern Lights roadhouse, 7, 51, 54–57, 89
photographs, *plate xiii*
rathskellerian act headed by, 3, 5–6, 8–11, 35, 41, *plate xi*
in vaudeville shows, 41–42
on vice in cabarets, 35
at White City Amusement Park, 4–6, 8–11, 35
Blanco, Marcella Bennett, 135, 143, 156, 210*nn*147–148, 211*n*173
Blanco, Virginia, 135, 156, 157
Bock, Annie Sara, 138, 210*n*152
Bohemian neighborhoods, 107, 116, 138, 147, 193
Bouche, Albert "Papa," 43, 45–53, 58–59, 200*n*23, 202*n*53
Brockman, Slayter, 5, 42, 144, 146
Browne, Burton, 209*n*139, *plate xxix*

burlesque theaters, 4, 7, 165–167

cabarets. *See also specific cabarets*
anti-cabaret ordinance, 29–30, 36–40
atmosphere of, 6, 35, 75
clientele serviced by, 22, 38, 87–89
closure of, 37–39, 104
gangsters in, 88
introduction to Chicago, 6, 9–10
lid laws for, 163–165
married women in, 32–33
minors in, 22, 23, 27–32
Nesbit in, 75, 76, 80–81
owl privileges for, 165
patron misconduct in, 27
raids conducted in, 22–25, 27, 30–32, 39
rathskellerians in, 9
reform efforts targeting, 13–14, 17, 27–32
taxation of, 180–181
warnings issued to, 33–35
Café Owners' Association, 36–37
Capone, Alphonso "Al"
in Chicago Outfit, 49, 58, 88, 162
Lyle on, 143
restaurants frequented by, 181
rivals of, 56, 140
St. Valentine's Day Massacre and, 116, 139
territory controlled by, 49, 116
Torrio as mentor to, 58
vagrancy charges against, 142
worldwide notoriety of, 188
Carlyle, Jean, 162

Carus, Emma, 42, *plate xv*
Casino Café, 27–28, 34, 38, 39
Castle, Hazel, 27–28
Chaplin, Mildred Harris, 151
Chez Paree, 183, 164, 207n116
Chicago (Illinois). *See also* cabarets; gangsters; saloons
  Bohemian neighborhoods of, 107, 116, 138, 147
  gambling in, 15–16, 18–19, 22, 116–117
  gangster wars in, 116, 139
  key clubs in, 124, 126, 207n116, 209n139
  lid laws in, 163–165
  prostitution in, 7, 17, 20, 170
  public influence of showmen in, 4
  reform efforts in, 13–20, 163–164, 170
  St. Valentine's Day Massacre in, 88, 116, 139
  standards of morality in, 17
  war on crime in, 56
  whoopee belt of, 123–126, 188
  World's Fair (1933–1934), 86, 147, 151, 173, *plates xxxvi–xxxvii*
Chicago Outfit crime syndicate, 49, 58, 88, 162
children, delinquency of, 22, 23, 27–34, 37, 41
Clifford, Jack (Virgil James Montani)
  dance partners of, 64, 84
  divorce, 65, 82–83, 123, 140, 150
  marriage, 64–65, 73, 76, 132, *plate xxii*
  private detectives hired by, 66

Club Alabam
  advertisements for, 163, 168, 171, 179
  apartments connected to, 108, 135–137, 159
  atmosphere at, 109, 115–116, 185–186
  burglary at, 143–144
  clientele serviced by, 25, 107, 111, 115
  decline of, 1, 186, 214n214
  doorman at, 152–153, 164
  entertainment at, 113–117, 123–124, 138–140, 143–152, 160, 163, 172–174
  Epicure Room at, 184, *plate xlix*
  fire ordinance violations at, 182
  gambling at, 116–117, 168–170, 174
  illegal alcohol sales at, 116
  lid laws impacting, 163–165
  location of, 106–108
  mob connections of, 141, 162, *plate xxxv*
  murder involving employees of, 160–163
  Nesbit at, 117, 123–124, 140, 143, 148–150, 163
  New Year's Eve celebrations at, 126, 146, 147, 181
  opening of, 88, 108, *plate xxxix*
  photographs, *plate xxxix, plate xlix*
  on prohibition agent watch list, 114
  raids on, 147, 169, 170, 174
  resilience of, 145–147, 174, 182–184
  unpaid back sales tax for, 181
clubs. *See* cabarets; *specific clubs*

cocaine, 17, 77, 78, 205*n*93
Coleman, Jack, 152–153, 164
Collins, Arthur, 10–11, 200*n*15
Colony Club, 165, 169–170, 173, 174, 212*n*194
Colosimo, Jim, 14, 16, 30
corruption, 17, 24, 25, 169–170
Craig, Andy, 7, 54, 55, 57, 89, 203*n*63
Crosby, Dorothy, 31–32
Crowe, Robert E., 103

dancing, alcohol in relation to, 36, 37, 40
Daniels, Jerry, 118, 120
David, Joseph B., 56–57
delinquency of minors, 22, 23, 27–34, 37, 41
Dever, William Emmett, 50, 55–57
Dillinger, John, 153
drugs. *See illicit drugs*
Drury, John
  on Bock's tea shops, 138, 210*n*152
  on Club Alabam, 146
  on Club Ambassadeur, 144, 209*n*137
  on Frolics, 206*n*102
  on Northern Lights renovation, 203*n*63
  on Turkish Village Café, 208*n*126
  on Vanity Fair, 208*n*126
Dryden, George Eastman, 154–155
Duvall, Irene, 151–152, 211*n*169

Eighteenth Amendment, 36, 41
Erdman, Ernie, 5, 6, 199*n*6
Essig, Charles, 123–124

Farwell, Arthur Burrage, 4
Fashion Club Pony Farm, 178, *plates xlvi–xlvii*
Fashion Club Stables, 175–176, 180, 213*n*201
Faulk, Bertha, 4–5
Fleming, Frank "Spiker," 23–24
Fontaine, Evan-Burrows, 81, 84, 206*n*96
Franche, James, "Duffy the Goat," 14
Franklin, Bernard A., 61–63, 84, 96, 101–103
Friar's Inn, 33, 87, 94, 103–106, 109, 114, 207*n*116
Fritzel, Mike, 87, 104, 114, 172, 206*n*102, 207*n*116

gambling
  at Club Alabam, 116–117, 168–170, 174
  mob-related operations, 139
  punch board, 15–16
  raids for, 118, 169, 170, 174
  reform efforts targeting, 18–19, 22, 170
  "26" dice game, 212*n*180, 213*n*212
gangsters. *See also specific gangsters*
  alcohol sales controlled by, 49, 54, 139–140
  in cabarets, 88
  in Chicago Outfit, 49, 58, 88, 162
  gambling operations run by, 139
  illicit drug sales by, 71
  at Northern Lights roadhouse, 54–55
  in North Side Gang, 58, 116, 139, 141

St. Valentine's Day Massacre and, 88, 116, 139
union operations infiltrated by, 53, 141
Garson, Thelma, 156, 210*n*148
Genthe, Arnold, *plate xxii*
Gibson, Sidney C., 11–12
Girl in the Red Velvet Swing, 195–196
Gleason, James, 15, 25, 28, 35, 38
Grand Café, 13, 22, 25, 31, 35, 41
Grant Beach School of Arts and Crafts, 193–195
Gray, Fawn, 101–102
Great Depression, 138, 145, 147, 156, 183
Green Mill, 88, 105, 124, 126, 139
Guinan, Texas, 126, 151, 173, 211*n*168

Hadley, Mabel, 137
Harcq, Clara, 102–103
Harlan, Byron G., 10–11, 200*n*15
Harpman, Julia, 82, 206*n*97
Harris, Aloisia "Babs," 1, 136, 159, 160, 182, 214*n*214
Harris, Bessie Agnes, 113, 136, 210*n*149
Harris, Clayton Eugene, 1, 111–112, *plate xxviii*
Harris, Elizabeth "Babe," 113, 182
Harris, Eugene Alexander "Gene." *See also* Club Alabam
  birth and early years, 1, 112
  Blanco as mentor to, 2, 159
  on customers at Club Alabam, 111
  death and obituary, 1, 159, 187, *plate x, plate xxxix*
  family background, 1, 111–112, 135

Fashion Club Stables owned by, 175–176, 180, 213*n*201
legacy of, 188–189
on lid laws, 164–165
on longevity of Club Alabam, 174
marriages, 113, 136, 210*n*149
in Military Order of the Guards, 179–180
New Wayside Inn opened by, 127–129, 159, *plate xxxii*
photographs and caricature, *plates xxvii–xxviii, plate xxix*
police apprehension of, 117
Shetland pony breeding by, 1, 176–178, 213*n*201, *plates xlvi–xlvii*
waiter experiences of, 88, 107, 112–113, 138
Harris, Merrilee (Merrilee Thomson), 182
Harris, Minnie. *See* Sanger, Minnie Harris
Harris, Ruth Wales, 1, 111, 112, *plates xxvii–xxviii*
Harrison, Carter Henry, Jr., 16, 18, 19
"Has Anybody Seen My Cat" (Blanco), 42, *plate xv*
Hellinger, Mark, 119, 132–133, 208*n*30
Hennessey, Thomas and Maurice, 24–25
Henri, Flo, 160, 168, 172, 186, *plate xliv*
Herrick, Genevieve Forbes, 98–99
"hippos," 94, 114
Houston, Charles E., 178, *plate xlvi*
Hoyne, Maclay, 15, 201*n*30

Hurlburt, George, 115, 125

illicit drugs
   cocaine, 17, 77, 78, 205n93
   gangsters in selling of, 71
   morphine, 17, 71–79, 81, 188, 205n93
   reform efforts targeting, 17

jazz music, 32, 186
Jirik, Aloisia "Babs." See Harris, Aloisia "Babs"
Jirik, Irene, 159, 182
Johnson, Enoch L. "Nucky," 80, 122, 205n94
Johnson, Eva, 29
Jones, Roy, 14–16, 201n29
Jordan, John J., 7, 14, 15, 199n8
juvenile delinquency, 22, 23, 27–34, 37, 41

Kelly, Mamie Lee, 131, *plate xxxiv*
Kelly's Ritz, 131, *plate xxxiv*
Kester, Dorothy, 54–55, 57
key clubs, 124, 126, 207n116, 209n139
"King of the Mafia" (Blanco), 5, *plate xiv*
Kirkland, Marcella. See Blanco, Marcella Bennett
Kissane, Anthony "Red," 141–143
Ku Klux Klan, 83–84
Kupcinet, Irv "Kup," 174

Lait, Jack, 99, 183, 192–193, 207n107
Lamont, Marie, 161–163
Langford, Albert and Marion, 191–192

LaPierre, Anita, 172–173
LaPierre, Geraldine, 172–173
LaPierre, Germaine, 146, 172–173, *plate xxxvi*
LaPierre, Paulette, 87, 146, 163, 172–174, *plate xxxvi*, *plates xl–xli*
Leblang (Le Blang), Daniel. See Blanco, Dan
Leonard, William "Will," 1, 183–185, 202n53, 214n214
lid laws, 163–165
Lingle, Alfred "Jake," 139, 141, 211n155
liquor. See alcohol
Little, Richard Henry, 8
Lowry, Ed, 86–88, 206n99, 207n110, *plate xxiv*
Lyle, John H., 141–143
Lyon, Herb, 137, 176–177, 186, 187

Magnussen, Erik, 138, 147
Mahoney, Bessie Agnes. See Harris, Bessie Agnes
Mandarin Inn, 45, *plate xvii*
Mann, Fred, 48, 114, 208n123
Martin, Jules, 119, 120
Matina, Bela and Matyus. See "Mike & Ike"
McCloskey, Ray, 13, 22, 25, 30–31, 35, 41, 201n34
McGovern Bros. cabaret and hotel, 18, 20–23, 25, 200n23
McGurn, Jack "Machine Gun," 88
McKelvey, Harry "Mack," 52, 53, 62, 202n54
"Mike & Ike" (twin midgets), 86, 90, 102, 151, 173, *plate xix*, *plate xxxvi*

Military Order of the Guards, 179–180
minors, delinquency of, 22, 23, 27–34, 37, 41
mob. *See* gangsters
Montani, Virgil James. *See* Clifford, Jack
Moran, George "Bugs," 116, 139–141, *plate xxxv*
Moran's Café, 28–29, 34, 38
Morgan, Gene, 9–10
Morgan, George. *See* Phillips, Johnny
morphine, 17, 71–79, 81, 188, 205*n*93
Moulin Rouge Café
   advertisements for, 47, *plate xvi*
   assault and battery case at, 102–103
   Blanco at, 43, 48–49, 63, 84, 89–91, 102, 203*n*68
   bombing at, 52–53, 62
   clientele serviced by, 87–89
   closure of, 50, 105, 106, 109
   entertainment at, 43, 48–49, 61–64, 84–91, 101–104, 173
   illegal alcohol sales at, 46–48, 62
   injunctions against, 47, 49, 50, 103–106
   Nesbit at, 63–64, 84–86, 90–91, 98
   ownership of, 45, 51, 59, 61, 84, 173
   raid on, 103
   reopening of, 51–54, 57
   shooting at, 49
   slander case involving, 103
Munn, Wayne, 177–178, *plate xlvii*
music
   alcohol in relation to, 18, 32, 37, 40

   jazz, 32, 186
   ragtime, 17–18, 200*n*15
   reform efforts targeting, 17–18, 28, 32, 37

narcotics. *See* illicit drugs
National Prohibition Act. *See* Volstead Act of 1919
Nesbit, Evelyn
   addiction to morphine, 71–79, 81, 188, 205*n*93
   affair with Stanford White, 119, 191, *plates xxi–xxii, plate xlv*
   Barrymore and, 167, 174, *plate xlii*
   Blanco's relationship with, 84–86, 98, 101, 150
   burglaries involving, 69–70, 88–89, 118
   in burlesque acts, 165–167
   cabaret comeback of, 75, 76, 80–81
   at Club Alabam, 117, 123–124, 140, 143, 148–150, 163
   death of, 197
   divorce, 65–66, 82–83, 123, 132, 140, 150
   film based on life of, 195–196
   at Grant Beach School of Arts and Crafts, 193–195
   health problems of, 148–149, 168
   Ku Klux Klan and, 83–84
   marriages, 64–65, 73, 76, *plates xxi–xxii*
   on mental state of Harry Thaw, 81–82
   mob connections of, 118, 149
   at Moulin Rouge, 63–64, 84–86, 90–91, 98

228 ••• THE BLACKEST SHEEP

at New Wayside Inn, 127–129, *plate xxxii*
ownership of clubs by, 80–81, 118–122
in Panama, 131–133
philosophy and religion of, 127, 130–131, 195, 196
photographs, *plates xxi–xxiii, plate xxx, plate xxxiii, plate xlv, plates l–li*
postcards from Atlantic City, *plate xxxi*
Prodigal Days, 154, 193, 205*n*93
publicity agent for, 137, 150
reconciliation with Harry Thaw, 117, 119–120, 122
retirement of, 168, 191
scandals involving, 63, 64, 75–76
as sculptor, 194–195, *plates l–li*
suicide attempts by, 71–74, 79, 96–101
tearoom opened by, 65–71, 73–75, *plate xxiii*
in vaudeville shows, 64, 78, 84–85, 120, 194, 207*n*114
New Wayside Inn, 127–129, 159, *plate xxxii*
nightclubs. *See* cabarets; *specific nightclubs*
Norman, Karyl, 104, 207*n*114, *plate xviii*
Norris, Harriet, 163, 172, 183
Northern Lights roadhouse
advertisements for, 51, *plate xx*
closure of, 55–56
entertainment at, 51
gangster activity at, 54–55
ownership of, 7, 54, 89

renovation of, 203*n*63
shooting at, 54–57
North Side Gang, 58, 116, 139, 141

O'Banion, Dion, 54, 56, 58, 116, 139
Orr, Ely H., 143
owl privileges, 165

Pegler, Westbrook, 169–170, 206*n*97, 213*n*196
Phillips, Johnny (George Morgan), 54–56, 58, 147
Phillips, Marcella. *See* Blanco, Marcella Bennett
Prohibition. *See also* alcohol; Volstead Act of 1919
cost of alcohol during, 105
criticisms of, 187
Eighteenth Amendment and, 36, 41
end of, 148, 152
illegal liquor sales during, 46–48, 62, 116, 124
key clubs during, 124, 126, 207*n*116, 209*n*139
raids and seizures during, 80, 83, 89, 103, 114, 147
speakeasies during, 121, 126, 172, 187
prostitution, 7, 17, 20, 170
publicity agents, 87, 137, 150

Raab, William "Frank," 161–163
ragtime music, 17–18, 200*n*15
Rainbo Gardens, 48, 94, 105, 114, 202*n*53, 208*n*123

Rasputin, Harry (Victor Weinshenker), 87, 137, 150
rathskellerians, 3, 5–6, 8–11, 35, 41, *plate xi*
Read, Hazel and Vera, 154–155
Roaring Twenties, 2, 88, 183, 185
Rohe, Alice, 73–75, 205*n*87
Romanoff, Ivan Alexievitch, 123
Rose, Kindred "Wesley," 112, *plate xxviii*
Rose, Pauline, 1, 112
Rose, Ruth. *See* Harris, Ruth Wales
Rothstein, William R. "Bill"
   closure of Moulin Rouge by, 105
   entertainers hired by, 85–87, 98
   financial partner of, 62, 101
   mob-connected clientele of, 88
   as proprietor of Moulin Rouge, 59, 61, 84, 173

St. Valentine's Day Massacre (1929), 88, 116, 139
saloons. *See also specific saloons*
   closure of, 38
   conversion into restaurants, 20–21
   prostitution in, 17, 20
   reform efforts targeting, 13–14, 17–19, 30
   Sunday closing order for, 20, 21
   in violation of public ordinances, 7, 15–16, 21
Sanger, Minnie Harris, 1, 111, 112
Schepps, Sam, 65, 66, 204*n*74
Schuettler, Herman F., 23–25, 28, 33–35, 38, 39
Sebastian, Nick, 46, 49
Seymour, Maurice, *plates xl–xli*

Shepard, Gerald, 26
Shetland ponies, 1, 176–178, 213*n*201, *plates xlvi–xlvii*
Sichy, Anna, 28–29
Sircy, Johnny, *plate xlvi*
South, Eddie, 87, 108, 114, 206*n*98, *plate xxxviii*
speakeasies, 121, 126, 172, 187
Stafford, Merrilee Harris, 182
stock market crash (1929), 123, 145
Sunday closing orders, 20, 21

Thaw, Evelyn Nesbit. *See* Nesbit, Evelyn
Thaw, Harry K.
   addiction to drugs, 205*n*93
   death of, 192, 193
   divorce, 65, 132
   female companions of, 102
   marriage, *plate xxi*
   in mental institution, 64, 81–82, *plate xxii*
   murder committed by, 63–64, 67, 85, 119, 192, *plate xlv*
   reconciliation with Evelyn Nesbit, 117, 119–120, 122
   The Traitor, 148
Thaw, Russell W.
   in car accident, 82
   education of, 63
   father's denial of paternity, 82
   grandmother as guardian of, 72, 78
   Los Angeles residence of, 193
   on mother's suicide attempt, 97–98
   in motion pictures, 74

paternity of, 82, 149
photographs, *plates xxii–xxiii*
in slander and libel lawsuit, 117, 208*n*127
Thompson, William "Big Bill" Hale, 20, 21, 23, 38
Torrio, Johnny, 16, 49, 56, 58
Touhy, Roger and Tommy, 162
"26" dice game, 212*n*180, 213*n*212

vaudeville shows
    lifestyle of performers in, 172–173
    at Moulin Rouge, 49
    Nesbit in, 64, 78, 84–85, 120, 194, 207*n*114
    popularity of, 10, 41–42, 64
    rathskellerians in, 3
    reform efforts targeting, 17, 18
    sideshow attractions in, 4
Volstead Act of 1919. *See also* Prohibition
    criticisms of, 110
    enforcement of, 93–94, 106, 109, 125
    nuisance clause of, 103
    violations of, 46–50, 55, 93, 121, 147, 202*n*52

Wade, Jimmy, 85–87, 89, 102, 108, 206*n*98
Wales, Ruth Belle. *See* Harris, Ruth Wales
Waller, Charles, 7, 136
Ward, Joseph, 121–123
Weinshenker, Victor. *See* Rasputin, Harry
Weisl, Edwin L., 104, 106
White, Bert, 7, 13–16, 35, 136, 199*n*7
White, Stanford, 63–64, 85, 99, 119, 191–192, *plates xxi–xxii, plate xlv*
White City Amusement Park, 3–6, 8–12, 35, *plate xii*
"white slavery" movement, 27
whoopee belt, 123–126, 188
Wicher, Ruth, 29
Williams, Max, 76–78, 80
Wilson, Rae, 25–26
World's Fair, Chicago (1933–1934), 86, 147, 151, 173, *plates xxxvi–xxxvii*

Yellowley, Edward C., 93–96, 105–106, 109, 114–115, 125, *plate xxv*
Young, Ernie, 61–63, 84, 203*n*67

Zuta, Jack, 139–141, *plate xxxv*

About the Author

PHOTO BY ANDY SNOW

After earning her doctorate in cinema studies at the University of Southern California, Joanne Yeck taught and wrote about film history for many years. She is the author of dozens of articles concerning Classic Hollywood and American Popular Culture, and is the co-author of *Movie Westerns* and *Our Movie Heritage*. Beginning in 1995, her interest in Virginia history became a full-time occupation. Years of research resulted in four books: *"At a Place Called Buckingham," Volume I* (2011) and *Volume II* (2015), *The Jefferson Brothers* (2012); and *Peter Field Jefferson: Dark Prince of Scottsville and Lost Jeffersons* (2018). From the geographical heart of Virginia, she followed her Harris family west to Leon, Iowa, birthplace of her great uncle Gene Harris, whose unconventional life provided a dazzling conclusion to her family history. Visit Joanne online at joannelyeck.com.

Also by Joanne Yeck

Without a doubt, Yeck truly provides her readers with much more than lessons about Buckingham's history. She offers them a connection, a bond, with the people who made this community what it is today....
  Tana Knott, *The Farmville Herald*

While doing research, Yeck had the opportunity to get to know her Virginia cousins. Being only the second person in her family to be born outside Virginia since 1617, returning to the state felt like a homecoming for her. She fell in love with both the county and its residents.
  Heather Harris, *Rural Virginian*

Joanne Yeck writes beautifully and is an instinctive storyteller.
  Carlos Santos,
  Publisher, Valley Publishing

Ms. Yeck is to be commended on what can only be described as a herculean effort to resurrect lost Jeffersons from the mists of time. As a result, we have not only an understanding of these folks, but also of the southern United States in a far distant and important time in our development as a nation. Well written and comprehensive, it is a must for anyone interested in American history.

Charles Culbertson, historian

"Peter Field Jefferson: Dark Prince of Scottsville & Lost Jeffersons" should be on every Virginian's bookshelf.

Sue A. Miles, *Buckingham Beacon*

slateriverpress.com

www.ingramcontent.com/pod-product-compliance
Lightning Source LLC
Chambersburg PA
CBHW030852170426
43193CB00009BA/576